RENAISSANCE DRAMA

New Series 33   2004

Renaissance Drama

NEW SERIES 33

Edited by Jeffrey Masten and Wendy Wall

Northwestern University Press

EVANSTON 2004

Copyright © 2005 by Northwestern University Press
All rights reserved
ISBN 0-8101-2199-9
Printed in the United States of America

10   9   8   7   6   5   4   3   2   1

Contents

Editorial Note

THE ESSAYS IN *Renaissance Drama*, volume 33, treat a range of current topics in the study of early modern drama and performance. An annual and interdisciplinary publication, *Renaissance Drama* invites submissions that investigate traditional canons of drama as well as the significance of performance, broadly construed, to early modern culture. We particularly welcome essays that examine the impact of new forms of interpretation on the study of Renaissance plays, theater, and performance; the cultural discourses that shaped and were shaped by drama and the institutional conditions in which it was produced; and the way that performance and performativity functioned both on and off the professional stage. Occasionally, special issues of the journal are devoted to specific topics of current interest.

Renaissance Drama conforms to the stylistic guidelines of *The Chicago Manual of Style* (15th edition), including endnote reference citations. Scholars preparing manuscripts for submission should refer to this book. Please submit an electronic file of manuscripts as an email attachment (saved in rich text, as an rtf file) to renaissancedrama@northwestern.edu, along with three hard copies sent to the address below. For initial review of manuscripts, legible photocopies of any illustrations are acceptable; authors of essays accepted for publication will be responsible for obtaining any necessary permissions. Manuscripts submitted with a stamped self-addressed envelope will be returned. The journal does not accept submissions of essays by fax. Please address all submissions and inquiries to:

> *Renaissance Drama*
> Department of English
> Northwestern University
> 1897 Sheridan Road
> Evanston, IL 60208-2240
> USA

Additional information on submissions, special issues, and forthcoming essays can be found at the Northwestern University English Department Web site, http://www.english.northwestern.edu/.

RENAISSANCE DRAMA

New Series 33   2004

Acts of Silence, Acts of Speech: How to Do Things with Othello and Desdemona

HARRY BERGER JR.

The word in language is half someone else's. It becomes "one's own" only when the speaker populates it with his own intention, his own accent, when he appropriates the word. . . . Prior to this moment of appropriation, the word . . . exists in other people's mouths, in other people's contexts, serving other people's intentions: it is from there that one must take the word, and make it one's own.

—Mikhail Bakhtin, *The Dialogic Imagination: Four Essays by M. M. Bakhtin*

The problem of why Iago casts himself in the role of the Vice . . . leads to the related problem . . . of why he succeeds so easily and totally in enacting that role. Why, that is, should Othello fall such easy prey to his snare? . . . Iago himself is somewhat surprised at . . . [his] success.

—Howard Felperin, *Shakespearean Representation: Mimesis and Modernity in Elizabethan Drama*

H ow to do things *with* Othello and Desdemona: two opposed meanings emanate from "with" and battle for control of the phrase. One is adversarial and the other conspiratorial. Iago obviously does things with Othello and Desdemona in the sense of doing things *to* them. But he wouldn't be able to do the things he does to them without their help. They are more than his victims; they are his accomplices. The words with which he poisons their greedy ears are words he appropriates from their mouths, their contexts, their intentions—and their acts of silence. Iago's speech acts are saturated with the silences of others—not only of Othello and Desdemona but also Emilia and Cassio. The adversarial sense of "with," which attributes full autonomy and instrumentality to Iago, gives the interpretation he and Othello prefer. But the conspiratorial sense gives the interpretation I think the text of the play features, and it is an interpretation that runs counter to arguments that position Iago as a genius and Othello a "lunkhead."[1]

3

Act 1 scene 1 opens up so deeply in medias res as to make viewers and readers feel like outsiders intruding on a conversation whose wandering course is hard to follow but obviously clear to the participants. Throughout this scene the speakers demonstrate their familiarity (and inhibit ours) with the topics under discussion by relying on personal pronouns rather than proper nouns. Othello's name is not uttered until two scenes later (1.3.49).[2] In 1.1 he is referred to only pronominally or by any of several invidious epithets. Desdemona is not mentioned until 1.1.66 and not named until 1.2.25. The effect of such conspicuous deferral combines with the stenographic (or stenological?) quality of the conversational interchanges to reinforce our sense that the speakers are insiders and we are outsiders. In that respect, they don't seem to be performing or speaking for anyone's benefit but their own. This is especially frustrating because it invites viewers and readers to wonder what went on in the prehistory (or, as they say nowadays, the back story) to which the deferral alludes. Some details of the prehistory get filled in during 1.1 and many more in 1.3 when Othello tells his story with assistance (or resistance) from Brabantio and Desdemona. But the most vital piece of information concerning the events that preceded 1.1 is not disclosed until more than halfway through the play, when we learn for the first time of a situation, a relational structure, a practice, that not only preceded the events unfolding from 1.1 on but was their hidden cause. The belated disclosure of this cause is the direct effect of the episodes leading up to it in acts 2 and 3. But the disclosure itself has uncanny causal force because it defamiliarizes and demands us to reconfigure, to reinterpret, everything that precedes it.

I'll disclose and discuss the disclosure in due time. I mention it now only to note that it will change the initial assessment we make, in terms of the information provided in 1.1, of who's in and who's out. At first, Iago's rhetorical attack on Othello the Moor and Cassio the Florentine has the effect of coupling them together as comical outsiders, while he represents himself as the quintessential insider. But there must be something wrong with this representation, since he failed in his suit to get promoted. When the disclosure forces us to reevaluate what we thought was going on in the early scenes, we discover that in the play's real scheme of things, Cassio and Othello have always been on the inside and Iago on the outside. Thus as the play proceeds, we don't move from early confusion to later clarification. Rather, one confusion is exchanged for another. The play's back story and its initial state of things simply, so to speak, get reconfused. We find out that having begun in medias res, the "res" turn out to be very different from what we first thought they were.

I noted above that at first glance Iago and Roderigo don't seem to be performing. A second glance changes this impression in the case of Iago. But like everything else in *Othello,* second glances and second thoughts are prompted belatedly. It isn't until we encounter Iago's first soliloquy at the end of 1.3 that we discover the extent to which he has been performing all along.

In 1.3, after Iago and Roderigo had heard Othello and Desdemona proclaim their love for each other in the presence of the assembled Duke and Senators, the lovelorn Roderigo threatens to drown himself. This draws from Iago a series of contemptuous harangues spanning some sixty lines and filled with the clichés of misanthropic discourse. While trying to restore Roderigo's self-confidence and hope, Iago seems at the same time to take pleasure in rubbing Roderigo's unmanliness in his face and increasing the sense of impotence that binds him to his diabolical savior. Since the threat of suicide seems little more than a melodramatic whine, the energy and volume of Iago's swash are gratuitous. This he all but acknowledges just after Roderigo's exit, as he steps forward and delivers his first soliloquy:

> Thus do I ever make my fool my purse:
> For I mine own gained knowledge should profane
> If I would time expend with such a snipe
> But for my sport and profit: I hate the Moor
> And it is thought abroad, that 'twixt my sheets
> He's done my office; I know not if't be true,
> But I for mere suspicion in that kind
> Will do as if for surety. He holds me well,
> The better shall my purpose work on him.
> Cassio's a proper man: let me see now,
> To get his place, and to make up my will
> In double knavery. How? How? let's see:
> After some time to abuse Othello's ear
> That he is too familiar with his wife.
> He hath a person and a smooth dispose
> To be suspected, framed to make women false.
> The Moor is of a free and open nature
> That thinks men honest that but seem to be so,
> And will as tenderly be led by th' nose
> As asses are.

> I have't, it is engender'd! Hell and night
> Must bring this monstrous birth to the world's light.
>   (1.3.382–403)

The opening word "Thus" points back to the preceding eighty lines of dialogue with Roderigo, and the words that follow make Iago sound apologetic. He speaks as one who has been and still is performing before an audience that was present throughout the scene. This must be a discriminating audience, since he defends against the imagined charge that his man-of-the-world outburst (312–73) was sententious overkill, wasted on "such a snipe" as his only onstage auditor.

The suspicion that he performs for another and better audience than Roderigo carries back to the first sixty-five lines of 1.1, which also featured the temptation to rhetorical overkill. Iago monopolizes that conversation with blather about himself and with generous dollops of cynicism that seem excessive to Roderigo's interlocutory demands. He is clearly enchanted with the rhetoric of villainy, with a discourse whose basic theme is not that of the victim, as in Lear's "I am a man / More sinned against than sinning," but that of the villain, "I am a man / More sinning than sinned against."[3] Something else, however, is going on in this performance. Iago is not only running the show but putting on a show, and since he treats Roderigo with a certain amount of impatience and disdain, you begin to wonder why Iago confides in Roderigo and what pleasure Iago gets in pushing him around. It isn't until the first soliloquy that we get some purchase on this question. Was it for Roderigo alone that Iago, in the first scene, pumped up his wickedness with the rhetorical verve of someone impersonating the stage villain?

> For when my outward action does demonstrate
> The native act, and figure of my heart
> In complement extern, 'tis not long after
> But I will wear my heart upon my sleeve
> For doves to peck at: I am not what I am.[4]
>   (1.1.60–64)

It is as if Iago has been using Roderigo not only as a factor in his revenge but also as a kind of stand-in or dummy against which to bounce a performance of the villain's discourse destined for an invisible gallery of discerning spectators, whom, from now on, I'll refer to as "supervisors," borrowing a term Iago himself uses later to taunt Othello: "Would you, the supervisor, grossly gape on, / Behold her topp'd?" (3.3.398–99). Although my use of the term will emphasize its innocent etymological sense, "an onlooker who looks down from above" (as if from the gallery or "lords' rooms" in the upper level of the public stage), I want to keep in play the edgier sense contextualized by Iago's usage—the sense of this invisible audience as a potential victim or dupe being invited by its deceiver to watch itself being betrayed.

We can now see that from the start Iago has been performing as if he were a needy actor who hogs the platea and continuously solicits the audience's admiration.[5] But which audience? Does he perform *like* an actor or *as* an actor? Brian Vickers misses the point by taking the direct address of Shakespearean villains personally and then getting huffy about it: Iago, he grumbles, thrusts his intentions on us, and this makes Vickers nervous because it "leads to an intimacy which we would willingly avoid, if we could. There is no one in the world whose confidence I would rather less share than Iago's."[6] But, first, the audience constituted by the soliloquy of a character preexists—and thus can't be identical to—any particular theater audience addressed by the actor who plays the character. Iago is not forcing himself on Vickers any more than on me. And second, I, for one, very much enjoy Iago's confidential nasties and can't get enough of them. I would be tickled to be a member of the ideal audience he addresses, and, in addressing, constructs.

What Iago bestows on this audience after the opening apology is unexpected. It has nothing to do with motiveless malignancy. As A. D. Nuttall well expresses it, Iago "is not just motivated, like other people. Instead, he *decides* to be motivated."[7] The very arbitrariness of the decision puts his manliness and autonomy on parade even as it mischievously airs a possible threat to them in the suspicion of cuckoldry. He dares the imaginary audience to accuse him of defeating his "favor with an usurp'd beard" (341–42) and then proceeds to disarm the threat by converting the mere suspicion to a sufficient motive for revenge. Among his onstage interlocutors, Iago had honestly flaunted his dishonesty with only Roderigo, taking the calculated risk that he might at some point be exposed by the poor snipe. Now he appears to have staged this risk for the approval of the audience who could appreciate his intrepidity, his masterful control, and, above all, the suave dishonesty of his frank avowals to Roderigo. He represents himself as a plain-speaking, disenchanted, resentful, satirical rogue—a "me-firster" who "tells it as it is." But can this be any more honest as a confession of knavery than his pledge of friendship to Roderigo? Iago's audience is encouraged to giggle along with Iago at everyone's stupid persistence in enlisting him as a trusty mediator and pinning medals of honesty on his chest.

Such moves make you wonder whether Iago's self-disclosure to the supervisors is any more reliable, genuine, or disinterested than his self-disclosure to Roderigo. Suppose it is just another conspicuously dishonest pretense of honesty, which he puts on to remind the supervisors that they're dealing with a consummate actor, and villain. To be thought of as honest in Venice serves his purposes but may also be a little humiliating. He wants more respect, more appreciation, for the rogue he knows himself to be. Perhaps he's looking for an audience he can shock and awe in frontal assault, or an audience of superior wit and judgment capable of rewarding him with the applause and execration he deserves.

"I am not what I am": Iago protects his absence—his freedom—from the honest Iago that confines him in Venice by pretending he is like an actor on a stage (which, of course, he isn't), escaping to the platea, clinging parasitically to the fantasy that he performs his villainies before the imaginary gallery of supervisors whose hero is dishonest Iago. But if it is possible to be dishonestly honest in Venice, is it equally possible to be honestly dishonest in the imaginary theater? In 1.1 Iago confides that he hates the Moor because he passed him over and gave Cassio the military office for which he himself is more qualified. In 1.3 Iago confides to the supervisors that he has disingenuously taken Roderigo into his confidence only for the "sport and profit" connected with his hatred of the Moor, who is rumored to have usurped his sexual office. Is the second confidence any less disingenuous than the first? Immediately after having suggested that so far as hatred and revenge are concerned the truth of the rumor is irrelevant—the mere fantasy "Will do, as if for surety"—Iago notes that he expects to succeed because Othello "holds him well."

This casual remark doesn't square with the story of being passed over for Cassio, and Othello's subsequent displays of confidence in Iago hardly substantiate the truth of the story.[8] Maybe, then, the story he tells in 1.1 has the same doubtful status as the story of cuckoldry. If so, he leaves it up to the supervisors to make that determination. He doesn't tell them much more than he discloses to Roderigo about his villainy, and his teasing obfuscations tend to diminish the implied contrast between taking the poor snipe into his confidence and confiding in the supervisors.

Iago delivers nine soliloquies in verse in addition to the two prose asides in 2.1.[9] Four of the soliloquies occur before 3.3—as we'll see later, this is an important dividing line—and five after. The first four, which vary in length from sixteen to thirty-two lines, stand out as rhetorical performances because each follows and precedes passages of prose. The remaining five are shorter—they vary from thirteen to one and a half lines—and with one exception they are surrounded by verse and thus not so clearly set off.

The speaker of the four soliloquies Iago delivers before 3.3 is in performative heaven. He coaxes, cajoles, confides, confesses, gloats, and sneers. In the fourth soliloquy, he can barely contain himself. He has just counseled the disgraced Cassio to enlist Desdemona's aid as mediator, and now, with Cassio's "Good-night, honest Iago" in their ears, the supervisors are treated to fourteen lines in which he mockingly performs everyone else's honest Iago in scare quotes:

> And what's he, then, that says I play the villain?
> When this advice is free I give and honest,
> Probal to thinking, and, indeed, the course
> To win the Moor again? For 'tis most easy
> Th' inclining Desdemona to subdue
> In any honest suit. She's framed as fruitful
> As the free elements: and then for her
> To win the Moor, were't to renounce his baptism,
> All seals and symbols of redeemed sin,
> His soul is so enfetter'd to her love
> That she may make, unmake, do what she list,
> Even as her appetite shall play the god
> With his weak function. How am I then a villain
> To counsel Cassio to this parallel course
> Directly to his good?
>
> (2.3.331–45)

In short, "All I'm doing, folks, is trying to push the right buttons and do my level best to help Cassio get back into Othello's good graces." And then, with a scarifying shift of tone at line 345, he makes sure the supervisors appreciate what he has just really done: "Divinity of hell! / When devils will the blackest sins put on / They do suggest at first with heavenly shows / As I do now."[10]

As he continues to unfold his devilish plot, exhilaration and self-delight spill out in a three-line rush:

> So will I turn her virtue into pitch
> And out of her own goodness make the net
> That shall enmesh them all.
>
> (2.3.355-57)

At this point, Roderigo has the bad taste to interrupt his iambic villainizing with a prosy complaint (lines 358-64). Iago impatiently counsels patience, hustles him off stage, and calls the supervisors back to attention to complete his briefing:

> Two things are to be done:
> My wife must move for Cassio to her mistress,
> I'll set her on.
> Myself the while to draw the Moor apart
> And bring him jump when he may Cassio find
> Soliciting his wife! Ay, that's the way!
> Dull not device by coldness and delay!
>
> (2.3.377-83)

The excitement pulsing through the nervous rhythm—the short line, the run-over lines terminated by a stagy "Eureka!" and followed by a burst of alliteration that adds zing to an already peppery couplet—is *performed* for the supervisors' pleasure. To borrow a figure of speech from another arena, Iago tries to get the crowd into the game by dramatizing the process of villainous *inventio* and stumbling on the solution before their very eyes and ears. What he fails to consider in this euphoric moment is the boomerang lurking in his triumphant vaunt, "out of her own goodness make the net / That shall enmesh them all": his victims' ability—painfully on offer in the very next scene—to beat him to the punch; or, to restate this in more elevated terms, their ability to put into play the principle of redistributed complicities.

According to this principle, the self-proclaimed villain is being run, or manipulated, by his victims more than he knows or would like—certainly more than they know or would like. If there is something they deeply and darkly desire but would never acknowledge (especially not to themselves), something they would never lift a finger to bring about, they get their villain to do it for them. Nothing could humiliate Iago more than to have his special audience of supervisors watch him being reduced to the tool of his victims.[11]

There is a moment in the play when you begin to wonder whether this reduction is taking place, an exchange between Desdemona and Othello in which you're casually let in on a little secret that turns everything in the play upside down. But the exchange is belated. It doesn't happen until the third scene in act 3. It's the moment of belated disclosure I referred to at the beginning of this essay, and it all but guarantees Iago his victory. The soliloquy I just glanced at is the last he delivers before that moment. The five that follow it differ in tone. They show him spinning his wheels, redundantly preparing new snares for an Othello already trapped, nervously keeping the supervisors up to date on his plans and progress. They are less consistently performative, less expansive, more hurried.

What happens in 3.3 is that Desdemona reminds Othello, in Iago's presence, that Cassio "came a-wooing with you." Snap! Just like that, we learn for the first time that the three principals have been choreographed in René Girard's dance of mimetic desire since before the play began.[12] Girard himself notes that Othello resorts to a go-between because he's an outsider who lacks confidence and who sees in Cassio everything that he himself "is not: white, young, handsome, elegant, always at ease among the likes of Desdemona." Othello's jealousy, Girard concludes, "is rooted neither in what Desdemona does nor in what Iago says, but in the internal weakness that forces him to resort to a go-between in the first place."[13] The triangle of mimetic desire puts Othello in competition with Cassio from the start— and at a disadvantage. Cassio has a daily beauty in his life that makes Othello ugly. Girard mistakenly calls Cassio "a true Venetian aristocrat." Shakespeare departs from his source, the novella by Cinthio, in making Cassio a Florentine, an outsider like Othello. But Girard's mistake is useful because it suggests two reasons for Shakespeare's departure: first, it picks out an impression Cassio would like to make, and second, it suggests that Othello may have chosen Cassio in part because he saw him as a successfully assimilated outsider.

Given both Girard's own development of his concept in subsequent work and the continuing critique of his work, from early issues of *Diacritics* to Eve Sedgwick's *Between Men* and beyond, a word of explanation is in order.[14] What I find useful for *Othello* is Girard's emphasis on the motive of victimage in the erotic triangle—on a condition of preemptive victimization in which the lover establishes and maintains control over the possibility that he will be or can get himself betrayed. Othello's fear of Desdemona, the character of which is first exposed in his reference to her "greedy ear" at 1.3.150 (see p. 22), is inscribed in the diffidence conveyed by his decision to seek the help of a go-between. Explicitly, the go-between's function is positive: to help the lover woo the beloved. Implicitly, the go-between literally "gets between" the lover and the beloved in the sense not merely of *mediation* but of *insulation.* Cassio will protect Othello from whatever the "greedy ear" symbolizes even as he "feeds" the ear, supposedly whetting its appetite for Othello.

In his comments on *Othello,* Girard ignores the dramatic impact produced by deferring the information that Cassio was the mediator, the traditional and sometimes infamous Lover's Friend, the Don Pedro who helped Othello win Desdemona. This means that the triangular structure of fantasy, desire, and distrust was already in place before the play began. It is part of the play's back story. As Graham Bradshaw notes in *Misrepresentations,* all this is news to Iago as well as to spectators and readers.[15] It is also a major addition to and departure from the tale by Cinthio that is Shakespeare's source. Yet when Desdemona mentions Cassio's role in the heat of the moment with Emilia and Iago present, she doesn't treat it as privileged information, and a few lines later Othello shows no hesitation in satisfying Iago's curiosity about it. He freely divulges that Cassio knew of their love "from first to last," was well acquainted with Desdemona "and went between us very often," and "was of my counsel, / In my whole course of wooing" (3.3.95-97, 101, 115-16). It is apparently no secret. Yet it is not something any member of the triangle has mentioned before. The play doesn't present it as something that troubles them or preys on their consciousness. They speak of it rather as something they take for granted and have put behind them. But the play shows that this itself is their mistake. What they casually recall and openly mention is a latent structure that mediates all their dealings with each other and Cassio: a structure of contaminated intimacy in which they have inscribed themselves. This previously unmentioned shadow plot now emerges and starts to haunt the play. Something that has never been said, a dark silence, becomes retroactively audible, slips beneath, and shakes, the floor of all their prior interactions. And the context into which it intrudes is a renewal of the original triangle in a dangerously skewed form: Cassio has replaced Othello as the suitor, and Desdemona has replaced Cassio as the go-between who promises to give Othello no peace until he grants "Cassio's suit." The first triangle featured Othello as the outsider and Cassio as the insider, the authority, in the practice of courtship. Although Cassio becomes the outsider in the second triangle, the shade of the first triangle malingers within the second.[16]

It was Iago who first suggested that Cassio should appeal for help to Desdemona (2.3.309-20) and who, in his subsequent soliloquy, planned to make Emilia "move for Cassio to her mistress" and to arrange for Othello to find Cassio "soliciting" Desdemona (2.3.378, 382-83).[17] Act 3 opens with Cassio asking Othello's Clown to notify Emilia that he'd like an interview and then reporting this to his honest friend, her husband, who obligingly offers "to draw the Moor / Out of the way" (3.1.37-38). Up to now, Iago remains comfortably in charge of the campaign in which attempts at reparation will lead to tragic consequences. But this balance of power begins to change immediately. After Iago leaves, Emilia enters and assures Cassio "all will . . . be well" because "[t]he general and his wife" are already "talking of it, / And she speaks for you stoutly; the Moor replies" that although Cassio's offense was serious and can't be ignored, "he protests he loves you / And needs no other suitor but his likings" to find the opportunity to reinstate him (3.1.42-52).[18] Desdemona need not take on herself the role of Cassio's suitor: Othello loves him enough for both of them. The (still undisclosed) shadow of triangulated desire falls across Emilia's report.

The importance of this critical moment in the play has been sharply illuminated by Bradshaw: one "effect of Emilia's report is to make Desdemona's subsequent appeals in 3.3 redundant, and even offensive"; another "is to suggest how, at this crucial moment, Othello is to be the victim not only of his ensign's brilliantly malignant improvisations but also of the two people he most 'loves' and trusts." Had Cassio abandoned "his (or Iago's) plan of involving Desdemona as soon as he heard Emilia's report . . . the play, or the play Iago is now staging, would stop."[19] Since, as Bradshaw notes, Emilia's use of the present progressive tense indicates that the discussion she reports occurs as she speaks,[20] Desdemona must just have come from her talk with Othello when she opens 3.3 by greeting Cassio with the promise that "I will do / All my abilities in thy behalf."

Bradshaw's analysis makes what follows even stranger. In spite of the good news Cassio hears from Emilia, and in spite of "Othello's insistence that . . . [Desdemona's] role as 'Suitor' is . . . inappropriate," both Cassio and Desdemona persist.[21] First, Cassio implores Emilia to set up an interview "with Desdemona alone" (3.1.53–54). The interview takes place after the brief interval of a seven-line scene guarantees it will be undisturbed by showing Othello on his way to work. Desdemona vows to make Othello's life miserable until he agrees to reinstate Cassio: "Thy solicitor shall rather die / Than give thy cause away" (3.3.27–28). As Bradshaw notes, these requests and assertions seem gratuitous and even perverse. Having been advised by Othello to butt out, Desdemona "encourages Cassio to believe that she is the general's general" and that his reinstatement depends on her success in "overcoming Othello's resistance with her own eager and relentless suit."[22] From this moment on, the trouble the trio make for themselves facilitates and exceeds the trouble Iago makes for them.

One reason the uncanniness of this episode may not have received the press it deserves is that critics have been too busy asking about two other odd features of the play: the uncertainty about the sexual relation between Desdemona and Othello, and the temporal anomalies that motivate the double time theory. These are of course closely interconnected. The two parts of the first question are, did they or didn't they have sex, and, if they did, when did it first happen? The second question is motivated by a concern for at least minimal psychological realism: unless Othello is totally mad, it would have to be possible for him to believe that there had been time and opportunity for the illicit affair to develop. Therefore, even though Shakespeare presents "an unbroken series of events happening in 'short time,'" it would be necessary for him "to present them against a background of events not presented but implied, which gives the needed impression of 'long time.'"[23] Specifically, a longer period of time than the play suggests must have elapsed between the events of acts 3–5 and those of 1–2. Reduced to its essentials, which I give in Joel Altman's paraphrase, the original justification for the theory was that "long time is needed to convince the audience that what Othello imagines has taken place could have taken place; short time is needed to make Othello's gullibility credible."[24]

Altman briefly discusses and dismisses the genetic theory Ned B. Allen cooked up to account for the inconsistencies.[25] Allen speculated that Shakespeare first wrote acts 3–5, largely based on material from the source tale by Cinthio, and then wrote acts 1–2, in which he introduced new and discrepant material not found in the source; that he intended to integrate the two parts by revising acts 3–5 in terms of "the new idea he was using" in acts 1–2; but that he never got around to it because he assumed the discrepancies wouldn't "destroy the illusion of reality" when the play was staged.[26] The idea of writing the play backwards suggested to Jay Halio that if the play were read backwards, acts 1–2 would provide a moral commentary "on the action that Shakespeare presents in acts 3–5."[27] In his much more rigorous and imaginative account, Altman demonstrates the needlessness of the Allen hypothesis by analyzing the signs of Shakespeare's "careful preparation for the transition into acts 3–5."[28] But Halio's idea of reading the play backwards remains attractive on other grounds, and I'll take that up in the next section.

From the belated disclosure in 3.3 augmented by Othello's narrative to the Duke and Senators in 1.3, we can establish a simple sequence of events in the play's prehistory, a sequence that tells us all we need to know without having to resort to complex time schemes.[29] First, Othello met Desdemona while visiting Brabantio and regaling him with the stories that she, eavesdropping, devoured "with a greedy ear" (1.3.150–51). Second, Othello seems to have taken up the suggestion she coyly made while sighing over his stories (1.3.164–67) and invited a friend to help him woo her. Third, in 1.1 Iago expresses anger because Othello promoted Cassio instead of him. Between the first and second event as well as between the second and third, no specific periods or relations of time are, or need to be, given. We learn from Othello that Cassio "went between us very oft" and "was of my counsel / In my whole course of wooing" (3.3.100, 114–15). But we know neither how long after the reported period of early encounters with Desdemona the wooing began nor how long it went on. Weeks? Months? It isn't important. Causal relevance trumps chronology. The lack of temporal indications allows enough flexibility and latitude to obviate the need for a special theory of time without which Othello's susceptibility to jealousy would be improbable.

The double time theory is therefore a distorted response. But it is a response to a real problem. Critics who solicit its assistance to make sense of inconsistencies overlook the pattern of multiple disorientations produced by the belatedness of the disclosure. This confers primacy on an entirely different structure of temporality, not double time but inverted time, that is, *preposterity,* or the preposterous, in which what happens later is treated as the cause of what it follows—the radicalization and consequence of the critique of the interpretive method generated by commitment to the logic of *post hoc ergo propter hoc*. The various aspects of this structure have been brilliantly explored by Altman and Patricia Parker.[30] They focus on the grammatical, rhetorical, logical, genealogical, and chronological aspects of the preposterous—on linguistic, causal, and temporal inversions exemplified in hysteron proteron, metalepsis, and the larger structures of deconstructive historiography, or "genealogy," associated with Nietzsche and Foucault. In what follows, my indebtedness to Altman and Parker will be obvious. But my attention will be directed toward another aspect of *Othello*'s preposterous structure: the reinterpretation, necessitated by the disclosure in 3.3, of everything that occurred before it. Why does it surface so belatedly and briefly, and then disappear, as if it has done its work? But what *is* its work? Is it only Iago who was looking for the opening it provides?

The idea that Othello is in Cassio's debt for premarital services shines a new light on his jumpy reaction to seeing Cassio leave Desdemona a few lines earlier. Retroactively it invites us to reconsider earlier moments in the play. Cassio's laconic performance in his first appearance in 1.2, for example, provides an interesting contrast to Iago's spirited high jinks. Like 1.1, the scene begins in medias res with Iago inveighing against the animosity toward Othello of some unidentified "he"—whom we assume to be either Roderigo or Brabantio—and then warning Othello that Brabantio is out to get him. Othello is in the midst of defending his pedigree with studied diffidence and hauteur when Cassio makes his first appearance, along "with Officers and torches." He tells Othello that the Duke and Senate require his presence "haste-post-haste" concerning some news from Cyprus. But as soon as he enters, and before he can say a word, Iago brilliantly sees and seizes an opportunity for mischief. He misidentifies Cassio's party as Brabantio's—"Those are the raised father and his friends" (1.2.29)—thus removing Cassio from the martial to the marital context and from the party of Othello's public supporters to the party of his private enemies. This wicked misdirection is underlined twenty-five lines later, when Brabantio's party does indeed appear, again "with Officers and torches."

Since Cassio adds to his message from the Duke the news that "three several quests" have been sent to find Othello (1.2.36–38 and 39–47), his must be the first of the three parties to make contact. Presumably, this is because he knew where to look. Othello responds, "'Tis well I am found by you," that is, "by *you* rather than the others" outside the lovers' trysting place. This suggests that Cassio is in on the secret he pretends to hide (1.2.47). Othello then exits, and Cassio turns to Iago with a series of questions that my reading of the Girardian plot makes me construe as disingenuous and intended to forestall any suspicion of his complicity in the elopement: "Ancient, what makes he here?"; "I do not understand"; married "To whom?"[31] Cassio speaks once more in this scene: as the group headed by Brabantio and Roderigo enter, again "with Officers and torches," he tells Othello, "Here comes another troop to seek for you" (1.2.54).[32] Cassio surely knows why. He then falls silent until 2.1.

That silence is especially noticeable in 1.3. Cassio is listed among those who enter at line 48 in both Quarto and Folio.[33] Brabantio, Othello, Iago, Roderigo, and Officers are the others. Cassio remains onstage during most of the scene. He is onstage, for example, when Othello exploits the inability topos in order to distinguish his soldierly self from the run of Venetian suitors:

> . . . Rude am I in my speech
> And little blest with the soft phrase of peace,
>
> . . . .
>
> And therefore little shall I grace my cause
> In speaking for myself. . . .
>
> (1.3.81–89)

"The soft phrase of peace" denotes a facility easy to associate with what the perplexed Brabantio referred to earlier as "the wealthy, curled darlings of our nation" (1.2.68) whom Desdemona unaccountably rejected for Othello. Here the opposition is between the rudeness of the simple unspoiled soldier and the decadence of overcivilized and "super subtle" Venetians. This changes later when Othello speculates on the motives for Desdemona's unfaithfulness: his blackness, age, and lack of "those soft parts of conversation that chamberers have" (3.3.268-69). The echo retroactively brings out the blade sheathed in the euphemism, "the soft phrase of peace," and redirects it toward its initially hidden target, Cassio.

At 1.3.115 Othello asks the Duke and Senate to bring Desdemona from "the Sagittary" so that she may verify his account, and when the Duke gives the order Othello turns to Iago with "Ancient, conduct them, you best know the place." Does he know the trysting place better than Cassio does? Othello apparently would have the auditors on stage think so, and he apparently prefers to have Desdemona accompanied by Iago rather than Cassio, who was available for this assignment.[34] Of these episodes, it should be noted that Iago's mischief and misdirections are on the surface, but Othello's and Cassio's are not. Cassio is poker-faced in 1.2, the soul of discretion. He behaves strictly as an officer and state functionary. Until 2.1, our sense of him is too limited to allow us to assess the truth of the picture of unmanliness Iago drew for Roderigo in 1.1 or of his remark to the supervisors that Cassio "hath a person and a smooth dispose / To be suspected, framed to make women false" (1.3.396-97).

Perhaps the most startling of the retroactive changes produced by the disclosure occurs during Othello's confessional speech before the Duke and Senators (1.3.129-71), which I discuss on pp. 22-24. First, he says nothing about Cassio's mediation. Second, Cassio is among those on stage silently listening to the narrative from which his part has been elided. Third, Othello reports a request by Desdemona that resonates through the indirect discourse of his conveyance as demurely coquettish but that contains the germ of the go-between idea:

> She wished she had not heard it, yet she wished
> That heaven had made her such a man. She thanked me
> And bade me, if I had a friend that loved her,
> I should but teach him how to tell my story
> And that would woo her.
>
> (1.3.163-67)

As reported by Othello, Desdemona's "if I had a friend that loved her" seems at first glance to be similar in tone to her wish "That heaven had made her such a man." Both statements are coyly distanced acknowledgments that Othello is on the right track: his wooing is having its effect. But, since the statements are Othello's, they register his apprehension, repeated later in the scene, that she is more than half the wooer (1.3.261-75). The optative playfulness in which his report invests her suggestions doesn't prevent them from sounding like suavely aggressive innuendoes. This investment conforms with the general diffidence Othello displays in his utterances in 1.3: an anxiety about her forwardness, an effort to protect or at least dissociate himself from her frank avowals of desire.

"She . . . bade me, if I had a friend," can be construed figuratively or literally: either, "she urged me to act as a friend to myself" (to do myself a favor) or else "she urged me to find a go-between." The former is obviously what Desdemona must have intended, since she referred to "a friend that loved *her*." The latter is a demonic inversion of the former, an erotic analogue of the lieutenancy whose potentially ironic structure has best been characterized by Julia Genster: "In choosing a subordinate a captain is, in effect, choosing a second self; he is empowering someone to play him, to be him in his absence."[35]

Had Desdemona intended the go-between suggestion to be taken literally, one would expect Othello to report her as saying and implying " 'if I [Othello] had a friend that loved *me*,' I should enlist him as my go-between." Oddly, then, and even perversely, Othello opted for the go-between plan in spite of the strange proviso, "a friend that loved her."[36] Or perhaps *because* of it? His decision produces the triangular instability that this proviso structurally and conventionally guarantees. The go-between will become the Friend/Rival whose threat reanimates Othello's potentiality to be victimized: defending against Desdemona's desire, he exposes himself to the danger of being betrayed and replaced by his courtly place-holder.

When the light of the disclosure is turned toward the first scene of act 2, it casts shadows over the good-natured banter and flirtation that precede Othello's entrance. The effects are at once subtle and devastating. As the venue shifts from Venice to the storm-battered isle of Cyprus, we learn that the storm has destroyed the Turkish fleet and separated the Venetian ships, one of which carries Othello, another Cassio, and a third Desdemona, Emilia, Iago, and Roderigo. Cassio enters first, followed by the company of four, whom he greets. He tenders Desdemona a respectful and slightly flowery greeting, then he salutes Iago ("Good ancient, you are welcome"), approaches Emilia to punctuate his "Welcome, mistress," with a kiss, and immediately turns to apologize to Iago: "Let it not gall your patience, good Iago, / That I extend my manners; 'tis my breeding / That gives me this bold show of courtesy." This initiates an episode of about one hundred lines of good-natured banter and flirtation that precedes Othello's entrance. At one point Desdemona and Cassio move upstage, and Cassio apparently redirects his extended manners from Emilia to Desdemona. According to the stage directions embedded in Iago's excited aside, they paddle palms and kiss fingers until Othello shows up: "He takes her by the palm. . . . Ay, smile upon her, do: . . . good, well kiss'd, . . . yet again, your fingers at your lips?" Sneering villainously at his pathetic victims, Iago whets his audience's appetite for the spider's inevitable triumph ("as little a web as this will ensnare as great a fly as Cassio," 168-69).

I imagine that the actors playing Cassio and Desdemona would exhibit the behavior Iago describes in gestures that are more restrained—more conventionally courtly—than his description. The idea that there may be something going on between Desdemona and Cassio is at first sight ridiculous: we tend to discount Iago's spidery glee as an outburst of irrational exuberance. You may well find Cassio's brief display of courtly palaver with Desdemona and Emilia strenuous, perhaps a little silly, but this tells you something about Othello. He sought advice from someone who has "those soft parts of conversation / That chamberers have"; someone to whose "smooth dispose" he entrusted gallantries he didn't consider himself either capable of or comfortable with. Cassio's boorish treatment of Bianca after the disclosure may be explicable in terms of the Venetian code that the play foregrounds. Nevertheless, it reflects on Othello's taste in go-betweens, and on his sense of what it would take to persuade Desdemona. He must think her vulnerable to the sort of solicitations Bianca responds to, at least up to the incident with the handkerchief in 4.1.

Returning to these scenes after the disclosure, we also take more notice when Cassio replies guardedly to the insinuations with which Iago ferrets out signs of his sexual desire for Desdemona (2.3.15-26). He refuses to speculate about the wedding night and insists on her modesty. Yet this diffidence *does* reflect his own tendency to describe her in romantic terms that conspicuously displace a response to her sexual attractiveness, as when his references to the "divine Desdemona" who is "our great captain's captain" receive an erotic charge from his subsequent references to Othello's "tall ship" and "quick pants in Desdemona's arms." The charge may owe no more to Cassio's self-representation as a man of extended manners than to her enjoyment in receiving compliments and commanding attention. Nevertheless, a stray note escapes from his reference to "our great captain's captain," a hint of courtly condescension, possibly a sidelong glance at Othello's uxoriousness. This is something Iago himself glances at directly, later on in the same scene, and it is an impression Othello had taken care to defend against in Venice.

The disclosure in 3.3 retroactively recasts Cassio's mild flirtation with Desdemona in Girardian terms: the familiarity, the intimacy, of the erotic triangle lingers on, even if only in the form of good-natured mimicry or fond memory. What Iago excitedly anticipates is something that has, in a sense, already happened.

But after his salacious account of their dumb-show is interrupted by the trumpet announcing Othello's arrival, the question of what may be going on between Cassio and Desdemona mutates into the related question of what may (or may not) be going on between Desdemona and Othello. This question sails into full view at their reunion when Desdemona meets Othello's "O my fair warrior!" with a more reserved "My dear Othello" and Othello comes back with a heady burst of runover lines that climax in a fantasy of *Liebestod:*

> If it were now to die
> 'Twere now to be most happy, for I fear
> My soul hath her content so absolute
> That not another comfort, like to this
> Succeeds in unknown fate.
>   (2.1.187–91)

Like to what? *What* is he talking about? Is he only expressing relief that they both made it through the storm? "Nothing good that happens to us in the future can match this orgasmic moment." What about the comfort of sex, the enjoyment of which they're still looking forward to at the beginning of 2.3? Beneath the intensity of expression is an ominous prospect that draws from Desdemona a mild rebuke: "The heavens forbid / But that our loves and comforts should increase, / Even as our days do grow." She sensibly redirects him toward a future of lovemaking, affection, and family life. Is that the anticlimax he fears?

Othello hurriedly acknowledges her correction ("Amen to that, sweet powers!") and blathers on: "I cannot speak enough of this content, / It stops me here, it is too much of joy," a too-much that irrupts in kisses: "And this, and this, the greatest discord be / That e'er our hearts shall make!" (198–99). But if this is said to his "fair warrior," and kisses are part of their warfare, shouldn't he look forward to greater and more pleasurable discord? Isn't that what it means to be "fast married" (1.2.11)? He calms down a few lines later, announces that the Turkish "wars are done," and assures Desdemona she will "be well desir'd in Cyprus."

This reunion occurs on a crowded stage before Montano, two Cyriots, Iago, Roderigo, Emilia, Othello's attendants—and Cassio. In other words, it isn't a private conversation but a public performance. Does Othello say what he feels or what he thinks he ought to say, what he has been taught to say? There are some family resemblances between his and Cassio's hyperbolic utterances to and about Desdemona in this scene. It's worth noting that we never see or hear Desdemona and Othello alone together until after the turning point in 3.3: for sixty-two lines of bitter talk in 4.2, and for eighty-three lines before he smothers her in 5.2. Prior to 4.2, their exchanges take place either in public with Cassio present (1.3, 2.1, 2.3) or in the domestic setting that always includes Emilia and sometimes Iago. The disclosure retroactively surrounds both the silent presence of Cassio in 1.3 and his speaking presence in 2.1 with the disquieting aura of the other silence he shares with Othello and Desdemona.

If, as Stanley Cavell argues, Othello has a use for Iago in 3.3, we learn from the disclosure in the same scene that he has had a use for Cassio since before the beginning of the play. He seems to have used Cassio both to stir up Desdemona's desire and to keep his own distance from it. He desires her desire but is troubled by it. The marks of his diffidence are clearly inscribed in the courtship account he gives the Senators, in 1.3.

Let's turn to that story and look at the strangely twisted tale of who does what to whom that unfolds between lines 146 and 156:

> Her father loved me, oft invited me,
> Still questioned me the story of my life
> From year to year—the battles, sieges, fortunes
> That I have passed.
> I ran it through, even from my boyish days
> To th' very moment that he bade me tell it,
> Wherein I spake of most disastrous chances,
>
> . . . .
>
> Wherein of antres vast and deserts idle,
> Rough quarries, rocks and hills whose heads touch heaven
> It was my hint to speak—such was my process—
> And of the cannibals that each other eat,
> The Anthropophagi, and men whose heads
> Do grow beneath their shoulders. This to hear
> Would Desdemona seriously incline,
> But still the house affairs would draw her thence,
> Which ever as she could with haste dispatch
> She'd come again, and with a greedy ear
> Devour up my discourse; which I, observing,
> Took once a pliant hour and found good means

To draw from her a prayer of earnest heart
That I would all my pilgrimage dilate,
Whereof by parcel she had something heard
But not intentively: I did consent. . . .

(1.3.129-56)

Here is a rough paraphrase of the critical section, the characterization of Desdemona's response beginning at line 146 ("This to hear . . ."): observing her "rapacious appetite" for my discourse, I found means to persuade her to implore me to retell the whole story, only parts of which her household chores had allowed her to hear; I then consented and was often able to beguile her of her tears with my accounts of one or another bad thing—"disastrous chances" (135)—that befell me in my youth.[37]

The unexpected vividness of the figure, "greedy ear," its reductiveness, its weight as a synecdoche, register a moment of recoil. It glances back to his mention in line 144 of "the cannibals that each other eat," and since Othello's language also betrays his complicity in taking advantage of Desdemona's appetite, it binds them closely together in mutual cannibalism. At least in the defiles of his rhetoric, their courtship falls under the shadow of the beast with two backs.

It is from this shadow that his narrative strives to escape by shifting the cause of their burgeoning desire from sexuality to stories: his prowess as a raconteur combined with vivid little sketches of himself as the victim of "most disastrous chances." These evoked from Desdemona not groans of lust but sighs of pity, a proper Aristotelian response by a proper Venetian lady seated next to a crackling fire as if in some novella by Henry James. Nevertheless, discernible beneath the appeal to the register of romance are traces of the fear of monstrosity that give the appeal the value of defensive sublimation. Othello uses his report to the Senators to continue dealing with the fear. But he only half succeeds. The triumphant noblesse oblige of "I did consent" comically disowns responsibility for the manipulativeness betrayed in the statement that it was *he* who "found good means / To draw from her" a request for more stories. A note of pride in his powers of narrative seduction is sounded by the phrase in line 157, "often did beguile her of her tears," and in lines 160-67 he savors his conquest by mimicking the labored coyness with which she archly invites him to pop the question.

What this performance registers is the speaker's sense of the deviousness and underlying horror of their mutual seduction, but a sense also of the gradual shift of power in which his narrative dilation strives both to satisfy and to domesticate the desires of her greedy ear, to redescribe their discourse in terms of prayer and pilgrimage. And all this happens with Cassio standing quietly by, along with Iago, whose subsequent comment on the performance is characteristically mordant and one-sided but contains a grain of truth: "Mark me with what violence she first loved the Moor, but for bragging and telling her fantastical lies—and will she love him still for prating? let not thy discreet heart think it" (2.1.220–23). An earlier comment, uttered in the soliloquy (quoted on p. 5) that concludes 1.3, floats one of the play's teasingly ambiguous pronominal references: "After some time to abuse Othello's ear / That *he* is too familiar with his wife" (1.3.394–95, my italics). In the context of Iago's planning, the referent of "he" is more likely to be Cassio than Othello. But the preceding interpretation suggests that whatever we think Iago intends to say, in the context of Othello's reaction to Desdemona's greedy ear, the "he" drifts in his direction.[38]

Looking back from 3.3, we're inclined to wonder about the silent presence of Cassio during this account, especially since the story Othello tells is selective and has a defensive function. More is involved in winning Desdemona than telling stories about himself in her father's house. Cassio's role in the courtship is not expressly mentioned. But it is clearly laid out, and it glides past like a dark shape when Othello reports Desdemona's suggestion about a friend who could be taught to tell his story. Cassio listens silently. And at the end of the scene Othello chooses Iago and Emilia rather than Cassio to escort Desdemona to Cyprus.

"If she confess that she was half the wooer," Brabantio states when Desdemona appears, his "bad blame" will not fall on Othello: if she is half the wooer, the blame is wholly hers (1.3.175–78). And she proclaims from the start that she was and still is half the wooer. Critics who argue that Othello subscribes to Brabantio's misogynist article of faith are partly right: his language represents him representing her (to himself) as half the wooer. It already glances at the pornographic fantasy Iago will concoct later. It registers his fear of the desire—hers more than his—that could jeopardize his effort to escape the stigma of the Venetian stereotype of the "lascivious Moor."

That he is the sole object of Desdemona's desire and she is so eager to publish the fact only makes matters worse. She insists on accompanying Othello to Cyprus because if she should be left behind when he goes to war, "The rites for which I love him are bereft me" (1.3.248, 257). Even as Othello seconds her request, he's at pains to emphasize that the sexual "will" motivating the request is hers, not his, and the very phrase he later uses to affirm her faithfulness also reaffirms his insistence that Desdemona of the greedy ear was the primary mover in their relation: "For she had eyes and chose me" (3.3.192). I think Nuttall was the first to argue that this is what throws Othello off balance and perplexes him "in the extreme."[39] In Cavell's words, Othello is surprised "at what he has elicited from her. . . . Rather than imagine himself to have elicited that, or solicited it, . . . [he] would imagine it elicited by anyone and everyone else."[40] It's the role he imagines for Cassio, the role he had, so to speak, *pre*selected Cassio to play in choosing him as go-between and advocate. Cassio is his alibi, ready in the wings along with honest Iago should the need arise for Othello to persuade himself it wasn't he who stained her.

Cassio, Iago, Othello: this too is a Girardian triangle, one of envy rather than jealousy, with Othello choosing, apparently arbitrarily, to promote the outsider Cassio instead of Iago. But the choice was arbitrary only to Iago. His exposition in 1.1 suggests that Othello gave Cassio his commission during roughly the same period that Cassio was his go-between and second in the courtship. But did Othello choose Cassio as his officer before or after he chose him as a go-between? The implications both in Iago's irritable report and in Othello's account of the courtship suggest that he was a go-between before Othello gave him his commission. The disclosure throws an ironic shadow over Iago's complaint in 1.1 that Othello "Nonsuits my mediators" (1.1.15–16). Iago didn't know that Othello has a mediator of his own to reward.

This scenario is supported by positional logic. A lieutenant is second in command and a substitute or "placeholder" roughly comparable in the domain of Mars to that of the second or go-between in the domain of Venus. The difference is that in the military hierarchy the lieutenant is safely subordinate to his superior—there can be no rivalry between them—but the suitor's friend is traditionally, notoriously, a site of concealed rivalry and betrayal. I think it's interesting that the triangle, Cassio/Iago/Othello, is featured by Iago in skewed form after the disclosure. For Othello's benefit, he pictures himself in bed with the sleeping Cassio who kissed him and boarded him because he dreamed Iago was Desdemona. Iago as Othello's beloved getting screwed by Cassio; Iago, soon after, replacing both Desdemona and Cassio in Othello's affection and being rewarded with a field commission, albeit a commission in the wrong field: "I greet

thy love . . . with acceptance bounteous. . . . Now thou art my lieutenant."
Iago submits: "I am your own for ever" (3.3.472-73, 481-82). As Genster finely puts it, they celebrate "their newly wrought alliance as sexual
avengers within the structures of military rank,"[41] a comment that reminds
us "Othello's occupation" has been revived—again in the wrong field, the
field of domestic warfare in which his new lieutenant has also appropriated
the spousal role. Toward the end of the play when Iago says, "I bleed, sir, but
not killed" (5.2.285), he strangely represents himself as a truer Desdemona,
one whom Othello has deflowered but lets live.

At the beginning of this essay I said that Iago doesn't merely do things *to*
Desdemona and Othello; the things he does *to* them he does with their
help. In conclusion, I want to suggest that if this is true, if what he does
to them he also does *for* them, then it follows that what they do *for* him
they also do *to* him. What they do *to* him is reflected in the sequence of his
soliloquies. In the first two, which I briefly discuss on pp. 7-8, his worries
about being cuckolded are so obviously off the wall that I find it hard to
take them as personal complaints rather than as mimicry of the structure of
suspicion and castration known in Venice as manhood. The play shows us a
Venetian culture dominated by a misogynist discourse governing relations
between men and women, fathers and daughters, and wives and husbands,
in and out of marriage. At this point, Iago isn't airing his own suspicion
so much as making fun of the insecurity of Venetian males in general—the
sexual and proprietary insecurity of husbands and fathers in a culture that
promotes the distrust of wives and women.

   Things change after the fateful disclosure in 3.3. Iago begins to question Othello shortly after Desdemona mentions it. By the time he leaves
the stage some 150 lines later, Othello shows himself ready to supplant
him by stepping up to the platea and batting out the first of *his* three
soliloquies. But Iago now faces more than one competitor in this practice.
Othello's soliloquy segues into the handkerchief episode that leaves Emilia
standing alone on the platea armed with the power of soliloquy, with the
handkerchief, and with knowledge of its meaning. Her protracted silence,
her protracted lying, is the power behind Iago's throne from 3.3 to the
play's last scene.[42] This thought throws a strange backlight on the diabolical
chortles of the soliloquy he delivers after she gives him the handkerchief
and he dismisses her. The dismissal is curt: "Be not acknown on't, / I

have use for it. Go, leave me" (3.3.322-23). He wants to be alone with his supervisors so that he can inform, instruct, and entertain them:

> *I will in Cassio's lodging lose this napkin*
> *And let him find it.* Trifles light as air
> Are to the jealous confirmations strong
> As proofs of holy writ. *This may do something.*
> *The Moor already changes with my poison:*
> Dangerous conceits are in their natures poisons
> Which at the first are scarce found to distaste
> But with a little art upon the blood
> Burn like the mines of sulphur.
>
> [Enter OTHELLO]
>
>   I did say so:
> Look, where he comes. Not poppy nor mandragora
> Nor all the drowsy syrups of the world
> Shall ever medicine thee to that sweet sleep
> Which thou owedst yesterday.
>
> (3.3.324-36, my italics)

This is Iago at his most pompous: each of the two italicized statements—one voicing an intention and the other an observation—is followed by a pedantic little gloss instructing the supervisors in the fine points of the psychology of jealousy. When the already devastated victim rages into view, the villain commends his own insight ("I did say so") and points to the evidence of his art ("Look, where he comes"). He then melodramatically turns from the supervisors to Othello and shows them the proper way for villains to spook their victims.

Although it has the self-satisfied ring of the master villain this little performance feels gratuitous, feels like overkill, for two reasons. The first is that Iago depends, and will continue to depend, more on Emilia's complicity than he knows. The second is the shadow cast on Iago's platea strut by the belated discovery of Cassio's role. We now know that of the four major characters, Iago was the only one who was out of the loop up to the moment of discovery, and that during the time he was out of the loop, he was playing the villain in the most outrageous and engaging manner.[43] The soliloquies delivered before the discovery are both more sustained and more conclusive. Three of them end scenes, four terminate in couplets, and all have more rhetorical juice and spirit in them than the last five. The latter are shorter and seem more hurried, partly because Iago is trying hard to keep up with the different plots he has going, and partly because he gets interrupted by other characters—Othello in the one just discussed and Cassio in the next three.

The same combination of spookery and sententiousness animates the sixth soliloquy, which is uttered in grotesque circumstances. After Iago has mercilessly trashed Othello and all but reduced him to the horned blabberer and goatish monster he most fears to be, Othello falls into a trance and Iago seizes this opportunity to favor the supervisors with a brief sample of Doctor Evil's mumbo jumbo followed by another of the cynical bromides he periodically recycles for their edification:

> Work on,
> My medicine, work! Thus credulous fools are caught,
> And many worthy and chaste dames even thus,
> All guiltless, meet reproach.—What ho! My lord!
> My lord, I say, Othello![44]
>
> [*Enter CASSIO.*]
>
> How now, Cassio?
>
> (4.1.44–48)

This hand-rubbing assertion of malignant agency is a bid for the kind of approbation poor Othello in fact bestows on him several lines later. After Iago belabors him with such morale-building recommendations as "Would you would bear your fortune like a man!" and "Good sir, be a man" (4.1.61, 65),[45] he congratulates him for having escaped (thanks to Iago's vigilance) the plight of the millions of cuckolds who are unaware their wives are cheating on them (4.1.65–72). To this Othello gratefully replies, "O, thou art wise, 'tis certain" (4.1.74). The only thing more embarrassing than Othello's abjectness is Iago's obvious relish in laying it on well beyond necessity. But according to the principle of redistributed complicities, Iago's bullying may be considered compensatory if indeed, as I've been arguing, Othello has been "working on" Iago to get himself undone since early in act 3. From this standpoint, even the Folio stage direction, "Falls in a trance," suggests the transitivity of a self-induced breakdown that catachrestically figures the process he has been using Iago to facilitate.

The seventh soliloquy is especially interesting in dramatic terms because of the way it is contextualized. Preparing to set Othello up with his Cassio-Bianca charade, Iago instructs him to assume the supervisors' position as an eavesdropper:

> . . . Do but encave yourself
> And mark the fleers, the gibes and notable scorns
> That dwell in every region of his face;
> For I will make him tell the tale anew
>
> (4.1.82-85)

Once again, he concludes by inviting his interlocutor to leave: "Will you withdraw?" (4.1.93). He then turns so eagerly to the real supervisors that the invitation to withdraw seems motivated primarily by impatience to get back to his fans and impress them not only with his latest brainstorm but also with his deep insight into the folly of strumpets:

> Now will I question Cassio of Bianca,
> A housewife that by selling her desires
> Buys herself bread and clothes; it is a creature
> That dotes on Cassio—as 'tis the strumpet's plague
> To beguile many and be beguiled by one.
> He, when he hears of her, cannot refrain
> From the excess of laughter. Here he comes.
>
> [*Enter CASSIO.*]
>
> As he shall smile, Othello shall go mad.
> And his unbookish jealousy must construe
> Poor Cassio's smiles, gestures and light behavior
> Quite in the wrong. How do you now, lieutenant?
>
> (4.1.94-104)

The supervisors must enjoy his calling Cassio "lieutenant" as much as Cassio hates it—"the addition / Whose want even kills me" (4.1.105-6). For Iago the crowning moment of this interlude occurs when Othello hears Bianca mention the handkerchief and believes he has all but seen the "ocular proof" (147-56). But because Cassio independently repeats an idiom Emilia introduced, "take out the work," and Bianca angrily echoes it, we're freshly reminded at this crucial moment that the silent Emilia retains the power behind the villain's throne, the power she gained access to when Othello and Desdemona "lost" the handkerchief and themselves with it.

Iago's penultimate soliloquy differs from those it follows because the circumstances of its delivery are barely under his control, and even the directions for staging it are underindicated. In addition, he has to share the platea with, of all people, Roderigo, who dares to soliloquize for three lines before the villain reclaims his rightful place and tells the supervisors

Roderigo must die. Act 5 begins with Iago positioning a reluctant Roderigo
for the attack on Cassio.

> RODERIGO
> I have no great devotion to the deed
> And yet he hath given me satisfying reasons:
> 'Tis but a man gone. Forth, my sword: he dies.
> IAGO
> I have rubbed this young quat almost to the sense
> And he grows angry. Now whether he kill Cassio
> Or Cassio him, or each kill the other,
> Every way makes my gain. Live Roderigo,
> He calls me to a restitution large
> Of gold and jewels that I bobbed from him
> As gifts to Desdemona:
> It must not be. If Cassio do remain
> He hath a daily beauty in his life
> That makes me ugly; and besides, the Moor
> May unfold me to him—there stand I in much peril.
> No, he must die. Be't so! I hear him coming.
>   [*Enter CASSIO.*]
>   (5.1.8–22)

Since no exits are marked in either the Quarto or Folio texts, each of
the successive soliloquies is apparently delivered with the other speaker
present (at a distance) but not listening. This setup conveys an impression
of permeable and therefore insecure boundaries that affects the tone and
development of Iago's speech. The speech itself seems less like a bravura
performance than its predecessors and more like a harried series of rapid-
fire assessments and decisions. He begins by expressing a concern about
Roderigo, which he then shrugs off, but the mood darkens when a pair
of conditional utterances, "if either Roderigo or Cassio lives I stand to
lose," leads to the obvious conclusion, "both must die." This soliloquy lacks
the performative high spirits that marked Iago's previous addresses to the
supervisors. He speaks as if he has painted himself into a corner. And he
strikes a new note with the first of the two reasons he gives the supervisors
for deciding to kill Cassio: "He hath a daily beauty in his life / That makes
me ugly." Why at this juncture does he so oddly identify himself with his
victim and appropriate Othello's deepest feeling as his own?

In the hugger-mugger that follows, he seems on the verge of losing control of the situation. Roderigo botches his assignment and gets wounded

by Cassio, whom Iago then stabs but fails to kill. With the arrival of
Lodovico and Gratiano, he regains his form, suavely orchestrates the death
of Roderigo and rescue of Cassio, and is joined by Emilia for a brief moment
of bonding (their last) at Bianca's expense. But the scene ends in a rush
with Iago sending his companions off in different directions:

> Kind gentlemen, let's go see poor Cassio dressed.
> Come, mistress, you must tell's another tale.
> Emilia run you to the citadel
> And tell my lord and lady what hath happed.
> Will you go on afore?
>
> (5.1.124-27)

"Will you go on afore" (or the Quarto variant, "Will you go on, I pray?")
expresses polite impatience—compare the use of the hortatory idiom,
"Please," to usher others out—as he hurries them off in the hopes of
squeezing in a quick communiqué to the supervisors, his ninth and last
and shortest soliloquy: "This is the night / That either makes me or fordoes
me quite" (128-29).[46] Anticipation or deflation, the matter is out of his
hands; he can do no more.

As if to celebrate the success that induced this failure, Othello at this
moment all but shoulders Iago aside as he thunders on stage with his
second and most resonant soliloquy: "It is the cause, it is the cause, my
soul!" (5.2.1). Compare the mad and unwaveringly murderous force of "Yet
she must die, else she'll betray more men" (5.2.6) with the plaintive and
calculating tone of

> If Cassio do remain
> He hath a daily beauty in his life
> That makes me ugly; and besides, the Moor
> May unfold me to him—there stand I in much peril.
> No, he must die.
>
> (5.1.18-22)

Iago has lost the supervisors, the power of soliloquy has shifted to Othello,
and by the end of the play the villain is reduced to the figure of castration
he had initially mocked. Because he cannot get Emilia to keep silent,
he threatens her with his sword. And if we follow the Quarto stage
direction a few lines later—"*The Moore runnes at* Iago. Iago *kils his
wife*"—the prescribed action is fuzzy enough to make Honigmann think

Iago stabs Emilia while trying to avoid Othello (5.2.223–32). However you visualize it, it's a copycat crime and signifies the disempowerment already demonstrated by Othello killing Desdemona. Iago's subsequent "I bleed, sir, but not killed" (5.2.285) is taunting but tinny, pert but puerile: he sticks out his tongue as if to say "you missed." But rustling within that retort is the shade of the wounded Cassio, the shade of Desdemona's desire to bleed and live. He declines into the position of the morality Vice, but with a difference. The Vice is not merely a maverick individual but the embodiment of cultural norms of evil. The wickedness this figure represents is not his own but everyone else's. Shakespeare inserts the villain into this position in such a way as to set up an ironic structure of agency. He transforms the idea that the Vice *represents* everyone else's evil desires and purposes into the idea that the villain *is empowered* by them, but empowered in a such a way as to be disempowered. He is undone, his claim to autonomy compromised, by the efficiency with which his victims have used him to undo themselves. And even Iago's last defiant stand undoes itself: "Demand me nothing. What you know, you know. / From this time forth I never will speak word" (5.2.300–301). Mum's the model housewife's word.

But there's nothing to demand. Victims and survivors, the dead and the quick, know everything he knows. And yet—it was all so easy. There must be so much more to know than he knows. Surely Othello and Desdemona, and maybe Emilia, know things he doesn't know. He must have done something not only *to* them but also *for* them, something they got him to do to and for them.

They must have had a use for him.

They must have used him.

Notes

Epigraphs at the beginning of the essay are from Mikhail Bakhtin, *The Dialogic Imagination: Four Essays by M. M. Bakhtin,* trans. Caryl Emerson and Michael Holquist (Austin: University of Texas Press, 1981), 294–95, and Howard Felperin, *Shakespearean Representation: Mimesis and Modernity in Elizabethan Drama* (Princeton: Princeton University Press, 1977), 75–76.

1. The sort of argument I have in mind is well exemplified by Brian Vickers's theoretically sophisticated but dramatically simplistic reading of the play in *Appropriating Shakespeare: Contemporary Critical Quarrels* (New Haven: Yale University Press, 1993), 74–91. "Lunkhead" is Stanley Cavell's term: Stanley Cavell, *Disowning Knowledge in Six Plays of*

Shakespeare (Cambridge: Cambridge University Press, 1988), 133. But Cavell introduces it in the course of denying that it is applicable to Othello, whereas Vickers—in a mean-minded critique of Cavell's *Othello* essay (*Appropriating Shakespeare,* 308-20)—asserts merely that Cavell "calls Othello" a lunkhead.

2. William Shakespeare, *Othello,* ed. E. J. A. Honigmann, Arden Shakespeare Third Series (Walton-on-Thames, Surrey: Thomas Nelson and Sons, 1997). All references to the play are to this edition unless otherwise noted.

3. See William Shakespeare, *King Lear,* ed. Kenneth Muir, Arden Shakespeare First Series (Cambridge: Harvard University Press, 1959), 3.2.59-60.

4. Since one expects "I am not what I seem," "I am not what I am" doesn't merely replace it but is defined by it: "what I seem *is* what I am."

5. On the needy actor as a model, see in general Meredith Skura's remarkable *Shakespeare the Actor and the Purposes of Playing* (Chicago: University of Chicago Press, 1993). On the meaning and significance of the *platea* and the *locus* as, respectively, a downstage area reserved for interactions between characters and an upstage area where self-contained action among fictional characters occurs, see Robert Weimann, *Shakespeare and the Popular Tradition in the Theater: Studies in the Social Dimension of Dramatic Form and Function,* ed. Robert Schwartz (Baltimore: Johns Hopkins University Press, 1978), 73-85 and passim. See also my "The Prince's Dog: Falstaff and the Perils of Speech-Prefixity," *Shakespeare Quarterly* 49 (1998): 40-73, esp. 47-50.

6. Vickers, *Appropriating Shakespeare,* 79.

7. A. D. Nuttall, *A New Mimesis: Shakespeare and the Representation of Reality* (London: Methuen, 1983), 143.

8. See Marvin Rosenberg, *The Masks of Othello: The Search for the Identity of Othello, Iago, and Desdemona by Three Centuries of Actors and Critics* (Berkeley: University of California Press, 1961), 168-69.

9. Verse soliloquies: 1.3.381-403, 2.1.284-310, 2.3.45-60, 2.3.331-57 and 377-83, 3.3.324-36, 4.1.44-48, 4.1.94-104, 5.1.11-22, 5.1.129-30. The two prose asides occur at 2.1.167-78 and 2.1.198-200. Arden 3 and the 1622 Quarto format the second aside as verse, but I follow the Folio in treating it as prose.

10. "As I do now" is just too much, a self-delighting metatheatrical twinkle best uttered in a tone that makes it a deictic comment on the high-toned spookery it follows.

11. I wouldn't make too much of the oft-noted presence of "hell" and "demon" in the protagonists' names. They are caricature signifiers. But there they are.

12. A dance, incidentally, that gets performed in the shifting shadows of another triangle, the one in which Desdemona vies with her father for Othello's attention.

13. René Girard, *A Theater of Envy: William Shakespeare* (New York: Oxford University Press, 1991), 290.

14. See, for example, the interview with Girard published in *Diacritics* 8(1) (Spring 1978): 31-54; Toril Moi, "The Missing Mother: The Oedipal Rivalries of René Girard," *Diacritics* 12(2) (Summer 1982), 21-31; Eve Kosofsky Sedgwick, *Between Men: English Literature and Male Homosocial Desire* (New York: Columbia University Press, 1985), 21-27 and passim.

15. Graham Bradshaw, *Misrepresentations: Shakespeare and the Materialists* (Ithaca, N.Y.: Cornell University Press, 1993), 160. And if it is news to Iago, it is also news to Emilia.

16. Space doesn't permit discussion of such prior triangular complications as Othello's threat to the bond between Brabantio and Desdemona and Desdemona's threat to the bond between Brabantio and Othello.

17. That Iago carried this plan out is indicated by Emilia's remark at 3.3.3–4: Cassio's plight "grieves my husband / As if the cause were his."

18. In view of subsequent developments centered on the handkerchief, it's worth noting that Emilia's complicity with Iago and distance from Othello is suggested here when she follows Iago in referring to Othello as "the Moor."

19. Bradshaw, *Misrepresentations,* 174–75.

20. Ibid., 149–50.

21. Ibid., 175.

22. Ibid. Strictly speaking, what Desdemona promotes and Othello resists is not reinstatement per se but simply a face-to-face interview.

23. M. R. Ridley, *Othello,* Arden 2 (1965; repr. London: Methuen, 1971), lxx.

24. Joel B. Altman, " 'Preposterous Conclusions': Eros, *Enargeia,* and the Composition of *Othello,*" *Representations* 18 (Spring 1987): 145.

25. Ned B. Allen, "The Two Parts of 'Othello,' " *Shakespeare Survey* 21 (1968): 13–29.

26. Ibid., 20.

27. Jay L. Halio, "Reading *Othello* Backwards," in *Othello: New Critical Essays,* ed. Philip C. Kolin (Routledge: New York, 2002), 391. Halio tries to show that Othello's behavior in 1.2–3 establishes "a standard of behavior and judgment for a satisfactory and just resolution of conflict," and the question then becomes, "why does Othello fail to act later according to those procedures he had followed earlier and in fact himself helped to establish?" (395).

28. Altman, " 'Preposterous Conclusions,' " 146–48.

29. Bradshaw argues compellingly that it can't be rationalized in terms of the theory of the double time scheme, which, he demonstrates, is redundant: *Misrepresentations,* 156–63.

30. Altman, " 'Preposterous Conclusions,' " 129–57; Patricia Parker, *Shakespeare from the Margins: Language, Culture, Context* (Chicago: University of Chicago Press, 1996), chap. 1, esp. 48–52. See also the related discussion of "dilation" in *Othello* in chap. 7, esp. 248–52 and 268–70, and the earlier more expanded version of these pages in "Shakespeare and Rhetoric: 'Dilation' and 'Delation' in *Othello,*" in *Shakespeare and the Question of Theory,* ed. Parker and Geoffrey Hartman (New York: Methuen, 1985), 54–74.

31. "Certainly," Bradshaw notes, "no spectator watching the play for the first time could know that Cassio has reason to be discreet when he asks, 'To who?' " (*Misrepresentations,* 157).

32. Whether or not we're supposed to assume this is one of the three "quests" sent by the Duke and Senate is not clear. The Duke's subsequent impatience with Brabantio and insistence that he not interfere with state matters suggest that Brabantio's "quest" is a fourth party.

33. His name is oddly omitted by Muir in the New Penguin edition.

34. Cassio's departure from the stage is not specified in either Quarto or Folio. We can be sure he leaves before Iago and Roderigo begin their scabrous conversation at 1.3.301. The "Exeunt" (Quarto) and "Exit" (Folio) indicated after Brabantio warns Othello that Desdemona will deceive him (1.3.294) are open (not followed by names) and thus encourage editorial

improvisation. Honigmann specifies "Duke, Brabantio, Senators, Officers," but not Cassio. The Folger edition adds Cassio to this group; Muir oddly omits Brabantio; McDonald leaves an opening for Cassio by adding "etc." This is probably a good moment for Cassio to exit. If he does, he will not hear Othello entrust Desdemona to Iago for the second time. But what if he remains and hears? He would certainly understand. But he would then have to exit at line 301 in the company of Othello and Desdemona (who are named in the Quarto but not in the Folio).

35. Julia Genster, "Lieutenancy, Standing In, and *Othello*," *English Literary History* 57 (1990): 786.

36. In Othello's version of this plan, as Desdemona implies in 3.3, he may have told Cassio his story but surely didn't teach him *how* to tell it.

37. The phrase "rapacious appetite" is borrowed from Stephen Greenblatt, *Renaissance Self-Fashioning: From More to Shakespeare* (Chicago: University of Chicago Press, 1980), 239.

38. The reference to Othello is most tellingly justified by Greenblatt, *Renaissance Self-Fashioning,* 233. For an excellent critique of responses to the passage see Edward Pechter, *Othello and Interpretive Traditions* (Iowa City, University of Iowa Press, 1998), 94-95.

39. Nuttall, *New Mimesis,* 138-39.

40. Cavell, *Disowning Knowledge,* 136.

41. Genster, "Lieutenancy, Standing In, and *Othello*," 788.

42. On Emilia's lying, that is, refusal to tell Othello and Desdemona about the handkerchief, see my "Impertinent Trifling: Desdemona's Handkerchief," *Shakespeare Quarterly* 47 (1996): 235-50.

43. Was Emilia in on this secret? If so, she apparently didn't tell Iago. But since the text gives no indication whether or not she knew of Cassio's role, and nothing rides on this question, there is no point speculating about it.

44. This is Honigmann's variant of the Folio version, which begins, "Worke on, / My Medicine workes." The difference between the two versions is that between incantation and exultation, Honigmann borrows the variant from the Quarto, which prints the passage in prose.

45. See also 4.1.78 ("A passion most unsuiting such a man") and 4.1.89-90 ("all in all in spleen / And nothing of a man").

46. Honigmann's Folio reading of the last two lines. The Quarto differs: "Will you go on, I pray? This is the night / That either marks me, or fordoes me quite."

The Social Logic of
Ben Jonson's Epicoene

ADAM ZUCKER

N EAR THE END of act 4 of Ben Jonson's *Epicoene* (1609), Dauphine, one
of the play's three heroes, is sized up by Lady Haughty, the dean of
a women's club known as the Collegiates: "He seems," she claims, "a very
perfect gentleman" (4.6.12).[1] Haughty's tastes are often bitterly ridiculed in
Epicoene, but here she issues a judgment that jibes neatly with those of the
play and its most privileged characters. With one unexpected gesture at the
end of act 5—the removal of a boy actor's wig—Dauphine reveals himself
to be the most perfect, powerful gentleman in the play's social world. The
action that inspires Lady Haughty's rather conventional compliment is similarly noteworthy. While being watched by a small sequestered audience
that includes Haughty, Dauphine doles out a series of kicks and tweaks
to two helplessly deceived characters who assume they are being abused
in private by one another. Having been told that Dauphine has personally
arranged the plot that permits these blows to go unpunished, the women
who witness his performance immediately turn their erotic attention to
him. Lady Haughty's pronouncement, then, uses the commonplace status
designation of "gentleman" to express an allocation of sexually invested
social power to Dauphine, and the scene as a whole works to establish
his position of privilege within the world of the play.[2] In and of itself,
this process is not remarkable: social identity is always partially a product
of the intersection between performance and interpretation, and in the
early modern period, status was often explicitly linked to material forms

of public appearance and behavior.[3] But as Dauphine's specific actions might suggest, Jonson's engagement with this process in *Epicoene* is far from routine. By what set of standards could tweaking a blindfolded man in the nose lead to the title of "perfect gentleman"? What sort of status is this?

In order to answer questions like these, it is necessary to look beyond the common analytical frameworks used to make sense of status difference in early modern London.[4] The most familiar methods of expressing and ordering the heterogeneous social relations of sixteenth- and seventeenth-century England are not up to the task: neither the traditional hierarchy of orders and degrees with its political and occupational rankings nor the economic categories of a more modern class-based understanding of status seem to have much to do with the logic that ratifies Dauphine's authority in *Epicoene*. Sirs John Daw and Amorous La Foole (the kicked and the tweaked, respectively) are, like Dauphine, titled; all three men are knights, and thus all possess a form of privileged political status. None of them work for wages, yet all maintain residences in a fashionable neighborhood in London; all three would thus seem to possess a form of privileged economic status.[5] But while Dauphine is a "perfect gentleman," it is obvious from the moment Daw and La Foole appear on stage that the social power that should adhere to their titles and incomes is completely absent. They are abject characters, and by the time audiences and readers reach act 4, the abuse Daw and La Foole receive at the hand (and foot) of Dauphine fits seamlessly into the comic imperatives of the play. A different sort of status formation is at work in *Epicoene*, a logic of social power that uses differences in taste, differences in cultural competence,[6] to supplement, compete with, and at times disguise the developing economic and political relations of early modern London.

The social logic set out in *Epicoene* is partially based on individuals' relationships to and within the vast field of acts, objects, spaces, and knowledge that constituted Jacobean urban culture. Jack Daw's lack of status, for example, is articulated through his aesthetic judgments and his literary ignorance: on the most basic level, he deserves to be kicked because he "pretends only to learning" (1.2.73). Early in the play, Clerimont and Dauphine goad Daw into a discussion of classical authors during which he first ridicules Seneca and Plutarch as "Grave asses! Mere essayists!" (2.3.46) then runs through a catalog of no fewer than twenty other authors in order to dismiss them (53–65). The responses of the gallants to this list are telling:

> DAUPHINE
> What a sackful of their names he has got!
> CLERIMONT
> And how he pours them out! Politian with Valerius Flaccus!
>
> (2.3.66–67)

Daw ends up seeming foolish for two obvious reasons. First of all, he has bad taste, or, at least, he has standards that are so indiscriminately negative that they seem to be no standards at all. Second, he is unable to arrange knowledge into historical categories; the gallants rip into him for including Politian, a fifteenth-century humanist, in a list of classical authors. But beyond these academic quibbles, Dauphine and Clerimont also attack Daw through metaphor; they figure his relationship to culture as one of blind accumulation. Authors' names become commodities in a sack, goods to be poured out and displayed as the occasion arises. When Dauphine asks Daw which writers he appreciates as "authors," he responds with a sequence of four titles, three in Latin and one, "The King of Spain's Bible," in English, presumably to drive home the joke to audience members with small Latin (73–74). Daw's already benighted status is further degraded as it becomes evident that he has misread the simplest material elements of print culture. In short, it is not bad enough that Daw commodifies knowledge—he can't even consume these commodities correctly.

Whereas John Daw fails to parlay into status his investment in early modern literary culture, the oft-praised Truewit is a mogul of taste. Instead of blindly accumulating and randomly displaying signs and commodities of sophistication, Truewit has an active relationship to them; he reworks knowledge for his own ends and, in doing so, sets himself apart from those who lack his performative skill. Take, for example, his cynical exhortations to Morose suggesting that suicide would be preferable to marriage (2.2.19–31). The Juvenalian source of this particular diatribe reads in part, "Can you submit to a she-tyrant [domina] when there is so much rope to be had, so many dizzy heights of windows standing open, and when the Aemilian bridge offers itself to your hand?"[7] Truewit's formulation recasts the arcane in familiar terms:

Marry, your friends do wonder sir, the Thames being so near, wherein you may drown handsomely; or London Bridge at a low fall with a fine leap, to hurry you

down the stream; or such a delicate steeple i' the town as Bow, to vault from; or a
braver height as Paul's.   (2.2.19-23)

A similar transformation takes place in Truewit's discourse on cosmetics
as he puts forth the Ovidian position that women, while they should do
everything in their power to enhance their appearance, must not let their
lovers see them preparing themselves (1.1.108-21; based on passages from
Ars Amatoria, III). But rather than merely letting Ovid speak for him,
Truewit supports a classical argument with a contemporary example:

How long did the canvas hang afore Aldgate? Were the people suffered to see the
city's *Love* and *Charity* while they were rude stone, before they were painted and
burnished? No. No more should servants approach their mistresses but when they
are complete and finished.   (1.1.116-21)

This urban refiguration of classical sentiment speaks to Truewit's improvisa-
tional skill, his capacity to resituate knowledge so as to make it rhetorically
useful; in short, it marks him as "witty" in all the ways that Daw fails to be.
And just as Daw's problems are partially based on his inappropriate relationship to the objects and exchanges of the print marketplace, Truewit's
status is inflected by the material city to which he constantly refers. His
claim to social power is signified by his ability to remap the rhetoric and
content of classical texts onto common social and physical topographies
of London.[8]

This observation runs counter to a line of reasoning that has—up until
quite recently—dominated analyses of the play's comic heroes.[9] Beginning
with John Dryden's claim that Truewit "seems mortified to the world by
much reading" and that "the best of his discourse is drawn not from the
knowledge of the town, but books,"[10] critics have tended to focus on
the ways in which Truewit and his cohorts are disconnected from the
day-to-day matrices of London life. One modern reader of *Epicoene* has
stressed the "playful detachment" of the gallants, noting their "indepen-
dence" from "all positions, values, and convictions";[11] another points out
that they have "no commitment to the larger social hierarchy of which
they are nominally a part";[12] a third distances the gallants from economic
relations by calling them "above mercenariness, mere gain" and goes on
to depoliticize their status, claiming, "The king might create a duke, but
not even he could create a gentleman."[13] By mystifying the link between
cultural competence—or "wit," as both the play and the majority of its

readers call it—and other kinds of social and economic relationships, claims like these reproduce one of the primary ideological fantasies of the play.[14] *Epicoene* is widely regarded to be the first "West End comedy," or the first play to deal exclusively with the concerns of "polite society." It is also, however, the first English play set in London to imagine that wit and taste might exist apart from or eclipse entirely other structures of city life that generate status. Contemporary critics, vested in well-developed forms of the cultural capital that was only beginning to emerge in Jonson's London, have tended to take this premise of the play at face value, treating tastefulness as a transparent sign of inherent status, or as a social form detached from the material world. But while Truewit's knowledge is drawn from books, this knowledge becomes socially functional in the play only when it is projected onto the familiar landmarks that structured Jacobean urban space. As the local details of Truewit and Daw's performances begin to suggest, wit, even in Jonson's fictional version of London, always has a material historical context.

Though this may seem to be a fairly self-evident point, the playful, offhanded quality of witty performance often works to mask the link between cultural competence and broader social relations, especially under the gaze of the tasteful literary critic. Jonas Barish, for example, an extremely skilled close reader of the play, argues that Truewit's multiple rhetorical positions make him resemble "a disembodied intelligence flickering over the action" of *Epicoene*, "lighting up its dark corners."[15] Here, wit is figured as a sort of will-o'-the-wisp: visible, powerful, but without material substance. On the opposite end of a theoretical spectrum is the sociology of Pierre Bourdieu, which positions wit and taste as essentially materially determined phenomena: "The ideology of natural taste owes its plausibility and its efficacy to the fact that, like all the ideological strategies generated in the everyday class struggle, it *naturalizes* real differences."[16] These "real differences," for Bourdieu, are always economic: the flow or "distribution of symbolic capital" masks the distribution of "legitimate capital" so that "the balance-sheet of a power relation" is misrecognized as differences in taste.[17] While one would be hard-pressed to find signs of a late capitalist "class struggle" in Jacobean London, the terms of Bourdieu's argument should push us to examine the material relations that are implicated in and help produce both early modern cultural competence and the social power it signifies. After all, a great deal of social labor goes into the organization of taste and its appearance as an effortless or playful form of status. My reading of the intertwined roles of literary culture, urban space, and gender in *Epicoene* is an attempt to excavate some of this labor, to denaturalize early modern wit and taste by attending to the multiple intersections between "disembodied intelligence" and "real differences" that constituted status in the changing scene of seventeenth-century London.

Recent work in social history can help to clarify why a logic of power organized around cultural competence might have first dominated a dramatization of London in 1609. Historians charting out expressions of status have stressed an emerging dynamism in Tudor and Stuart England's understanding of social power, and with good reason.[18] Early modern texts repeatedly engage with forms of social difference by experimenting with the structure of status hierarchies,[19] by exploring how status itself might be signified or produced,[20] and, at times, by bitterly critiquing or attempting to regulate those who disregarded the boundaries of conventional hierarchies.[21] The causes and effects of this dynamism are multiple and always subject to debate, but it seems clear that conservative forms of social description became increasingly unwieldy with the expansion of a market for nonessential commodities. As Joan Thirsk has argued, this expansion, which began in the 1540s and was still underway in the early seventeenth century, was characterized not just by an increase in the sorts of goods available in the shops and stalls of London but also by a diversification in the quality of these goods such that a wider economic range of producers and consumers was able to participate in commodity exchange.[22] Although the emphasis in recent scholarship has been on mobility in the upper echelons of society,[23] it's worth keeping in mind that simple goods such as lace and starch had many more buyers and sellers in early modern London than did an estate in Essex. Despite the difference in degree, the acquisition of a brass pot or a pair of worsted stockings by an apprentice bowyer could have a social effect analogous to the purchase of a silk doublet by a young student at the Inns of Court or a knighthood by a wealthy goldsmith: with each purchase, an individual altered his or her position within the increasingly complex and ultimately interdependent social, cultural, and financial economies of the city. The classical hierarchy of degrees did not disappear, as Keith Wrightson notes,[24] but it was simply unable to encapsulate the flows of power within this early form of consumer society. Other ways of imagining and expressing status began to develop alongside the political or occupational categories of older classification schemes, at times supplementing the social relationships described within them, at times offering more flexible or adaptable alternatives, and at times obscuring older modes of status entirely.

City comedy, the group of plays to which *Epicoene* belongs, is notorious for its interest in the ways in which the explosive elaboration of London's markets affected social relations in the city.[25] Earlier examples of the genre usually invoke a political hierarchy of orders and degrees to structure their populations (we always know who has a title, for example, and who doesn't), but these conservative expressions of rank are often complicated by scenes that explicitly stage acts of commodity production, consumption, and exchange, linking marketplace savvy and wealth to the acquisition of social power. In Thomas Dekker's *Shoemakers' Holiday* (1599), for example, Simon Eyre's astonishingly rapid rise through the hierarchy of city government is fueled by the purchase and sale of the undervalued contents of a single Dutch carrack, and in Thomas Heywood's *2 If You Know Not Me* (1605), Thomas Gresham's stature in a nascent global marketplace is instantly consolidated as he buys from a Russian trader a pearl equal in value to the average yearly wage of 750 journeymen cloth-workers, grinds it into a powder, mixes it with wine, and, with a toast to the onlooking Queen Elizabeth, literally consumes it. Other city plays tone down the economic hyperbole that made Eyre and Gresham early modern urban legends, but they always foreground the ways in which social power might be produced or dissipated through the material practices of London's marketplaces. The transformations of Frank Golding in Heywood's *Fair Maid of the Exchange* (1602) and Richard Easy in Thomas Middleton's *Michaelmas Term* (1606) are representative: although both characters lack general authority at the outset (the former is the youngest of three brothers vying for the hand of the same woman, and the latter is a naive out-of-towner destined to be parted from his rentier income), propitious marketplace alliances permit both to achieve a noticeable level of control by the end of their respective plays. Golding joins forces with the Cripple of Fanchurch, a heroically hardworking East End pattern maker, allowing him to outsmart his older brothers and win the hand of the eponymous Fair Maid, who had been in love with the Cripple and his work ethic; Easy, partnered with the savvy wife of the merchant who had swindled him out of his land, is by the end of *Michaelmas Term* a member of the *re*landed gentry (a rare breed on the Jacobean stage), the juridically sanctioned lover of the merchant's wife, and an unexpected beneficiary of the binding contracts of early modern credit finance. Both Golding and Easy, then, gain an element of status that has nothing to do with degree but is instead contingent on a successful, active relationship to the practices of the marketplace.

The logic of social difference laid out in *Epicoene* often competes with—if not masks entirely—the economic logic that structured earlier city plays. Prefiguring the interests of later Jacobean, Caroline, and Restoration London comedies in a way that no play had before, *Epicoene* stages a city devoid of material labor. The workers, shops, and commodity exchanges that help to organize the status narratives of almost every city comedy written before 1609 (and many written after) do not appear on stage in the play, and the intricacies of London's literal marketplaces, while they are referred to at various points in the dialogue, are never explicitly acted out. In fact, it sometimes seems that social power in *Epicoene* is contingent upon the ability to ignore economic activity entirely.[26] Daw's trouble with literary culture is again a case in point. When Dauphine and Clerimont question him about the clunky lyric poetry that he composes and proudly recites, Daw anxiously insists on the difference between himself, one of a number of "Wits that write verses and yet are no poets" and the "poor fellows that live by it" (2.3.100-101). As the two gallants make clear, however, a different sort of relationship to textual production is possible:

DAUPHINE
Why, would you not live by your verses, Sir John?
CLERIMONT
No, 'twere pity he should. A knight live by his verses? He did not make 'em to that end, I hope.
DAUPHINE
And yet the noble Sidney lives by his, and the noble family not ashamed.

(2.3.102-6)

Daw's bad taste stems in part from his inability to distance textual production from its material manifestations; he threatens the play's fantasy of effortless wit and laborless status by constantly letting the acts and objects of financial exchange and commodity consumption shape his relationship to the cultural sphere. For Dauphine and Clerimont, however, poetic text can produce a form of social power that has nothing to do with a literal marketplace. By punning on "live," the tasteful duo deflect attention away from the commercial aspects of authorship and position a lasting reputation as the desired effect of verse, a quantity clearly tied up in the production of status both for authors and for readers who stake their own claim to sophistication by constructing and properly invoking a literary hierarchy.

Although the play can imagine a literary text (and a form of status) unspoiled by the drab realities of buying and selling, that is, while it can fantasize about a form of social privilege imagined in direct opposition to what is presented as crass financial concerns, in some ways the economic engine of the print marketplace makes the gallants' cultural investments possible in the first place. Dauphine's nod to the reputation of Philip Sidney is particularly suggestive here, since Thomas Newman's 1591 edition of *Astrophil and Stella* paved the way for a broad range of authors to bring their own lyric work to the press.[27] This surge in print publication made its mark on the cultural scene of London by permitting the relatively widespread dissemination of the durable texts that came to be read as literary. Were it not for certain marketing decisions by publishers such as Newman to print and sell lyric verse, or, from the demand side, were it not for the desire of a viable number of consumers to purchase printed lyric verse, there might have been no broadly accepted literary status system in 1609 London. The printer's devils and reams of paper—or more generally, the labor and materials—that helped to create Tudor and Stuart literary culture have no place in the dramatic action of *Epicoene,* and it might seem somewhat pedantic to bring them up at all. But their absence, as natural as it may seem to be, is a facet of the play's comprehensive urban fantasy. Mirroring some of the broader social processes at work in the play, the economic logic of the print marketplace is obscured by a logic of cultural distinction.

Despite Jonson's notorious interest in the link between literary text and social authority (a link, it has been argued, that he himself was partially responsible for forging in the seventeenth century),[28] cultural competence in *Epicoene* is not only a function of its characters' familiarity with things bookish. Rather than simply setting out a series of differently literate Londoners, *Epicoene* consistently situates its characters in relation to the spaces of London itself to render and reinforce its social hierarchy. Truewit's analogies between his city and ancient Rome gesture toward this dynamic as they transform abstruse intellectual knowledge into functional wit. But, as *Epicoene* amply demonstrates, urban space is not just something to be cataloged or described in playful orations. It is lived in and moved through, the a priori site of social interaction and thus the physical matrix of the performances that produce cultural competence. Henri Lefebvre has famously argued that social space is both "a *product* to be used" and "a *means of production.*"[29] Though the terms of his analysis are taken from political economy, they hold true for the mechanisms of status formation put to use in *Epicoene.* If, as Lefebvre goes on to suggest, "networks of exchange and flows of raw materials and energy fashion space and are determined by it,"[30] the same might be said of the early modern struggle to forge an understanding of status that was responsive to a physically, socially, and economically expanding urban scene. To rephrase Lefebvre: a social logic of cultural competence fashions certain kinds of space and is likewise determined by them. As it transforms this social logic into the stuff of comic narrative, *Epicoene* reveals some of the ways in which conceptions of and relationships to the material spaces of the city can structure and be structured by emerging modes of wit or taste.

Like most city comedies, *Epicoene* is filled with references to specific London streets and place names. But while the plays written before it (and, again, many written after) tend to focus on the streets and shops in the central and eastern parts of the city, the action of *Epicoene* is limited to the small stretch of land between the city wall and Westminster that would come to be known as the West End.[31] This neighborhood has developed a reputation in recent historiography as a magnetic center of early modern financial and cultural capital.[32] With the concurrent growth of centralized markets for land, luxury goods, marriages, and legal services, the Ward of Farringdon Extra and points west became over the course of the late sixteenth and early seventeenth centuries the seasonal, if not permanent, home of a significant portion of England's moneyed population. But—and this fact often gets lost in readings of city plays in general and *Epicoene* in particular—the neighborhood between the court and the city was home to more than just a collection of law students, courtiers, landowners, and recently knighted grocers. Bridewell Prison was one of Farringdon Extra's more prominent civic landmarks, and much of the residential development in the area (as in the rest of the city) took the form of tenement subdivisions that housed poorer laborers.[33] Of course, this economic range is completely absent in *Epicoene*—or flattened—as it must be, if the social fantasy of the play is to hold up. Power relations in *Epicoene* are staged through an emphasis on taste, not on economic or political status, and if a play based on this premise is going to engage with urban space, it must do so in an exclusive fashion. Part of the work of the play, then, is the evacuation of social variety from Farringdon Extra.

Predictably, the lack of economic and political difference in the spaces of the city clears the way for an exploration of the ways in which those spaces might be invoked in the creation of a sense of taste. Though written in a more sarcastic vein, Thomas Dekker's mock courtesy pamphlet, *The Gull's Hornbook* (1609), makes a similar move. The subjects of Dekker's satire— the young social aspirants of London—are advised to walk relentlessly about the city in order to prove their reputation; from St. Paul's to the theater to a tavern and to bed (these are just a few of the locations noted), a route through urban space helps Dekker map out possible motions through social space. Each location provides an opportunity to stake a claim to cultural competence by being observed engaging in one or more of the leisurely pursuits Dekker simultaneously lists and ridicules, among them smoking, eating oysters, and conspicuously cleaning one's gums.[34]

The most well-known stop along Dekker's suggested route is an un-named indoor theater. Dekker advises his fictional readership[35] to pay the higher entrance fees necessary to acquire a seat upon the stage of a playhouse,[36] and, recommending a combination of loud conversation, gaming, and general rowdiness, he puts his readers on the path to achieving a "conspicuous eminence":

As first, all the eyes in the galleries will leave walking after the players, and only follow you, the simplest dolt in the house snatches up your name, and, when he meets you in the streets, or that you fall into his hands in the middle of a watch, his word shall be taken for you; he'll cry "He's such a gallant," and you pass: Secondly, you publish your temperance to the world, in that you seem not to resort thither to taste vain pleasures with a hungry appetite; but only as a gentleman to spend a foolish hour or two because you can do nothing else.[37]

With tongue firmly in cheek, Dekker outlines a program of self-production that will lead to the creation and maintenance of a particular identity, named first "gallant" then "gentleman" above. Instead of the explicitly sexual power encoded in Lady Haughty's similar appraisal of Dauphine, a modicum of practical urban power is acquired along with these labels: those who have publicly established themselves as gallants in the theater will not, Dekker snidely suggests, be subjected to inconvenient questioning by London's night watches. The acquisition of this status and its attendant element of power is made possible in part by a spatial dynamic (i.e., where an audience member sits in relation to the stage) that in turn relies on a logic of expenditure (i.e., how much one paid to occupy that space). But rather than emphasizing this economic logic, Dekker presents the rather thin division between those who attend plays "to taste vain pleasures with a hungry appetite" and those who attend "to spend a foolish hour or two" because they "can do nothing else" as a function of how one (mis)behaves from an expensive place on stage. Since *The Gull's Hornbook* is primarily a satire, the work of public performance is framed as fantasy or entertainment: "observe your doors of entrance, and your exit, not much unlike the players at theaters," Dekker advises, "keeping your decorums in fantasticality."[38] But the joke here shows that managing one's relationship to urban spaces—knowing when, where, and how to display one's self—could help produce and signify forms of cultural competence that competed with or obscured entirely a hierarchy made possible by money.[39]

Social difference in the seamlessly elite West End world of *Epicoene* is similarly linked to spatial practice in a way that tends to render irrelevant political and economic modes of status. But where *The Gull's Hornbook* is primarily concerned with sites in which large numbers of people gather, most of *Epicoene* takes place in private chambers and homes.[40] On one level, the possession of a private residence in London would have been a sign of status in and of itself due to the wealth needed to buy or rent personal quarters in the city. But, as is the case with the audience members sitting on stage in Dekker's theater, distinctions are drawn between wealthy characters in *Epicoene* based on how they act within their privileged space. The play famously opens in Clerimont's bedroom, and for the entire first act his servants and friends come and go bearing news from around the city as he dresses himself (1.1.sd 1). The singing, the leisurely debates over leisure itself, and the gossip of the scene all work to create a sense of privilege for the gallants. Beyond these behaviors, as Emrys Jones has argued, the different ways in which people enter and exit Clerimont's private room also help order the social world of the play. Truewit and Dauphine are welcomed unannounced, whereas La Foole is admitted only after he requests permission; Jones claims that this regulation of entrance creates a sense "of inner and outer" that he links to the opposition between "superior and inferior" and "élite and multitude."[41] But while Clerimont properly polices the boundary between public and private space, *Epicoene* features two characters, Morose and La Foole, whose styles of urban living are less than socially successful. The former is a residential introvert, the latter an extrovert, and their relationships to urban space, or, more precisely, the types of permeability they allow between public and private spaces, distance them from cultural competence and the social power it brings.

Though one of the obviously moneyed characters in the play, Morose's status is most blatantly figured through his inappropriate hermetic desires. He lives on a street too narrow for coaches to pass by, limiting his social engagements, and he does everything in his power to shut out the noise of the city that surrounds him. The image of a man with nightcaps piled high on his head, a man sequestered in a house with a "flock bed" padding its front door and "quilting" on its staircase (2.1.10, 26), pushes the boundaries of humorous hyperbole, even for Jonson. But the more details we learn about Morose's phobias, the more it becomes clear that they have less to do with noise itself and more to do with the material practices that create that noise. He is described as detesting all manner of tradesmen, from a "costardmonger" to a "pewterer's prentice" (1.1.143-54); he has violent hysterical fits at the sound of a public entertainer, like a "bearward" or a "fencer" (1.1.166-73); the constant ringing of church bells commemorating plague deaths "has made him devise a room with double walls and treble ceilings" (1.1.175-80); the tumult of his wedding feast drives him to the uppermost reaches of his attic (4.1.18-23); and finally, the "several voices of citations, appellations, allegations, certificates, attachments, intergatories, references, convictions, and afflictions" that make up the scene at the law courts force him back to the relatively "calm midnight" that is the feast back in his home (4.7.12-18). Indeed, when Morose himself ticks off a few of the major landmarks of London, he does so with an agenda quite different from Truewit's:

And that I did supererogatory penance, in a belfry, at Westminster Hall, i' the cockpit, at the fall of a stag, the Tower Wharf—what place is there else?—London Bridge, Paris Garden, Belinsgate, when the noises are at their height and loudest.
(4.4.12-16)

While Morose, like Truewit, seems to have a good grasp of "the knowledge of the town," there is a crucial difference in the way these two characters perform that knowledge. What emerges in the case of Morose is a portrait of a man isolating himself from an entire system of behaviors, from the markets, entertainments, juridical establishments, and general social practices and locations that constitute seventeenth-century London. The lengths to which he goes to shelter himself from everything around him mark him as a type of urban monster, a metropolitan hermit, deserving not

only of scorn but also of humiliation. Morose is an emblematic figure in a
play obsessed with sidestepping various material relations. His hysteria is
a hyperreactive mode of taste, a sense of distinction so minutely receptive
to the possibilities of the urban scene that it has been crushed by the mass
of cultural products and production that flood the world around him. By
positioning Morose as an oppositional figure against the aims of its heroes,
and by punishing him mercilessly, *Epicoene* helps mediate the pressures of
this mass, subsuming them under the seemingly laborless forms of wit that
bring the gallants their social authority, and that permit them to dominate
their satirized other.

Whereas Morose is ridiculed for his attempts to seal himself within
his home, La Foole is guilty of failing to contain himself (or, at least, of
failing to allow his apartment to contain him). His own particular brand of
foolishness results in part from being excessively talkative (1.3.49–1.4.64),
but along with his tendency to run off at the mouth, the play inflects and
defines La Foole's social behaviors by imagining him in his urban element:

> He does give plays and suppers, and invites his guests to 'em aloud out of his
> window as they ride by in coaches. He has a lodging in the Strand for the purpose,
> or to watch when ladies are gone to the china-houses or the Exchange, that he may
> meet 'em by chance and give 'em presents, some two or three hundred pounds'
> worth of toys, to be laughed at. He is never without a spare banquet or sweetmeats
> in his chamber, for their women to alight at, and come up to, for a bait. (1.3.32–40)

As opposed to the tasteful Clerimont, whose chambers are open to friends,
but who is shown simply receiving his guests as they arrive, La Foole
expends all of his effort trying to drag guests into his home. The boundary
between his lodging and the public spaces of the West End is repeatedly
broached in all the wrong ways as he shouts out his window, chases after
potential visitors, and brings serving women up to his rooms with promises
of food. If Morose is too isolated from the city in which he lives, La Foole,
even from within the confines of his home, is too much in it. He is a "windfucker," as Clerimont's bitter epithet has it (1.4.74), a character who stands
to gain little satisfaction from his rapid movements through urban space.[42]

The extrusion of La Foole out of his residence and into the main public thoroughfare of the West End combined with his verbosity and his
laughable expenditures distance him from social power by marking him as
tasteless. But, less obviously, they also do so by marking him as feminine.
Karen Newman has read the early modern commercial zones of Farringdon

Extra—the Strand, the New Exchange—as sites in a gendered discursive network that produces images of unruly femininity in part by linking excessive "female talk" with the conspicuous consumption of luxury commodities.[43] La Foole's low status is articulated through this network, registering the ways in which the tropes of gender can circulate within expressions of cultural competence. This discursive interpenetration becomes especially prominent later in the play as the men whose social performances are lacking are branded with a form of sexual lack: Daw and La Foole undergo a symbolic castration when their swords are taken away from them (4.5), and Morose is made to proclaim his own impotence (5.4.41: "I am no man, ladies").

Gender was, of course, a fundamental element of status in early modern London, and like other forms of social power the codes and performances around which masculinity and femininity were organized were slowly transformed along with the spaces and economic relations of the city. Newman traces out the signs of a cultural anxiety evoked by the entrance of women into the public spaces and financial transactions of early modern London's developing commodity markets; she reads in *Epicoene* a "discursive slippage between women's talk, women's wealth, and a perceived threat to male authority" under early capitalism.[44] With the conspicuous lack of outright commodity exchange on stage, however, the dramatization and mediation of this threat in *Epicoene* often takes place in the arena of taste. The play constantly reminds its audience that if urban social power is based in part on performances that express cultural competence, then it is available to women, who could take on the role of the sophisticate and co-opt its attendant privilege. One of Truewit's misogynist rants meant to persuade Morose to remain unmarried plays off of this possibility. Here, fears of sexual and economic excess are linked to a less familiar concern that one's wife might become too witty, too tasteful, and thus, by implication, too powerful:

If [your wife is] learned, there was never such a parrot; all your patrimony will be too little for the guests that must be invited to hear her speak Latin and Greek, and you must lie with her in those languages too, if you will please her. . . . [S]he may censure poets and authors and styles, and compare 'em, Daniel with Spenser, Jonson with tother youth, and so forth; or be thought cunning in controversies or the very knots of divinity, and often in her mouth the state of the question, and then skip to mathematics and demonstration, and answer religion to one, in state to another, in bawdry to a third.   (2.2.71–75, 112–20)

The Collegiates, Mistress Otter, and the disguised boy Epicoene act out
this fantasy almost to the word, encroaching upon the privileged position
of the three gallants: Haughty, upon meeting Epicoene, proclaims tŏ her
associates, "and she have wit, she shall be one of us!" (3.6.49–50), establishing the women of the play as potential arbiters of taste. With this in
mind, Truewit's famous pronouncement that the Collegiates "cry down or
up what they like or dislike in a brain or fashion with most masculine or
rather hermaphroditical authority" (1.1.75–77) seems to register an anxiety
generated not only by new possibilities for women in an expanding public
sphere, but by the more specific possibility that once in this public sphere,
women might use taste, "what they like or dislike," to stake a claim to a
traditionally masculine authority.

Epicoene negotiates this threat to some degree by calling on the cultural
matrix that inarguably brings all of its characters together: the spaces of
the city of London. We never learn precisely where the Collegiates reside
(Truewit locates them "i' the town" and claims that they "live from their
husbands" [1.1.72–74]), but the way in which they manage the relationship
between their private residences and the social scene outside of them is
more important than topographical realism here. As with Morose and La
Foole, the permeability of the boundary between public and private space
becomes emblematic of an individual's position in a social hierarchy. In
the case of the Collegiates, however, residential penetration is linked to
sexual penetration, creating a forcefully eroticized urban identity. In act
5, Haughty, Centaure, and Mavis all attempt to seduce Dauphine, and all
of them do so by offering him access to their "chambers" (5.2.18–19, 35–
36, 57–59). The bawdy overtones are not coincidental. Private space, an
expensive sign of wealth or economic status, becomes a figure for the
Collegiates' private parts, linking this form of social power to fears of
feminine sexual excess. The space of the "chamber" is a transfer point
where the social or economic control implicit in a woman's possession of
a private room is reinscribed as unruly desire or immorality. Drawing on
the same discursive network that permits Truewit's vision of the culturally
adept woman to touch on both economic and sexual anxiety, *Epicoene*
uses emerging elements of urban culture to discredit the Collegiates as
licentious.

Along with this eroticization of the Collegiates' private spaces, *Epicoene*
mediates the threat to masculine authority posed by feminine judgment
by putting that judgment itself to work in the consolidation of the social

order of the play. I began this discussion with evidence of Lady Haughty's discerning eye: at one point, she calls Dauphine "a perfect gentleman" (4.6.12). As I briefly noted, this seemingly simple assessment is the result of the complex plot staged by the three gallants in the fourth act that leads to the humiliation and physical debasement of Daw and La Foole. Truewit uses the language of theater to describe the plot, calling it a "tragicomedy between the Guelphs and the Ghibbelines" (4.5.27–28), and he insists it be performed in front of a particular audience:

CLERIMONT
Shall I go fetch the ladies to the catastrophe?
TRUEWIT
Umh? Ay, by my troth.
DAUPHINE
By no mortal means. Let them continue in the state of ignorance, and err still; think 'em wits and fine fellows as they have done. 'Twere sin to reform them.
TRUEWIT
Well, I will have 'em fetched, now I think on't, for a private purpose of mine; do, Clerimont, fetch 'em, and discourse to 'em all that's past, and bring 'em into the gallery here.
DAUPHINE
This is thy extreme vanity now; thou think'st thou wert undone if every jest thou mak'st were not published.
TRUEWIT
Thou shalt see how unjust thou art presently.

(4.5.215-25)

Truewit's "private purpose" is to manipulate the women in the play, to shift their erotic attachment from Daw and La Foole to Dauphine. The very fact that the Collegiates and their followers would accept the attentions of two social pretenders casts aspersions on their taste; likewise, their susceptibility to Truewit's ploy becomes the grounding for the play's most blatant critique of feminine judgment: "all their actions are governed by crude opinion, without reason or cause; they know not why they do anything" (4.6.58–59). This scene, however, has more significance than its narrative use as a proof of feminine caprice. As Jonson's stage directions indicate (4.6.sd 1–3), Clerimont leads every single female character in the play (including the one whose boyish identity will be explicitly revealed) to the tarras above the main stage, where they serve as a dramatized audience for Truewit's "tragicomedy." The scene has all the makings of an Elizabethan play within a play, and like similar components in *Hamlet* or *The Spanish*

Tragedy, it functions as a moment of revelation. *Epicoene* is no revenge tragedy, however, and the revelation here is of a cultural crime or aesthetic imposture, rather than of physical violence.

As Truewit directs the entrances, exits, and mock battles of Daw, La Foole, and Dauphine, the women, silent perhaps for the only time in the play, take in the show. Lady Haughty's first lines following the small drama register its efficacy: "Centaure, how our judgements were imposed on by these adulterate knights!" (4.6.1–2). The overall effect of the scene is to reaffirm the social order of the play, not only by placing Dauphine at the center of attention but also by assigning theatrical roles to the characters on stage. Whereas Truewit and his cohorts are marked as producers of a disciplinary plot, or as tasteful agents, the women are integrated into the social hierarchy as spectators—spectators who ultimately conform to the standards of taste imposed by the three protagonists and who read their performances precisely as they are meant to be read. Like the groundlings in Dekker's unnamed theater in *The Gull's Hornbook* who recognize the "conspicuous eminence" of a boisterous man on stage, the women of *Epicoene* underwrite a cultural economy by being the complicit audience through which the status of Truewit, Clerimont, and Dauphine is made manifest.

This quasi-theatrical scenario nicely articulates the basic social logic of the play: the three gallants move smoothly through their urban world, ordering their environment and the people in it. Their privilege (and other characters' lack thereof) is contingent on a series of performances that are bound up in the material exchanges, spaces, and discourses of the city around them. But the intricate convolutions of this tie are usually pushed out of focus in *Epicoene,* as its denouement makes clear. As the play nears its end, Dauphine, promising his uncle relief from matrimonial discomfort, removes the wig of the actor playing Epicoene. The metatheatrically obvious suddenly becomes an unexpected twist in the narrative: Morose has married a boy and is thus not legally married. With the nullification of his wedding vows, the terms of a contract Morose has just signed are met; Dauphine becomes his heir, receiving a yearly allowance of £500, or one third of Morose's income (the details of the contract are carefully recited at 5.4.164–76). Truewit reads this revelation and its results as a decisive gesture of waggish triumph: "Well, Dauphine, you have lurched your friends of the better half of the garland, by concealing this part of the plot!" (5.4.208–10). Like many of the textual moments I've described here, Truewit's exhortations would make an immaterial sort of wit out to be the natural, obvious determinant of status in the play. From his perspective, the unveiling of the boy Epicoene is a masterstroke, the epitome of the sort of playful gesture that throughout the play has emblematized the gallants' control within their environment. If his lines are taken at face value, Dauphine's power would appear to be the result of nothing more than some delightful trickery. As I have been arguing, however, performances of wit, taste, and/or cultural competence are constantly in tension with and made meaningful by a vast field of objects, spaces, and knowledge that produce social power or make status recognizable. The sudden appearance of paper contracts on stage and the explicit discussion of income and inheritance in the final scene begin to register this tension by reasserting economic practice and financial need—so often obscured by the demands of tasteful performance—as crucial elements of the play's narrative. Dauphine may be witty, but his status, his "garland," is equally proven by the allowance he has won for himself by the end of the play.

Further undermining the breezy tone that colors Truewit's declamation, the decisive effects of Epicoene's transformation suggest that Dauphine's success is a product of his ability to manipulate the signifiers of gender upon the body of a boy. In this way, the end of *Epicoene* elaborates on the social potential of the open sexualities set out in its first scene. If Clerimont's bedroom is a space that helps signify a tasteful hierarchy in the play, then contributing to his own leisured power in the scene is his "ingle" (1.1.23), a youngish boy who, when he's not too busy warbling love songs penned by Clerimont, slips in and out of bedrooms and erotic scenarios with both men and women. In the active life of this ingle, the transferable materials of gender inspire a number of homoerotic arrangements: in a woman's wig, the boy is kissed by women (1.1.14-15); in a boy's apparel, he lies "above a man" (1.1.10). Clerimont seems nervous about his ability to compete with the academy of women and their dresses ("you shall go there no more, lest I be fain to seek your voice in my lady's rushes a fortnight hence" [1.1.19-21]), and his lack of control over the costumes and visitations of the boy puts their master/servant relationship in danger of sliding into the disorderly realm of the sodomitical.[45] Dauphine, on the other hand, as Mario DiGangi points out, has proven his own status in part by successfully manipulating both the gender and the desire of his own retainer: he "has chosen his young companion wisely and it pays off in his intellectual, social, and financial mastery over all the wits and asses of the play."[46]

Ultimately, then, the fashioning of Epicoene is Dauphine's crowning performance. It's a move that amplifies and in some sense literalizes the social process that brings meaning to Truewit's Londonization of Juvenal and Ovid: a seemingly abstract form of knowledge is made (in)to matter as out of the obscure grammatical term "epicoene," which refers to Latin and Greek nouns that can "denote either sex."[47] Dauphine tastefully materializes Epicoene, an eroticized body that, by carrying the properties of two genders, permits his social successes. True to form, however, the labor invested in the fashioning of Epicoene is never explicitly staged. The audience first learns of Dauphine's efforts in his easy flourish as he uncovers his creation at the end of the play, and the sudden shock of the revelation itself shifts attention away from the work, the scheming, the rehearsals that would have made that shock possible in the first place. Like the labor and materials of the print shop, this sort of work has no place in the master plot of *Epicoene*. Other characters discuss their machinations at length, from Clerimont's page, who sends noisy entertainers under Morose's windows to provoke him (1.1.166–73), to Truewit himself, whose project for effecting the punishment of Daw and La Foole is charted out step by step (4.4.159ff.–4.5). But the "better half of the garland" belongs to the character in *Epicoene* whose efforts at trickery are completely absent from the play, and whose social power thus appears to be an entirely laborless production.

In this final scene, then, a form of status made legible through a seemingly effortless performance of wit or good taste is structured by—and mystifies—an intersection of economic and erotic practice. To be a "perfect gentleman" in the world of *Epicoene* is to exist at the nexus of elaborate intersections like this one, intersections that frequently work to obscure the materials out of which they are composed. But as natural or playful as they may seem to be, the triumphs of Dauphine and his fellow gallants are never the result of some kind of socially aleatory cleverness. In *Epicoene*, as in the many later English plays that would take up its social logic, cultural competence depends on an ability to successfully manage the fluid set of knowledge, objects, and behaviors that could be put to use in the formation of status in the spaces of an ever-expanding London.

Notes

Thanks to Alan B. Farmer, Zachary Lesser, and especially Jean Howard for their thoughtful readings of earlier drafts of this essay.

1. All citations of the play are from *Epicoene, or The Silent Woman,* ed. R. V. Holdsworth, *The New Mermaids* (New York: W. W. Norton, 1990).

2. By "social power" I mean to suggest a general manifestation of privilege that takes the form of control over and within a given environment. Discussions of this element of power often invoke a "status" hierarchy in order to systematize for logical analysis what is in practice a nearly infinite set of fluid relationships. I have no interest in creating a static set of categories, however, so I will use the term "status" primarily to refer to social power itself, rather than to the specific classifications or ranks of a given hierarchy.

3. See, for example, Alan Hunt's discussion of sumptuary legislation in *Governance of the Consuming Passions: A History of Sumptuary Law* (New York: St. Martin's Press, 1996), and Frank Whigham on the rhetorical performances of courtly contestation in *Ambition and Privilege: The Social Tropes of Elizabethan Courtesy Theory* (Berkeley and Los Angeles: University of California Press, 1984).

4. The authority on early modern expressions of social difference is Keith Wrightson, whose broader analysis in *English Society, 1580-1680* (New Brunswick: Rutgers University Press, 1982) is refined in two essays that attempt to chart out the meanings and social purpose of what he terms "the language of sorts": " 'Sorts of People' in Tudor and Stuart England," in *The Middling Sort of People: Culture, Society and Politics in England, 1550-1800,* ed. Jonathan Barry and Christopher Brooks (New York: St. Martin's Press, 1994), 28-51, and "Estates, Degrees, and Sorts: Changing Perceptions of Society in Tudor and Stuart England," in *Language, History and Class,* ed. Penelope J. Corfield (Cambridge, Mass.: B. Blackwell, 1991), 30-52.

5. Economic status as I'm defining it here is not based on financial wealth alone (Dauphine cannot be considered wealthy until the end of the play), but on relationships to and within shifting modes of early modern production. In this regard, Daw, La Foole, and Dauphine are on equal footing; they all fit into the *economic* category of "gentleman" put forth by William Harrison as those who "live without manual labor." William Harrison, *The Description of England,* ed. Georges Edelen (Ithaca, N.Y.: Cornell University Press, 1968), 114.

6. I've taken the term "cultural competence" from Pierre Bourdieu's work in *Distinction: A Social Critique of the Judgement of Taste,* trans. Richard Nice (Cambridge: Harvard University Press, 1984), a book that I'll have the opportunity to discuss in more detail both in the main body of this piece and in notes, below. The idea is used in a number of ways in Bourdieu's sprawling discussion (see, for example, pp. 65-70, 85), but it generally suggests a skill made manifest in the performance of a critical relationship to cultural products— products that range from privileged forms of literature, art, architecture, and philosophy to less obviously valued (but still socially productive) texts, objects, spaces, and knowledge. To have cultural competence is to recognize the social value of these products and to make this recognition public in a seemingly effortless fashion. As may already be apparent, I will use the term "culture" in its broadest sense to refer to a set of socially determined and

determining acts, objects, spaces, and ideas that compose the material and textual traces of a given community. The breadth of this definition registers some of what might be at stake in the kind of analysis I've set out to perform here: "There is no way out of the game of culture," Bourdieu asserts at the beginning of *Distinction* (12), but left open to players is the option of rigorously examining the historical development and purposes of the rules.

7. Juvenal, Satire VI (30-32) in *Juvenal and Persius,* trans. G. G. Ramsay, Loeb Classical Library (Cambridge: Harvard University Press, 1940).

8. For a related discussion of the role of London topography in *Epicoene,* see Janette Dillon, *Theatre, Court and City, 1595-1610* (Cambridge: Cambridge University Press, 2000), 124-36. Dillon reads Truewit's references to city sites (along with those of Morose, which I discuss below) as "part of a nightmare that refuses to be suppressed" in the play (128): the knowledge that economic relations—linked conceptually to the idea of the "city" as opposed to the "court" or the "town"—always produce the value of the goods that structure the fashionable world of the West End. I am less concerned than Dillon with the moral thrust of *Epicoene,* and I am not sure that the spaces of the city are necessarily an incompletely repressed scene of anxiety in the play (as I've already begun to suggest, a proper engagement with them can have positive social effects), but the shape of her argument has positively influenced mine.

9. Along with Dillon, recent critics who have worked against this trend and shaped my own work include Karen Newman, "City Talk: Women and Commodification in Jonson's *Epicoene," English Literary History* 56(3) (1989): 503-18; Jonathan Haynes, *The Social Relations of Jonson's Theater* (Cambridge and New York: Cambridge University Press, 1992), esp. 34-98; and Mathew Martin, *Between Theater and Philosophy: Skepticism in the Major City Comedies of Ben Jonson and Thomas Middleton* (Newark: University of Delaware Press, 2001), 58-77.

10. John Dryden, *Of Dramatic Poesy and Other Critical Essays,* ed. George Watson (London: J. M. Dent and Sons Ltd., 1962), 180.

11. Michael Shapiro, "Audience vs. Dramatist in Jonson's *Epicoene* and Other Plays of the Children's Troupes," *English Literary Renaissance* 3 (1973): 416.

12. P. K. Ayers, "Dreams of the City: The Urban and the Urbane in Jonson's *Epicoene," Philological Quarterly* 66(1) (1987): 80. Ayers's essay is, in fact, more sensitive than most to the link between urbanity and a historical urban scene (see note 13 below).

13. Emrys Jones, "The First West End Comedy," *Proceedings of the British Academy* 68 (1982): 247, 232. Like Ayers (see note 11 above), Jones is generally an astute reader of the social relations set out in *Epicoene.* The fact that these critics would make these claims in arguments intelligently invested in the play's historical context speaks both to the endurance and the deep familiarity of the social processes structuring the play's engagement with modes of taste and wit.

14. The word "wit" had a wide range of reference in the early seventeenth century; I will use it here as it is mainly used in the play (and in modern criticism thereof) to denote a combination of intelligence, cleverness, and originality that creates a desirable social effect, or to label a person who possesses that combination of qualities (see *OED* defs. 5, 7, 9 and 10). Martin Butler, writing about Caroline plays heavily influenced by Jonson, makes a key distinction between different sorts of wit in city comedy, distinguishing between

" 'wit' as a social value ('accomplishment' or 'breeding')" and "the 'wit' of Middleton's heroes which represents their capacity to swindle." Martin Butler, *Theater and Crisis, 1632-1640* (Cambridge: Cambridge University Press, 1984), 159. Like *Epicoene* itself, I am more interested in the former definition, but as the end of the play suggests, these two kinds of wit are tightly interwoven in Jonsonian comedy. Readings of *Epicoene* that specifically take up the "wittiness" of Clerimont, Dauphine, and Truewit include W. David Kay, "Jonson's Urbane Gallants: Humanistic Contexts for *Epicoene,*" *Huntington Library Quarterly* 39 (1976): 251-66; L. G. Salinger, "Farce and Fashion in *The Silent Woman,*" *Essays and Studies* 20 (1967): 29-46; Michael Shapiro, "Audience vs. Dramatist"; Philip Mirabelli, "Silence, Wit, and Wisdom in *The Silent Woman,*" *SEL* 29 (1989): 309-36; and, more recently, Mario DiGangi, "Asses and Wits: The Homoerotics of Mastery in Satiric Comedy," *English Literary Renaissance* 25(2) (1995): 179-208. I would single out DiGangi's essay, to which I will return below, for its complex vision of the social relationships that allow an individual to be recognized as a "wit"; he uses the distinction between orderly homoeroticism and sodomy in master/servant relationships to do so—homoerotic mastery becomes a figure for social authority.

15. Jonas Barish, *Ben Jonson and the Language of Prose Comedy* (Cambridge: Harvard University Press, 1960), 157.

16. Bourdieu, *Distinction,* 68. Bourdieu's vocabulary should be approached with caution by cultural historians of Tudor and Stuart England, since the relevant portion of his work is based on the study of the practices of a bourgeois community in 1960s France and, therefore, its unqualified application to the population of seventeenth-century London runs the risk of being anachronistic. The economic mode fueling and mystified by the social dynamic laid out in *Distinction* had yet to fully develop in Stuart England, and the technologies and institutions of the twentieth century (mass media and public museums, for example) that have provided access across a broad social spectrum to aesthetic fields and cultural products were either nonexistent in the first half of the seventeenth century or, in the case of the book trade, in early stages of development. That said, elements of the dynamic under investigation in *Distinction* were clearly gaining purchase in Tudor and Stuart London as its population became more and more integrated into an expanding commodity marketplace (see my discussion on p. 42).

17. Bourdieu, *Distinction,* 172.

18. Keith Wrightson claims of "the language of sorts," a mode of social description that developed over the late sixteenth and seventeenth centuries: "Adaptable to context and responsive to change, it expressed the plasticity of social identity, the mutability of social alignments, the clash of interests, and the power relations of a dynamic society." Wrightson, "Estates, Degrees, and Sorts," 51-52. Wrightson's work implies that modes of social description are linguistic forms active within and responsive to their historical context, rather than being static, objective, and accurate reflections of power relations. See also Lawrence Stone, *The Crisis of the Aristocracy, 1558-1641* (Oxford: Clarendon Press, 1965), and "Social Mobility in England, 1500-1700," *Past and Present* 33 (1966): 16-55; and Whigham, *Ambition and Privilege.*

19. See, for example, Harrison, *Description of England;* Thomas Smith, *De Republica Anglorum* (London, 1583); Thomas Wilson, *The State of England Anno Dom. 1600* (London, ca. 1600).

20. The courtesy book or conduct manual is the most prominent example of the type. See Whigham's excellent analysis of the genre, *Ambition and Privilege,* and his useful catalog of editions of Elizabethan courtesy texts (199).

21. See, for example, the infamous polemic of Phillip Stubbes, *Anatomie of Abuses* (London, 1581), and, for a juridical perspective, Tudor sumptuary legislation, analyzed most recently by Hunt, *Governance of the Consuming Passions.*

22. Joan Thirsk, *Economic Policy and Projects: The Development of a Consumer Society in Early Modern England* (Oxford and New York: Oxford University Press, 1978). In an important admonition, Derek Keene notes that "something like a mass market in cheap manufactured goods had already come into existence in London by 1300." "Material London in Time and Space," in *Material London, ca. 1600,* ed. Lena Cowlin Orlin (Philadelphia: University of Pennsylvania Press, 2000), 59. However, the scale on which this market functioned was clearly transformed by the sixteenth-century developments charted out by Thirsk.

23. See Stone, *Crisis of the Aristocracy,* and F. J. Fisher, "The Development of London as a Center of Conspicuous Consumption," in *London and the English Economy, 1500–1700,* ed. P. J. Corfield and N. B. Harte (London and Ronceverte: The Hambledon Press, 1990), 105–18.

24. Wrightson, "Estates, Degrees, and Sorts," 44 and ff.

25. While there have been several notable attempts to mark out the definitive characteristics of Tudor and Stuart city comedy—see, for example, Brian Gibbons, *Jacobean City Comedy* (Cambridge: Harvard University Press, 1968 and 1980); Alexander Leggat, *Citizen Comedy in the Age of Shakespeare* (Toronto: University of Toronto Press, 1973); and most recently, Theodore Leinwand, *The City Staged: Jacobean City Comedy from 1603–1613* (Madison: University of Wisconsin Press, 1986)—I will use the designation in its broadest sense to denote a play obviously set in London that relies predominantly on comic narrative elements (i.e., romance, intrigue, the "untying of the knot of all the error") to produce and make sense of the complexities of an urban setting. (The knot metaphor is from a text widely read in Tudor and Stuart grammar schools, Donatus's "On Comedy," which can currently be found in *Medieval Literary Criticism: Translations and Interpretations,* ed. O. B. Hardison et al. [New York: Frederick Ungar Publishing, 1974], 45.) A broad definition is necessary here simply because comedies interested in London took on a variety of forms. Civic chronicle comedies such as *The Shoemakers' Holiday* (1599) and *2 If You Know Not Me* (1605) mythologize London sites and citizens as they imagine the interdependency and fantastical harmony of a vast spectrum of urban types ranging from manual laborers to the monarch (see David Scott Kastan, "Workshop and/as Playhouse," in *Staging the Renaissance: Reinterpretations of Elizabethan and Jacobean Drama,* ed. David Scott Kastan and Peter Stallybrass [New York: Routledge, 1991], 151–63, for a discussion of the social fantasy presented by *The Shoemaker's Holiday*), while plays often named as "typical" city comedies such as *Michaelmas Term* (1606), *A Chaste Maid in Cheapside* (1611), and *The Dutch Courtesan* (1603) devote a good deal of narrative energy to the agents of London's growing consumer marketplace (e.g., shopkeepers and their wives, retail customers, and usurers), repeatedly dramatizing moments of financial exchange and basing plot lines on the potential dangers thereof.

26. In this regard, *Epicoene* hints at the emergence of what Bourdieu has called the "aesthetic disposition," a facet of social power that is manifested by "a generalized capacity

to neutralize ordinary urgencies and to bracket off practical ends, a durable inclination and aptitude for practice without a practical function" (*Distinction,* 54). It's also worth noting that Mistress Otter, the only character in *Epicoene* with an immediate connection to mercantile exchange, is an object of particular scorn in the text. Like Daw, she makes obvious the labor of fashion, especially as she chastises her bear-loving husband for failing to wear his ruff and band, for his low-brow fetishization of his drinking cups, and for generally lacking the gentlemanly attributes she covets (3.1).

27. See Arthur Marotti, *Manuscript, Print, and the English Renaissance Lyric* (Ithaca, N.Y.: Cornell University Press, 1995), esp. 228-37, and David Scott Kastan, "Impressions of Poetry: The Publication of Elizabethan Lyric Verse," in *Approaches to Teaching Shorter Elizabethan Poetry,* ed. Patrick Cheney and Anne Lake Prescot (New York: Modern Language Association of America, 2000), 156-60.

28. See, for example, Richard Dutton, *Ben Jonson: Authority: Criticism* (New York: St. Martin's Press, 1996); and Douglas Brooks, *From Playhouse to Printing House: Drama and Authorship in Early Modern England* (Cambridge: Cambridge University Press, 2000), esp. 104-39.

29. Henri Lefebvre, *The Production of Space,* trans. Donald Nicholson-Smith (Oxford: Blackwell Publishers Ltd., 1991), 85.

30. Ibid.

31. See Jones, "First West End Comedy," 217-28, for a concise history of the neighborhood and, interestingly, its name, which predates the earliest reference in the *OED* (1807) by at least 140 years.

32. See Fisher, "Development of London," and R. Malcolm Smuts, "The Court and Its Neighborhood: Royal Policy and Urban Growth in the Early Stuart West End," *Journal of British Studies* 30(2) (1991): 117-49. For a broader view of the development of London, see the essays collected in A. L. Beier and R. Finlay, eds., *London, 1500-1700: The Making of a Metropolis* (Harlow: Longmans, 1986), especially R. Finlay and B. Shearer's work on demography, "Population Growth and Suburban Expansion" (37-59). Also, see Lawrence Manley, *Literature and Culture in Early Modern London* (Cambridge and New York: Cambridge University Press, 1995), esp. 1-21, 63-122, and 212-93, for his work on an urban culture predicated, in part, on different sorts of mobility.

33. See Norman G. Brett-James, *The Growth of Stuart London* (London: George Allen and Unwin, 1935), and A. L. Beier, "Engine of Manufacture: The Trades of London," in *London, 1500-1700,* 141-67. On the relations between rich and poor more generally in Covent Garden and surrounding West End parishes, see Jeremy Boulton, "The Poor Among the Rich: Paupers and the Parish in the West End, 1600-1724," in *Londinopolis,* ed. Mark S. R. Jenner and Paul Griffiths (Manchester and New York: Manchester University Press, 2000), 197-225.

34. Thomas Dekker, *The Gull's Hornbook,* ed. R. B. McKerrow (London, 1904; repr. New York: AMS Press, 1971). Of course, Dekker's pamphlet is a lengthy joke, and the information therein should be taken with a grain of salt. But since most printed satires rely on common knowledge to ground their humor, *The Gull's Hornbook* is likely a good indicator of the interests of the community for which it was published.

35. I use the word "fictional" here to differentiate between the readership Dekker invokes both in the prefatory material of the work and in his address throughout and the wide range of

book buyers who might purchase the pamphlet for entertainment value, or for a voyeuristic glimpse of a profligate world that may be condemned and/or envied.

36. Andrew Gurr, *The Shakespearean Stage, 1574-1642,* 3d ed. (Cambridge: Cambridge University Press, 1992), 158-59.

37. Dekker, *Gull's Hornbook,* 53.

38. Ibid., 34.

39. For more on this topic, specifically as it relates to a slightly more developed form of theater culture, see Michael Neill, " 'Wits Most Accomplished Senate': The Audience of the Caroline Private Theaters," *SEL* 18 (1978): 341-60.

40. Jones, "First West End Comedy," 240-47.

41. Ibid., 245.

42. The *OED* defines "windfucker" as a type of kestrel, or a windhover, a bird that beats its wings in midair but makes no forward progress.

43. Newman, "City Talk."

44. Ibid, 510.

45. On the link between "sodomy" and social disorder of various forms, see Jonathan Goldberg, *Sodometries: Renaissance Texts, Modern Sexualities* (Stanford: Stanford University Press, 1992). For a discussion relating Goldberg's work to the problem of master/servant relations as depicted in early modern drama, see Mario DiGangi, "Asses and Wits," 181-84. On the erotics (homo- and otherwise) of *Epicoene,* see DiGangi, "Asses and Wits," 184-87, and Bruce Barbour, " 'When I Acted Young Antinous': Boy Actors and the Erotics of Jonsonian Theater," *PMLA* 110(5) (1995): 1014-17.

46. DiGangi, "Asses and Wits," 186.

47. "Epicene," *OED,* def. 1.

Performatives and Performativity: Ben Jonson Makes His Excuses

JAMES LOXLEY

> it survives,
> A way of happening, a mouth.
> —W. H. Auden, "In Memory of W. B. Yeats"

> What happens, by definition, . . . couldn't care less about the performative.
> —Jacques Derrida, "Typewriter Ribbon: Limited Ink 2"

S INCE HIS JUVENILE labor on the garden walls at Lincoln's Inn, Ben Jonson's work has been intimately involved with the law.[1] At its baldest no more than a critical commonplace, this has been nonetheless a particularly fruitful and near-comprehensive concern for Jonson's readers in recent years. Whether the focus is on a determining relation to prerogative ambitions and procedures, a familiarity with the business or the inhabitants of the Inns, or the birth pangs of the institution of authorship, the intelligibility of the Jonsonian text can hardly be established without recourse to juridical categories and concepts.[2] Indeed, even the most superficial readings will inevitably run up against the connotations of "law" or "rule" in a number of their permutations, while the subject of law has often seemed identical to the subject of Jonson's writings. Here, selfhood is conceived juridically, both as the locus of propriety, agency, and responsibility and as the capacity to make law, while language becomes an object as well as the medium of such conceptions. The said or written is figured as action, and therefore as actionable, and writing comes to feature in the mutually dependent pairing of doer and deed. At the same time, writing as the legislative word becomes an instance of power.

To this extent, both the intra- and extradiegetic addresses of the Jonsonian corpus demand to be read as speech acts, as so many events or occurrences: a taking place, a happening, that can described in the language of *force*. In its persuasive or perlocutionary manifestations, this force can be described in the classical terms of rhetoric, though the connotations of "persuasion" are likely to make that a much less simple operation than it sounds. However, insofar as it is considered as a work in itself and not an affective *working on,* the proprietary terms of speech act theory suggest themselves. Long ago, J. L. Austin acknowledged that the kind of performativity on which certain kinds of ordinary language philosophy wished to focus was also an object of the law's interest, if not devising; more recently, Ian Maclean has returned the favor by identifying antecedents for Austin's concerns in Renaissance legal writing on the force (*virtus, vis, potestas*) of law.[3] Indeed, Maclean has suggested a tentative precedent for both Austin's discrimination between adequation and felicity and his tripartite distinction between locution, perlocution, and illocution in the work of the sixteenth-century jurist Alessandro Turamini.[4]

While Turamini, in Maclean's account, is concerned primarily with the power of the law, Maclean and other scholars have traced preoccupations and problematics that look very much like those of speech act theory through juristic analysis of the kinds of linguistic actions that might be subject to law. The work of legal historians on the development of contract law, for example, has paved the way for Luke Wilson's analysis of promises in literary texts in the same context.[5] Here, issues apparently central to speech act theory—the necessary conditions for the execution of a linguistic act, the relation between utterance and intention—appear reflected in the concerns of the juristic predecessors to whom Austin alluded. It is therefore no surprise to find Jonson's work illuminated by Wilson in just this way. In Wilson's account, the elaboration of the law of contract opens up a space (or rather, a time) in which the articulation of intention and action can be elaborated, and in Jonson's dramatic practice the effects of such a development can be traced.[6]

Though the influence of speech act theory is sufficiently pervasive to ensure the appearance of its terminology at points in Wilson's argument, his work seeks to demonstrate the extent to which the early modern juristic discourse of intention and agency joins other figurations of selfhood in providing a specifically early modern "spatial and temporal map of human purposiveness."[7] The possibility of the self, that is, is determined by the development and interaction of those discourses, the features on the map inscribed by a particular articulation of related sciences of the human. Wilson, of course, is neither alone nor controversial in proceeding in this manner, one that in its sophisticated versions is hegemonic in contemporary literary studies; a proximate example would be Lorna Hutson's tracing through *Measure for Measure* of the interplay between developments in a gendered law of slander and the early modern rhetorical practices of *ethopoeia,* or character writing.[8]

In making such claims, these kinds of reading also demonstrate both a renewed sense of the legislative or illocutionary force of these accounts of the human and, at the same time, the specific seductions of legal history for those concerned to produce them. This appears particularly starkly in the concluding sentences of a recent essay by David Harris Sacks on early modern contract law:

The modern law of contract was constructed from a variety of religious and philosophical sources and judicial precedents about which there was no firm consensus until Slade's case. Once Coke presented his own arguments as though they were the court's, his report shaped all future pleadings in the law of contract, molding the way promises and contracts were subsequently made, interpreted and enforced. The decision in turn reinforced the performative and internalist view of selfhood that underpinned it, and thereby endorsed a view that endowed the self with explicit and enforceable rights and liabilities. The selves we have are what they are because of the actions we can perform, and those actions are defined, in significant measure, by the laws, customs, and practices governing the social world in which we live.[9]

The law, for Sacks, defines the character of a subjectivity that is specifically human, the terrain of the lived, in determining the kinds of action that can be marked as the substance and limits—rights and liabilities—of a specifically human purposiveness or intentionality. Crucially, this definition is *itself* an action, a performative process of determination: these are the *customs* and *practices* that determine a conscious and human life through the constitution of the customs and practices in which it will come to be. To this extent, then, and despite the appeal to a mutuality of underpinning and reinforcement that marks Sacks's argument, the agency that here determines the agency of the human cannot itself be human according to the terms it defines, or internal to the human it actively defines as "internal": it cannot take place on the terrain of will, experience, or subjectivity, since its very performativity is the constitution of that terrain.

Such performativity might be characterized as radically historical. As a taking place that *makes* the place of the human, it necessarily involves an occasional dimension: we could list the occasions on which the law is made, and with it the persons for whom it is the law and who cannot be otherwise than the law makes them. The sheer givenness of custom and practice can only bolster this characterization and might perhaps incline us to see in it a highly distinctive kind of legal positivism. At the same time, however, the force of law apparently necessary for the establishment of a properly bounded liable subject cannot itself be sustained without an appeal to the more general regularity of custom or practice as such. And this cannot be a regularity the law might institute, since the law's performativity—its constitutive capability—is itself constituted by this regularity. Lawmaking and the production of legal subjects are themselves lawful in the sense of being necessarily procedural and rule-bound.

Attention is thus directed toward this more general performativity underlying that of the law, the very structure of "conventionality" itself, which alone is able to account for the productive power or force of a law that in fact generates what it claims to regulate. Such a generalized, rule-bound production might be approached through the Aristotelian category of *poesis,* the mode of making according to rules and patterns that informs the modern sense of the technical or mechanical. So the resort to the performative as productive convention reinvigorates a project of identifying culture as poesis, and the standpoint from which such a making of sense itself makes sense is once again that of a cultural poetics. Such a poetics is not just a mode of knowing what happens in culture, but free of any merely empirical remit is also the mode of knowing how culture happens, the conditions of its possibility. More than twenty years ago, Paul de Man recognized as much in his remark that "the characterization of the performative as sheer convention reduces it in effect to a grammatical code among others," and this is a grammar of the *event* of culture ("how culture happens") in the senses both of an object of knowledge and a kind of knowing.[10]

This might seem to make rather too much of Sacks's brief remarks. They do, however, and however briefly, exemplify the renewed resort to the performative that has informed social and cultural theory over recent years as part of the continuing effort to develop a satisfactory understanding of "cultural construction." They also illustrate a fascinating passage in a thinking of legal performativity between the two very different ways in which the concept of law is customarily invoked. There is a move here from the thinking of law as juridical obligation to its apprehension as regularity, a set of rules or constitutive conditions (scientific "laws," for example), and this is a move that matters for attempts to accommodate ethical or political questions within a thinking either of performative utterances or of cultural performativity in a more general sense. This essay aims, in part, to explore what happens when these differing senses of law come together in this way.

That such an exploration should proceed via the figure of Ben Jonson perhaps requires some justification. The exemplary and sustained—if far from unique—preoccupation with questions of justice, legality, and responsibility that is to be found in his writing, and in particular its sensitivity to the implication of language itself, as utterance and otherwise, in the machinations of the law, make it an obvious candidate for an examination in these terms.[11] His role here, though, is not merely illustrative: it is by taking seriously a problem Jonson explicitly bequeaths to us, his readers— the possibility of making one's excuses—that the essay is led to the work of some contemporary thinkers of language in action who have themselves stumbled across (and sometimes over) the peculiar difficulty of the excuse. To presume in this way to receive Jonson's addresses ensures that this cannot be a properly historicist account; furthermore, for reasons I hope will become apparent, this kind of anachronism inevitably precludes both an attempt to map out specifically early modern kinds of performativity and the ready utilization of a concept of performativity as a transhistorical critical instrument.[12]

It is, though, very difficult to begin without noting quite how many of Jonson's engagements with matters of law lend themselves to description in the terms of speech act theory. *Epicoene,* for example, is built around a wedding, one of Austin's paradigmatic speech acts; furthermore, much of the play's conclusion consists of an attempt to judge the felicity of that act, the discussion dominated by two minor characters playing the parts of the interpreters of "Canon-law" and "positiue Diuinitie" (5.3.41, 42).[13] Elsewhere, the question of seriousness or sincerity—a crux for juristic writing and speech act theory alike—is made an explicit focus of the drama. In *The New Inn,* for example, the structurally central last scene of act 4 features an exchange on this topic between Lady Frampul and Prudence, her maidservant. Lady Frampul insists that in the preceding "parliament of love," in which she has apparently toyed with the affections of Lovel, the protagonist, she was only initially sporting a "visor" or "masque" (4.4.294, 295) of mockery and rebukes Prudence for letting Lovel leave. The latter has done so because, she says, "I thought you had dissembled, Madam" (4.4.310), and she asks regarding the mask:

> But how do I know, when her Ladiship is pleas'd
> To leaue it off, except she tell me so?
>
> (4.4.296–97)

This might appear a not unreasonable question—but Lady Frampul insists that Prudence should have been able to tell what she really meant, and her anger at not being "vnderstood" (4.4.309) leads her into an outburst against her maidservant. Prudence's hurt at this is met with the Lady's insistence that she now does *not* mean what she says, that "it was a word fell from me, *Pru*, by chance" (4.4.325). Pru herself responds by claiming that it was this retraction that was in fact not meant, even if her mistress did not know that she did not mean it, and that she—Pru—*can* in this case tell the sincere from the nonserious:

> Good Madame, please to vndeceaue your selfe,
> I know when words do slip, and when they are darted
> With all their bitternesse . . .
>
> (4.4.326–28)

It is not clear whether Prudence is claiming that this intellectual capacity is in some way peculiar to her; Lady Frampul, though, is equally convinced that a common gender in fact ensures that women can know each other's intentions intuitively:

> One woman, reads anothers character,
> Without the tedious trouble of deciphering,
> If she but giue her mind to't.
>
> (4.4.300–302)

Given both their mutual and acknowledged incomprehension, and the dizzying complications introduced by Pru's confident invocation of Lady Frampul's unconscious, it is strange to find this accompanying and apparently contradictory insistence that utterances either *could* not or *should* not be misread (though the difference between "could" and "should" is itself a further complicating factor). Here, agency and its legibility are locked together in ways that point, as we will see below, to the crucial question of what can be *known,* and how.

In an influential reading of the poetry, Stanley Fish makes a prime example of Jonson's well-known "Epistle to Master John Selden." Here, he claims, Jonson institutes a "community of the same," a state "of epistemological immediacy and ontological self-sufficiency" that identifies its members with each other while preventing any opening to those excluded.[14] As such, it offers a security both of cognition and recognition in which its members participate without effort or loss—in short, without expenditure. The poem describes, and is, a process of "gifts reciprocally given and taken," of a "shared understanding . . . so total and so instantaneous, so independent of language or any other discursive form, that it need not be communicated."[15] Fish produces such an account, though, only by playing down the importance of the first twenty-eight lines of the poem in which, if Selden is addressed, it is not just from within the immediacy of a "community of the same." Instead, the opening statement—"I Know to whom I write"—is followed by a detailed reflection on the circumstances that call forth these kinds of addresses, where judgment on a work is asked for in order that praise might preface the printed book.

Given that the address to Selden is an instance of this kind of exchange functioning freely, honestly, and to the reciprocal benefit of the parties, happily aligning judgment and understanding on the one hand with obligation and benefit on the other, it cannot be begun without the establishment as context of different occasions on which the components failed to work reciprocally. As Jonson says:

> in most of workes it be
> A pennance, where a man may not be free,
> Rather then Office, when it doth or may
> Chance that the Friends affection proves Allay
> Unto the Censure.   (7–11)

This "so vitious Humanitie" (12) is something of which Jonson himself, so it transpires, has been not infrequently guilty:

> Though I confesse (as every Muse hath err'd,
> And mine not least) I have too oft preferr'd
> Men past their termes, and prais'd some names too much,
> But 'twas with purpose to have made them such.
>   (19–22)

Here, the language of contract appears only in its failure to contain judgment and obligation within the same frame. The responsibilities of friendship, the poem has already acknowledged, can lead to a sharp break between what is known and what is said or done; now, this and perhaps less "humane" vices are identified as a way of betraying the kind of equilibrium exemplified by the reciprocity of contract. And this failure calls forth other modes of obligation, debt, and settlement. First is the confession, in which the unity of knowledge and utterance may be reaffirmed; then comes the excuse, in which the disjunction itself can be redeemed as a means of remaking the lost unity.

That ought to be an end to the matter. But the poem immediately troubles its own excuse by offering another one:

> Since, being deceiv'd, I turne a sharper eye
> Upon my selfe, and aske to whom? and why?
> And what I write?
>
> (23-25)

This serves to make the position outlined in the previous lines almost untenable. Where in the first excuse understanding returned to make good its betrayal, here that betrayal outlasts the occasion and can only be ended by the "sharper eye" of a chastened hindsight. But can either excuse stand in the presence of the other? Is there a temporal sequence here that allows for the passage from the first to the second? Or do they nevertheless contaminate each other irreparably? Certainly, as far as the poem is concerned, both the ground and the author are cleared for a climactic declaration:

> So that my Reader is assur'd, I now
> Meane what I speake: and still will keepe that Vow.
>
> (28-29)

Under the circumstances, it is hard to imagine a less reassuring assurance. The reader—and is that here still only Selden?—is promised sincerity, the adequation of praise to judgment: the poet can here, now, finally be trusted once again. Or at any rate, the poet can be trusted once his promises can themselves be trusted, for to promise sincerity is to beg the question. This, perhaps, is why the promise is ineffectually redoubled in the vow to keep the vow, where that "will" hovers between a deontic and an epistemic future tense.[16] Though the equivocation is useful—if this last clause could simply be a statement, the poem could rescue itself from the promissory loop in which it has become caught—it also, fatally, ensures that even the limits of the epistemic cannot be properly known.

Having come this far, the poem then turns to address Selden as an intelligible "Object" (29) in precisely the terms that Fish suggests, but that it does so on the basis outlined here makes its evocation of "epistemological immediacy and ontological self-sufficiency" seem somewhat less confident. To the extent that the unity of judgment and performative is predicated on or—a necessary alternative—underwritten by a prior performative, it cannot proceed from such metaphysical foundations; it can only ever be a happy coincidence. At the same time, though, the poem insists on the intelligibility of the disjunction manifest in those instances when utterance broke its contract with knowledge. Excuse clears the way for the truthfulness that the promise is supposed to establish, and excuse involves a more or less forensic understanding of whatever action is to be its object. So before Selden can "Stand forth" (29) as a known object, those prior utterances must be made known for what they were. In this, the poem follows a pattern that forms one of the main modes of Jonson's engagement with the law, establishing the nature both of its dependence on and resistance to a thinking of language in action. Yet the significance of excuse for the address to Selden also recalls another set of Jonsonian utterances, epistles of another kind—the seven letters sent to powerful patrons following his incarceration in 1605, probably on account of the offense given by *Eastward Ho!*, that together make up a disproportionately large part of his surviving correspondence.

The familiar story, like much else in Jonson's biography, turns out to rest on some perhaps incautious interpretation of the available evidence.[17] The claims made in the letters, furthermore, do not tally with the account of the incident Jonson later gave to Drummond, hence offering further grounds for dispute. But interpreters are in broad agreement on the general outline: Jonson and Chapman are imprisoned for incurring the king's "high displeasure" with *Eastward Ho!*,[18] in mocking references to James's Scottish retinue (even to James himself) and perhaps in presenting the play without the necessary allowance at a time when the court was out of London.[19] They wait, unexamined, for the judicial process to do its work, while it appears that their collaborator, Marston, is somehow beyond the reach of the authorities. Both write a number of letters to those who might look favorably on their situation and have the power to influence the outcome—but while there is plenty of self-abasement in Jonson's accounts, and also an apology, the pleading is always special: there is no confession and no guilt, because there has been no crime. The note struck in the

first of the series (probably addressed to the Lord Chamberlain, the Earl of
Suffolk), where Jonson insists that "the cause is in us wholie mistaken
(at least misconstrued)" (193), is echoed in the rest. They accept and
acknowledge that offense was taken, but they seek to excuse Jonson from
the responsibility for that offense.

But excuse, as has already been noted, is not necessarily a simple matter.
The letter to Salisbury points up a potential difficulty: "being too diligent
for my excuse, I may incurre the suspicion of being guilty" (195). The fear
is that the more vigorously one exonerates oneself, the more ineffective
such exoneration may become. In whom, therefore, or in which procedure,
does the power to excuse reside? Is it appropriate to speak of it as a power
that might be wielded? And what is Jonson's excuse in the first place? Being
the victim of a mistake, as his letter acknowledges, is not the same thing as
suffering a misconstrual. The letter to Salisbury seems to suggest that it is
all Marston's fault, complaining that Jonson has had "othermens Errors . . .
made my Crimes" (195), while that addressed to Pembroke asserts that
the two prisoners are "vexed for other mens licence" (200). Even these
statements are not unambiguous, though, since they could be aligned with
the more frequently voiced suggestion that the troubling license has in
fact been exercised by those who have understood the play maliciously,
as demonstrating malice towards James, and therefore not understood it at
all. These already cloudy waters are further muddied by the translation of
some of these arguments to the Dedicatory Epistle prefaced to *Volpone:*
there, he seems to exclude his collaborations from the excuses advanced
to ward off criticism, yet he does so with terms and phrases borrowed
from the defense of one of those collaborations. But there is a consistency
among these various extenuations: unsurprisingly, it is the general form
of the excuse itself. Jonson can be excused because he is not at fault.
Perhaps it is only *"Rumor"* (195, 198), verifiably false. Or else Marston
wrote something offensive, but Jonson didn't, and he should not be held
responsible for that part of the play. But if it was something that he has
in some way signed, then they were not his words when they offended
but those of A. N. Other, a shadowy misunderstander. Excuse in this case
absolves in the sense not of pardoning but of declaring innocent.

It is the possibility of such absolution for words uttered that is of most
interest here, since it involves Jonson—as in the Selden epistle, or in
the exchange between Lady Frampul and Prudence—in evoking excuse
as a process of clarification, a performative whose force depends on

understanding and is thus derived from a properly constative core. Yet such a judgment does not appeal primarily to the facts of any particular situation, of whether or not some or other words were actually said or written, and not even ultimately to the malice of those who might wish to see Jonson hurt. Instead, excuse needs to account for the ways in which the accusation might be sustainable: it needs to clarify what it is in a work that gives the malicious their chance. Jonson seeks to establish this ground of excuse in a passage from the Dedicatory Epistle to *Volpone* that borrows directly from the letter addressed to Salisbury from jail more than a year earlier. Insisting that "it is not rumour can make men guiltie, much lesse entitle me, to other mens crimes" (60–62)—compare the letter to Salisbury: "suffer not othermens Errors, or Falts past, to be made my Crimes. . . . If others haue transgressd, let not me bee entitled to theyre Follyes" (195)— Jonson then announces an understanding of language in its generality:

I know, that nothing can bee so innocently writ, or carryed, but may be made obnoxious to construction; mary, whil'st I beare mine innocence about mee, I feare it not.   (62–64)

The word "obnoxious" has undergone a semantic reversal in recent centuries.[20] Here used in what the *OED* still gives as its primary sense, it implies not the power to harm or give offense but instead a *vulnerability*, a peculiar power to get hurt. This is clearly a form of inertia, appropriately following the "nothing" that is passively "writ or carried." At the same time, though, as a kind of receptivity it is a potential, oddly coupling lack of force with a tendency or drive toward self-mutilation. And this potent impotence is a property of *all* language, a general liability that thus reduces the liability of Jonson himself (indeed, without the preposition, "obnoxious" might mean precisely guilty or blameworthy[21]) while determining chance as danger.

Yet it is also as if this capacity of language had the power to render Jonson himself "obnoxious" (and we should perhaps remember that bodily mutilation was precisely the threatened punishment in this instance[22]): the more certain his innocence from malicious actions, the more insistent his guilty vulnerability. If the obnoxiousness of words has generated his difficulties, it is also that to which he must appeal if his excuses are ever to have a chance of being made. The stakes are made clear in an extraordinary passage from the letter archived as the first in the series. Like the others, this addresses itself to an aristocrat, a person of influence; it also, again like others in the series, calls God to testify to the author's sincerely held high opinion of the king. Yet there is another address here, too. A second paragraph begins:

And I appeale to posteritie that will hereafter read and Iudge my writings (though now neglected) whether it be possible, I should speak of his Maiestie as I haue done, without the affection of a most zealous and good subject. It hath euer bene my destenye to be misreported, and condemn'd, on the first tale; but I hope there is an Eare left for mee.   (194)

Not just the Lord Chamberlain's ear, then, nor even God's, but that of "posteritie," a future in which Jonson will be properly readable, justified, restored to the words whose vulnerability has produced his in making thinkable a severance of voice from affection. Whether such a severance is possible or not is the question—clearly a question of character, but in this context almost transcendental—that Jonson confides to the future. This would be an earthly last judgment that would give him the last word, allowing him to evade the destiny of the "mis-" he currently endures (a destiny to which even the first sentence of this passage recondemns him, if it can be read as answering the question it poses). And, of course, the ark that will carry him in pieces on toward this future is language. To postpone an answer is to give posterity the chance to redeem both language and Jonson in undoing his loss. But this redemption will happen only when Jonson is gone, indeed, on the condition that he—as both the "neglected" works and, with this address, his letter—become archivable. And if all language is obnoxious, such hopes might seem fragile. To appeal in making his excuses to this kind of linguistic potential is to put his trust in the very means that might prevent the establishment, documenting, and recording of his innocence, or at least to ensure that this will be an infinite labor. Posterity, that is to say, might never be in a position to announce that the question was merely rhetorical all along.

In these scenes of excuse we witness the necessary involvement and incompatibility of understanding and action: neither functions without the other, while their interdependence is never secured—it might rather be called an interference. Excuse here would be nothing without a grounding knowledge of the general structure of language in action, a knowledge that is other than or prior to any performative, precisely the knowledge of its preconditions; yet such knowledge appears to issue not in grounds but in the restless movement of contradiction or antinomy. Any understanding dissolves back into a claim to understand, an assertion of cognitive mastery that retains the unfulfilled status of a claim. What it knows, therefore, is an activity to which it can never be adequate and cannot comprehend, an activity that includes just this interference between understanding and action. If there is a proper performative in the customary sense, then, it is not an excuse; by the same token, if excuse happens, it does not (just) do so performatively. In this predicament—and as the echo of lines from the concluding scene of *Poetaster* in the letter to Salisbury makes clear—it parallels the activity of slander it is called upon to counter, in its particularly Jonsonian form of libelous misreading.[23] An insistent concern in the many works that make a topic of writing, slander is effective precisely to the extent that it goes unrecognized. It has force only for as long as it has the pure statement's irresistible lack of force: it ceases to happen as soon as it begins to appear as itself, as action.

From its beginnings in Austin, the thinking of the performative has come at once to rest and grief on the excuse (indeed, insofar as the concept is held to have philosophical antecedents, the difficulties have been traced back even further[24]). In "A Plea for Excuses," one of his better known essays, Austin treats it directly in setting out the variety of forms that a language of defense, justification, or extenuation might take. Excuse, he suggests, comes into play when "the mechanisms of the natural successful act" have broken down.[25] "It rapidly becomes plain," he continues, "that the breakdowns signalized by the various excuses are of radically different kinds, affecting different parts or stages of the machinery, which the excuses consequently pick out and sort out for us."[26] Here, the language of excuse is a means of comprehending the linguistic categorization of action, and it is happily set apart from the machinery of any action, marking the points where such a machine fails to function. Excuse comprehends action, without partaking of it. In *How To Do Things with Words,* however, matters are different. Austin is now investigating the machinery of language itself and in doing so confronts again, early on, the workings of excuse. This time, since it is linguistic action that is under investigation, one might expect excuse to be possible to the extent that one can appeal to a distinction between what was said and what was meant—the various ways in which something might be uttered inadvertently, unintentionally, unwittingly, and so on.

This, though, is not what happens. Instead, in a passage that has been a focus for recent discussion by Stanley Cavell and J. Hillis Miller, Austin cites a line from Euripides' *Hippolytus* as a paradigmatic example of an inadmissible excuse.[27] Of performatives, he says, "we are apt to have a feeling that their being serious consists in their being uttered as (merely) the outward and visible sign . . . of an inward and spiritual act." The "classic expression" of this, he suggests, is to be found in Hippolytus's statement regarding a prior promise, that "my tongue swore to, but my heart . . . did not."[28] Austin's immediate target is the metaphysics implicit in an understanding of any speech act as simply the constative description of an "interior" state. But he makes a scandal of this distinction, invoking an illocutionary force that marks *all* forms of insincerity (though any distinction between deliberate and accidental insincerity restates the issue) as inexcusable, beyond the reach of any effacing absolution. The philosopher who appeals to the breach between the exteriority of the tongue and the interiority of the heart may think that he is "surveying the invisible depths of ethical space" but in fact "provides Hippolytus with a let-out, the bigamist with an excuse for his 'I do' and the welsher with a defense for his 'I bet.' Accuracy and morality alike are on the side of the plain saying that *our word is our bond.*"[29]

The first consequence of this, as Cavell and Miller have pointed out, is that Austin cannot be read as identifying the seriousness or illocutionary force of an utterance with the intention of any conscious agent.[30] Quite the opposite, in fact: Austin insists here that a false promise—which is not the same as a lie—is not void, that it works or takes place and cannot be retracted by excuse. The "plain saying" to which he appeals is not an ethical "ought" or a breakable law but a rule, closer to what Cavell in an earlier work calls a "Categorial Declarative."[31] Words bind, necessarily: they are bound to bind; they can do no other. Austin pits the ordinary language philosophy to which his account of the performative belongs against a less accurate thinking of language that is apt only to lead us into epistemological error. That this erroneous thinking, though, is already at work in the ordinary, that it forms some of the kinds of inadvertence described in "A Plea for Excuses," might lead us to question the categorial status of this plain saying. If procedures for excuse can be extended to utterances, it is not necessarily the case that words bind and promises can come undone. On the other hand, as Cavell points out, if "the saying of words is not excusable the way the performance of actions is," then:

Saying something is after all, or before all, on Austinian grounds, not exactly or merely or transparently doing something. So Austin's theory of excuses cannot after all be incorporated tidily into the theory of performatives, hence releasing its grounding thought—that in certain critical instances saying something is doing something—into the open again.[32]

In Austin too, then, excuse reveals what is fraught in the analysis of performatives and performativity. Indeed, the dangers of the uncertain ground displayed in the equivocal place of excuse appear nowhere more starkly than in that brief quotation from the *Hippolytus*—something of a commonplace, already familiar enough in Plato's time to be cited twice in his works.[33] In Euripides, though, as Cavell insistently points out, it is not an excuse.[34] The tongue swore (not "lied" or "pretended to swear"), and Hippolytus dies in part because his word is his bond. Plato and Austin have misread him, inflicting exactly the injurious fate that exercises Jonson so strongly. In light of this episode Cavell reads Austin, *contra* Derrida, tragically: "not as denying that I have to abandon my words, create so many orphans, but as affirming that I am abandoned to them, as to thieves, or conspirators, taking my breath away, which metaphysics would deny."[35] That words bind, then, becomes "more a curse than a sensible maxim."[36] It can be such a maxim only to the extent that words, in the ordinary, must mean what they say, and the nature of the bonds is regular and knowable in advance. Austin, though, can only secure this ground by simultaneously excluding the subject of any utterance from its power to work and denying the difference between subject and saying. But if there is room in this realm for the kind of difference that might keep *falsity* meaningful, as Austin also avers, then the skies do darken dramatically. Whatever our words say that we have done, we have done. If they slander us—and it seems that they can—they slander us in the name of the law, to preserve its quasi-categorial functioning, to hold in place the properly calibrated distribution of responsibility, of guilt and innocence, without which we would be nothing. Such a destiny appears both as the matrix of our mundane language and the transfer of its vulnerability to the bodies of those by whom it lives. As in Jonson, it is the fracture exposed by excuse in the thinking of the performative that postulates both the plausibility of this fate and the hope of evading it.

The trajectory of these excuses revisits familiar theoretical topoi while invoking a disruptive power undimmed by any familiarity. Indeed, in marking this point in Jonson and Austin as a kind of disjunction between cognition and performance, we have approached, albeit from a different starting point, the disfigurement of excuse presented by Paul de Man in the concluding essay of *Allegories of Reading.* There, de Man reads Rousseau's *Confessions* and *Fourth Reverie* as particularly forceful instances of this disjunction. Analyzing Rousseau's narration of the scene of excuse that follows from the youthful theft of a ribbon, a scene culminating in the false accusation of a maidservant, de Man reads the disjunction as a sudden shift in the rhetorical mode of the excuse. Rousseau's initial formulation of excuse places it within the horizon of the desiring subject:

Knowledge, morality, possession, exposure, affectivity (shame as the synthesis of pleasure and pain), and the performative excuse are all ultimately part of one system that is epistemologically as well as ethically grounded and therefore available as meaning, in the mode of understanding.[37]

In de Man's reading, this abruptly gives way to an appeal to a language that speaks—or acts—entirely outside this tropological system, at the point where Rousseau claims to have made his accusation entirely without motivation. In asserting that he accused Marion accidentally, without meaning to, he produces what ought to be an unanswerable excuse:

For it is only if the act that initiated the entire chain, the utterance of the sound "Marion," is truly without any conceivable motive that the total arbitrariness of the action becomes the most effective, the most efficaciously performative excuse of all. The estrangement between subject and utterance is then so radical that it escapes any mode of comprehension.[38]

In his reading of the *Reverie,* this estrangement becomes generalized and radicalized as "fiction," a seemingly innocuous activity beyond all subject-centered determinations of guilt or innocence, which de Man provocatively reads back into the pure contingency Rousseau locates behind the accusation of Marion:

As a fiction, the statement is innocuous and the error harmless; it is the misguided reading of the error as theft or slander, the refusal to admit that fiction is fiction, the stubborn resistance to the "fact," obvious by itself, that language is entirely free with regard to referential meaning and can posit whatever its grammar allows it to say, which leads to the transformation of random error into injustice.[39]

The failure of some interpreters to read this passage as free indirect discourse has resulted in the lodging of strong objections since its publication, criticism reinvigorated by the revelation of crimes de Man never properly confessed, and for which he might have been seeking covertly to excuse himself.[40] Here, though, he retells *Rousseau's* appeal to the performativity of language as machine, precisely as a general, generative capacity that depends on no subject for its effects. Far from upholding this appeal as "the most efficaciously performative excuse," de Man's reading goes on to reinscribe the machine as a threat to the very possibility of excuse. Its relations to those who would be excused rendered completely arbitrary, excuse itself becomes in essence—as nothing but the performance of the letter—meaningless:

It is no longer certain that language, as excuse, exists because of a prior guilt but just as possible that since language, as a machine, performs anyway, we have to produce guilt (and all its train of psychic consequences) in order to make the excuse meaningful.[41]

In other words, as Jacques Derrida has noted in a recent commentary, the implication of excuse in such a radical technicity "engenders automatically a situation in which forgiveness and excuse are both automatic (they cannot not take place, in some way independently of the presumed living 'subjects' that they are supposed to involve) and therefore null and void. . . . [A]utomatic and mechanical pardons or excuses cannot have the value of pardon and excuse."[42] Yet as Derrida points out—and here we might be reminded both of Jonson's appeal to posterity and Austin's emphasis on the mundane necessity of the binding word—the authentic propriety of the excuse simultaneously depends on the regularity or technicity of a language considered in its grammatical aspect, as its *own* capacity to perform *us.* This moment is necessary if there is to be the linguistic event of excuse. The determining relation to the subject is stubbornly maintained, both as hope and as danger, and once again, in this context, an invocation of the power of language involves a threat figured as corporeal vulnerability, an openness to wounding or mutilation. Commenting on Rousseau's acknowledgment of "the lethal quality of all writing," de Man remarks:

Writing always includes the moment of dispossession in favor of the arbitrary power play of the signifier and from the point of view of the subject, this can only be experienced as a dismemberment, a beheading or a castration.[43]

The threat, though, does *not* arise from the disjunctive interference between the rhetoric of understanding and that of action. Indeed, though

on one level it puts in question the intelligibility of excuse, the invocation
of machinic language—as the specification of a general or constitutive
capacity—*restores* performance to cognition on another. In fact, it seeks to
close up the disjunction, "deciding or 'resolving' the question," as Cynthia
Chase suggests in an exemplary discussion,

> in favor of the cognition *of* performance. That is also the *aesthetifying* move: to
> perceive an arbitrary process as a recognizable, and in that measure a satisfying,
> formal whole. . . . It is the move that consists in the imaginary experience of
> beholding, and valorizing—as a single shape or "current"—an overdetermined,
> nondetermined, insolubly dual, contradictory and conflictual process.[44]

This is the trap nested in the thought of language as "radically formal, i.e.
mechanical": a vulnerability to the "aesthetic ideology" de Man describes
in his late essays, "its construction or construal as a whole, total, form,
a non-referential, because all-encompassing, self-sufficient system."[45] In
Cavell's reading of Austin, dismemberment and death are transfigured and
recognized as tragedy: this fate is only interrupted in de Man's text by the
unstoppable shuttling or temporal displacement across the disjunction—
the interference—that he calls irony.

What remains, then, is precisely this movement, this happening, irreducible to a thinking of performativity yet always at work within it
and marked only allegorically. For some interpreters it can for this reason be described as *a strange kind of* constitutive movement, a quasi-
transcendental condition of possibility that is never simply so.[46] In Derrida's
reading, drawing both on "Excuses (*Confessions*)" and the late essays, it
is named variously as a "work," "prosaic resistance," "force of resistance,"
and "materiality without matter":

> [I]t is not *something* sensible or intelligible; it is not even the matter of a body.
> As it is not something, as it is nothing and yet it works, *cela oeuvre,* this nothing
> therefore operates, it forces, but as a force of resistance. It resists both beautiful
> form and matter as substantial and organic totality.[47]

Such a work is related in this essay to the "cut" that is both the promise
of and threat to any performative event or subject, "at once a wounding
and an opening."[48] At the same time, it is the paradoxical precondition
of a machinic, purely grammatical language, marking the iterability that
both keeps it regular and necessarily contaminates it with an alterity—
even, perhaps, a spontaneity—it cannot foresee or master, preventing

it from settling into a generally and calculably determinative function. If Derrida can at this point assimilate the de Manian disjunction to his own quasi-concept of iterability, it is because both gesture in this way toward the necessary aporias of language thought as a fundamental poesis, as itself *properly constitutive* of anything. That is to say, both intimate a resistance to any—implicitly or explicitly—metaphysical understanding of a generalized linguistic performativity or technicity of illocution. Such a force can only be thought as necessarily undecidable, undetermined or overdetermined by the conceptual system that posits it; the system, that is to say, cannot account for its taking place and thus ground its own certainties. To call "performative" any of the kinds of linguistic taking place—none reducible to language *as such,* none necessarily substantial or felicitous— that such an account continues to imply, as de Man, Derrida, and others have done, involves a more or less thorough catachresis. This almost goes without saying: despite a long-established tendency to associate the work of both de Man and Derrida with a "linguistic turn," the tracing of these aporias is one of the most familiar movements in what has been known for more than thirty years as deconstruction.

But only *almost* without saying. We noted earlier the strong seductions for Sacks of a concept of generalized performativity in his account of the law's work, and it can be argued that such seductions are operative too in conceptual configurations of performativity that appear at first sight to come after deconstruction. Judith Butler's hugely influential deployment of the performative claims at least partial descent from Derrida's catachrestic rendering of the term,[49] yet in her account of the performative constitution of subjectivity it is a surprise to find more than a little evidence of this difficulty. It can be seen most clearly in the sustained engagement with Derridean iterability that makes up much of the concluding essay in *Excitable Speech,* itself the occasion of her most thoroughgoing examination of concepts of the performative. Butler's deployment of the term is to some extent problematic from the start, since her syncretic thinking of the performative event assimilates the (quasi-)transcendental register of Derrida's work both to Bourdieu's concept of the habitus and to a rather more Foucauldian emphasis on conditions of emergence—hence, perhaps, the troubling slippage between iterability and repetition that recurs throughout the essay.[50] The difficulty is most noticeable, however, in her insistence that the "breaking force" that Derrida identifies with iterability in his initial encounter with Austin is the same as "the force of the performative" in its productive, proper sense.[51] To make this equation is to transform the aporia of the iterable into a structural account of performativity, the determination of an event of force by positive conditions of possibility. It is this that allows Butler to speak of a "logic of iterability that governs the possibility of social transformation" and can be "enact[ed]."[52] The iterable serves here to supplement an account of performativity that attributes its "taking place" to its conventionality in order to make the possibility of change comprehensible within such a systematic account. There is nothing quasi- about this transcendental, nothing that points either to the necessary undecidability of performative events or to the equally necessary heterogeneity to the conceptual scheme of what it suggests must take place.

It is all the more perplexing, then, to find Butler arguing that the thinking of iterability ought itself to be supplemented by "a reading of the speech act that does more than universalize its operation on the basis of its putatively formal structure." If this accuses Derrida of formalism, it does so only to seek a more expansive formalism capable of furnishing "an account of the social iterability of the utterance."[53] Far from offering "an unanticipated political future for deconstructive thinking," as Butler suggests, such a theory would approximate more closely to a foreknowledge of the bounds of the political: it would be nothing other than the cognition of performance, the poetics of a poesis, an understanding of the machine.[54] The invocation by Derrida and de Man of a work at something like this transcendental level is the invocation of another kind of originary technicity or "originary performativity," an aporia that resists or renders vulnerable the very work of theorization.[55] There is, in other words, something of the obnoxious about such a force, something that at the same time affects a resort— such as Jonson's—to both the explanatory power of the obnoxious and the accusatory or exculpatory implications that can apparently be derived from it. Yet the ethical tenor of such implications is not thereby lost or abandoned, as de Man's critics too often supposed: Derrida's more recent work in particular has shown how far this predicament requires of theory a renewed consideration of the nature of the ethical and political, how far, indeed, it is opened up to the deontic modality of demands and injunctions precisely because its project of grounding an ethics or a politics cannot be secured on the terms it sets for itself. At any rate, a response to such a predicament cannot simply be sought in anything as grand as a poetics, or—which is the same thing—in a general theory of performativity. The question of our responsibilities, along with Jonson's questions regarding his, will not be so comprehensively settled: some kind of posterity still has work to do.

Notes

1. David Kay, *Ben Jonson: A Literary Life* (Basingstoke: Macmillan, 1995), 2.

2. See, for example, Jonathan Goldberg, *James I and the Politics of Literature* (Baltimore: Johns Hopkins University Press, 1983); Peter Womack, *Ben Jonson* (Oxford: Basil Blackwell, 1986); Richard Burt, *Licensed by Authority: Ben Jonson and the Politics of Censorship* (Ithaca and London: Cornell University Press, 1993); Joseph Loewenstein, *Ben Jonson and Possessive Authorship* (Cambridge: Cambridge University Press, 2002); and Richard Dutton, *Ben Jonson: Authority: Criticism* (Basingstoke: Macmillan, 1996).

3. J. L. Austin, *How To Do Things with Words* (Oxford: Oxford University Press, 1962), 19; Ian Maclean, *Interpretation and Meaning in the Renaissance: The Case of Law* (Cambridge: Cambridge University Press, 1992), 158-71.

4. Maclean, *Interpretation and Meaning,* 168-70.

5. P. S. Atiyah, *Promises, Morals and Law* (Oxford: Clarendon Press, 1981); J. H. Baker, *The Legal Profession and the Common Law: Historical Essays* (London: Hambledon Press, 1986); A. W. B. Simpson, *A History of the Common Law of Contract: The Rise of the Action of Assumpsit* (Oxford: Clarendon Press, 1979); Luke Wilson, *Theaters of Intention: Drama and the Law in Early Modern England* (Stanford: Stanford University Press, 2000).

6. Wilson, *Theaters of Intention,* esp. 68-148.

7. Ibid., 24.

8. Lorna Hutson, "*Ethopoeia,* Source-Study and Legal History: A Post-Theoretical Approach to the Question of 'Character' in Shakespearean Drama," in *Post-Theory: New Directions in Criticism,* ed. Martin McQuillan et al. (Edinburgh: Edinburgh University Press, 1999).

9. David Harris Sacks, "The Promise and the Contract in Early Modern England: Slade's Case in Perspective," in *Rhetoric and Law in Early Modern Europe,* ed. Victoria Kahn and Lorna Hutson (New Haven and London: Yale University Press, 2001), 45.

10. Paul de Man, *The Resistance to Theory* (Minneapolis: University of Minnesota Press, 1986), 19.

11. For an overview of his work, and indications of recent critical writing that might justify these assertions, see my *Complete Critical Guide to Ben Jonson* (London and New York: Routledge, 2002).

12. There are, inevitably, further exclusions, and one in particular calls for comment. My resort here to Jonson's letters, and the concerns that follow from a reading of those, mean that the important and fecund question of the relation between performativity and theatrical performance is not properly addressed. This is, as the history of the performative since Austin has shown, a topic of consistent interest and not a little disagreement, and one that sheds its own light on the concerns explored here. See, in evidence, the essays gathered in *Performativity and Performance,* ed. Andrew Parker and Eve Kosofsky Sedgwick (London and New York: Routledge, 1995).

13. References to Jonson's poems and plays, including prefatory matter, are from Ben Jonson, *Ben Jonson,* ed. C. H. Herford, Percy Simpson, and Evelyn Simpson, 11 vols. (Oxford: Oxford University Press, 1925-52).

14. Stanley Fish, "Authors-Readers: Jonson's Community of the Same," *Representations* 7 (1984): 35.

15. Fish, "Authors-Readers," 54, 54-55.

16. For the importance of this distinction within the late medieval and early modern deployment of the future construction, see Leslie Arnovick, *The Development of Future Constructions in English: The Pragmatics of Modal and Temporal* Will *and* Shall *in Middle English* (New York: Peter Lang, 1990).

17. Richard Dutton, *Mastering the Revels: The Regulation and Censorship of English Renaissance Drama* (Basingstoke: Macmillan, 1991), 171-79.

18. Jonson, *Ben Jonson,* I:193. Further page references are given parenthetically in the text.

19. Kay, *Ben Jonson,* 75-76; Dutton, *Mastering the Revels* 171-74.

20. *OED,* 2d ed., s.v. "obnoxious," def. 1.a.

21. Ibid., def. 2.

22. Jonson, *Ben Jonson,* I:140.

23. Compare *Poetaster,* V.iii.140-42, and Jonson, *Ben Jonson,* I:195, lines 22-24. In his edition of *Poetaster,* Thomas Cain traces the phrase to its roots in Martial: Ben Jonson, *Poetaster,* ed. Thomas Cain (Manchester: Manchester University Press, 1995), 231.

24. Rodolphe Gasché, *The Wild Card of Reading: On Paul de Man* (Cambridge and London: Harvard University Press, 1998), 11-47.

25. J. L. Austin, *Philosophical Papers,* 3d ed. (Oxford: Oxford University Press, 1979), 180.

26. Ibid.

27. Stanley Cavell, *A Pitch of Philosophy: Autobiographical Exercises* (Cambridge and London: Harvard University Press, 1994), 86-108; J. Hillis Miller, *Speech Acts in Literature* (Stanford: Stanford University Press, 2001), 28-40.

28. Austin, *How To Do Things,* 9-10.

29. Ibid., 10.

30. Cavell, *Pitch of Philosophy,* 106-8; Miller, 30-31.

31. Stanley Cavell, *Must We Mean What We Say? A Book of Essays* (New York: Charles Scribner's Sons, 1969), 25, 31-32.

32. Cavell, *Pitch of Philosophy,* 104-5.

33. Ibid., 181.

34. Ibid., 88, 101, 104, and 111.

35. Ibid., 125.

36. Ibid., 101.

37. Paul de Man, *Allegories of Reading* (New Haven and London: Yale University Press, 1979), 287.

38. Ibid., 289.

39. Ibid., 293.

40. See, for example, the discussions by Sandy Petrey, *Speech Acts and Literary Theory* (London: Routledge, 1990), 154-58, and Allan Stoekl, "De Man and Guilt," in *Responses: On*

Paul de Man's Wartime Journalism, ed. Werner Hamacher, Neil Hertz, and Thomas Keenan (Lincoln and London: University of Nebraska Press, 1989), 375-85.

41. De Man, *Allegories,* 299.

42. Jacques Derrida, *Without Alibi* (Stanford: Stanford University Press, 2002), 134.

43. De Man, *Allegories,* 296.

44. Cynthia Chase, "Trappings of an Education: Toward What We Do Not Yet Have," in *Responses: On Paul de Man's Wartime Journalism,* ed. Werner Hamacher, Neil Hertz, and Thomas Keenan (Lincoln and London: University of Nebraska Press, 1989), 59-60.

45. De Man, *Allegories,* 294; Chase, "Trappings," 61.

46. For two important and influential interpretations see Gasché, *Wild Card,* 34-47, and Geoffrey Bennington, "Aberrations: de Man (and) the Machine," in *Legislations: The Politics of Deconstruction* (London and New York: Verso, 1994), 137-51.

47. Derrida, *Without Alibi,* 150-51.

48. Ibid., 133-34.

49. See Vikki Bell, "On Speech, Race and Melancholia: An Interview with Judith Butler," *Theory, Culture and Society* 16 (1999): 164.

50. Judith Butler, *Excitable Speech: A Politics of the Performative* (London and New York: Routledge, 1997), 141-63. On Butler's debts to both Foucault and Derrida around this question, see Jeffrey Nealon, "Between Emergence and Possibility: Foucault, Derrida, and Judith Butler on Performative Identity," *Philosophy Today* 40 (1996): 430-49.

51. Jacques Derrida, *Limited Inc* (Evanston: Northwestern University Press, 1988), 9; Butler, *Excitable Speech,* 147.

52. Butler, *Excitable Speech,* 147, 148.

53. Ibid., 150.

54. Ibid., 161.

55. Jacques Derrida, *Specters of Marx* (London and New York: Routledge, 1994), 31. This phrase reprises—among other things—an account developed in the essay "Acts," included in *Memoires: For Paul de Man,* rev. ed. (New York: Columbia University Press, 1989), 89-154.

Livery and Its Discontents: "Braving It" in The Taming of the Shrew

AMANDA BAILEY

If therefore servants be attired unseemly, . . . all that see them will think their masters and mistresses are of such a mind as the servants are, or at least, too remiss and careless of their government.

—William Gouge, *Of Domestical Duties*

Was there ever less obedience in youth of all sorts . . . towards their superiors, parents, masters, and governors?

—Philip Stubbes, dedicatory epistle, *Anatomy of Abuses*

The Limits of Livery

One-half of the population of early modern London was at some point in their lives employed in service.[1] As part of their wages, live-in domestics or servants were provided with what was most broadly conceived of as "livery," nonmonetary payment that included food, board, and clothing.[2] Livery in the narrowest sense referred exclusively to the marked or colored clothing worn by household servants. Servants, who wore the customary "blue coats" of service or the more luxurious ensembles furnished by their masters, were not "freemen" but were visibly and bodily tied to the household in which they served.[3] Through the putting on of livery, servants became initiated into their corporate identities and positioned within the household hierarchy.[4] By the end of the sixteenth century, the system of livery, based upon a material mnemonics by which a servant's clothing daily reminded him and others of his corporate attachment as well as his place in the social order beyond the household, came under siege. Clothes, once the material signifiers of social obligation, were becoming the signs of fashion.

As Ann Rosalind Jones and Peter Stallybrass have recently argued, a marketplace of circulating fashions that realized items of apparel as exchangeable commodities dislocated traditional rituals of investiture by reintroducing cloth into a cash nexus.[5] Clothes in early modern England were not only socially valuable as the fabric that bound people to networks of obligation but also had economic value as exchangeable goods. Articles of clothing that were trimmed or embellished with costly materials such as velvet, ermine, precious metals, or pearl, for example, were detachable items that could be exchanged for cash on the increasingly popular secondhand markets that grew up within and around London.[6] Thus those very sartorial items that inscribed subjects into the realm of the social also enabled their wearers to reinvent themselves as consumers. By providing an alternate economy, the fashion industry and its outlaw secondhand markets created the conditions for new modes of sartorial fluidity that potentially unmoored not only clothes but also their wearers from the strictures of livery.

Shakespeare's *The Taming of the Shrew* addresses the increasingly vexed relation between the early modern household, an institution organized around "household stuff," and clothing, the stuff that made up the fabric of this institution.[7] Critics who have focused on the play's preoccupation with household stuff have placed *The Shrew* alongside various late sixteenth-century plays performed on the public stage that invoke the rhetorical and symbolic syntax of household manuals prescribing obedience to husbands, fathers, and masters as the principal duty of women, children, and servants.[8] As the household assumed a crucial role in the promotion of social stability and local governance in the period, scholars have demonstrated, authorities focused on those offenses that disrupted its working organization, most notably challenges to the gender hierarchy. The historical context of Shakespeare's play was, however, marked by competing discursive formations. *The Shrew* participates in a vast network of signification that includes not only householders' concerns about changing relations between men and women but also changing relations among men within the household.

The critical focus on gender politics in *The Shrew* has obscured the centrality of dependency, a key term in early modern culture.[9] In the late sixteenth century, the social place of every individual was determined by his or her relation to those above and below such that society was constructed by "an unbroken chain of service that stretched from the humblest peasant to the monarch who owed service only to God."[10] Service functioned as more than an analogy for relations among subjects, and the household, which ideally served as a microcosm of the larger social order, revolved around the symbolic and material rituals prescribed by an elaborate system of patronage and obligation. Good governance was exemplified by the seemly comportment of one's domestics, who through their gestures, posture, and clothing embodied the tenets of obedience. A broadening of the analytic framework with which we approach *The Shrew* brings into relief the stakes of domestic conduct for the social order within and beyond the household.

The innumerable instances in *The Shrew* in which superiors assert their authority through the distribution and transmission of clothes attests to the play's concern with the connection between domestic authority and the sartorial conduct of social inferiors. The recursive staging of investiture in *The Shrew* also, though, points to the contradictions surrounding livery and the impact of these contradictions on the early modern household. By attending to the tensions generated around clothing, a medium that simultaneously functioned as a means of self-fashioning and of social fashioning, the play interrogates the links between contestatory sartorial and social orders. Rather than attempting to resolve the tension between these two orders, however, Shakespeare's play presents a wholly unique perspective on the relation between sartorial practice and social power.

While the symbolic efficacy of livery may have been compromised by a developing global fashion industry, *The Shrew* demonstrates that the greatest challenge to the constitutive power of apparel came from within the system of livery itself. By staging how household order was realized through the micropolitics of sartorial incorporation, *The Shrew* reveals this order to be consistently undercut by an incoherent ideology of service. In order to serve their masters, domestics were required to appear elaborately attired at their masters' expense. Masters, though, were increasingly aware of the financial and social costs of maintaining sumptuous servants and yet continued to express their claims to social legitimacy through their own and their servants' sartorial majesty. An ideology of service and an ideology of gentility that relied on the vestimentary display was, moreover, articulated in the context of a household that was comprised of ambiguously positioned domestics who inhabited shifting erotic and pecuniary allegiances. The cultural fantasies and fears borne of the contradictions surrounding service inform *The Shrew*'s representation of servants performatively citing and irreverently transforming the processes of sartorial imprinting, even as their masters continue to look to clothes as the material reminders of status and primary means of social incorporation. By "braving it" in their livery, a practice I discuss in detail below, ambiguously positioned household subordinates, on and off the public stage, realized dress as an *embodied practice,* at once the material inscription of cultural norms and the mechanism of the re-signification of these norms.

The following discussion builds off of recent work that locates *The Shrew* in the context of a burgeoning commodity culture.[11] My intention is not to argue that the tenets of livery were unaffected by a new commercial logic. There can be little doubt that the circulation of clothes as commodities offered the wearer the opportunity to unmake and remake himself independent of the dictates of any specific social institution or role. An increasingly vital consumer culture and the impact of this new commercialism on the late sixteenth-century household serves as my jumping-off point, since I aim to demonstrate that the new social and cultural pressures associated with emergent market forces did not signal the end of the memorializing system of livery. Rather, as my reading of *The Shrew* will emphasize, the system of livery persisted even as dress became the site of embattled negotiations and complex strategies mobilized by those who occupied ambiguous social positions. By foregrounding the dissident ways in which subjects embodied their livery rather than charting the anarchic movement of commodities, I argue that *The Shrew* showcases an emergent mode of embodiment that shifted the onlooker's attention from clothes, or what subjects wore, to dress, or how they wore their clothes.[12] As a partial response to and reworking of the elite claim on manner, epitomized by the connection between proper comportment and the seamless grace of *sprezzatura,* this alternate mode of embodiment was distinguished by the wearer's flaunting the unseemly disjunction between who he was and what he wore.

My focus on the *how* rather than the *what* is grounded in the historical claim that status in this period was perceived less in terms of innate virtue or being and increasingly articulated by ritualized practices that evinced the doer's mastery of key codes of distinction. My theoretical approach presses on the supposition that complex sartorial strategies were the province of the elite or social aspirants attempting to pass as elite.[13] Most broadly, I hope to demonstrate that the sartorial strategies of the elite and nonelite alike cannot be adequately explained as merely reflections of contradictory market formations. "Spectacle and market, subjectivity and history converge . . . not as explanatory givens," Christopher Pye notes, but rather as "contingent phenomena actively constituted around their own volatile and mutually implicated limits."[14] Pye's cogent observation cautions us against automatically invoking the familiar syllogism that posits subjectivity as the function of the economic and the economic as the function of history and encourages us, rather, to explore the radical contingency of both objects and subjects. An engagement with Marx's understanding of historical analysis as the work of uncovering "the manifold uses of things" provides perspective on early modern men and women as occupying fractured and contradictory subject positions, which, in turn, inflected the complex ways that they used (and misused) objects.[15]

Braving It

David Evett asserts that *The Shrew* includes more sets of masters and servants than any other comparable dramatic text of the period, Shakespearean or otherwise.[16] The dynamic between masters and servants in *The Shrew* both reflects and participates in what was an ambiguous ideology of service, which grew out of changing perceptions of the role of the household, the nature of its head, and, concomitantly, the place of the male subordinates within the household.[17] An older notion of service based on a fraternal and militaristic notion of *comitatus,* exemplified by the retainer system, obligated servants to guard their master's person and protect him from bodily harm. By the end of the sixteenth century, this code of service was gradually replaced by a domestic ideal of personal service in which men were expected to represent their masters' prestige by dressing sumptuously and adopting what one popular manual describes as "a comely" or seemly demeanor.[18] While this newer ideology of service remained grounded in the traditional notion that servants were symbolically incorporated into the social body of the household, a conception of personal service that understood "Every Mans proper Mansion House and Home, being the Theater of his Hospitality," conceived of servants as extensions of their masters' couture.[19] As social privilege relied increasingly upon vestimentary display, the appearance of the household was regarded as tantamount to "the physical presentation of the attributes of the man."[20]

In accordance with the expectation that the luxurious household attested to the elevated status of its head, the elite household deployed large resources to promote its magnificence, such that the minimum standard for gentility rested on one's capacity to maintain sumptuously attired and visibly underemployed servants.[21] As one historian notes, "the size of a nobleman's house, the splendor of its furnishings, and the number and costly dress of his servants did two things: on the one hand, they advertised his wealth; on the other, they provided the material foundations of his power. Public power lay in the command of men, and the household was the institution through which that command was bought."[22] The key role that livery played in reflecting the master's wealth and status is indicated by sixteenth-century household records showing that grants of livery were "more than adequate" and that the value of finery awarded to servants often far surpassed the total value of their wages.[23] This is not surprising, since clothing was disproportionately expensive and, as Samuel Pepys noted as late as the mid-seventeenth century, even a secondhand velvet cloak cost as much as a domestic's annual wage.[24]

The decorative function of servants is discussed in *Of Civil and Uncivil Life,* whose anonymous author stresses that the work of the household servant is by no means "labor or drudgery." Rather, he observes, servants "take great scorn" at being requested to perform menial tasks "being comely personages," whose primary function is to adorn their master's personage by "attend[ing] upon [his] table, . . . follow[ing] [him] in the streets, . . . and furnish[ing] [his] halls at home."[25] Like the gentlemen they served, servants are expected to become "expert in sundry seemly, and necessary knowledges, without which they cannot . . . serve a noble man, or a gentleman." Among their areas of distinction, they should be practiced in how to "decently wear their garments, and chiefly their livery coats, their swords and bucklers," since they are expected to "carve very comely at [the] table." Servants entertain their masters with their wise and witty "table talk," since they, like the gentlemen they serve, are as well-versed in and ready to discuss either "pleasure or profit."[26]

Even the more modest households of the middling sort or professional ranks kept servants since there was a direct correlation between the social position of the head and the number of male domestics he employed. In the words of one contemporary, "no man will put off his cap or do him reverence" who "walk[s] in the city without servants attending on him."[27] Acknowledging that even members of the lower ranks kept men, I. M., author of *The Servingman's Comfort,* satirizes the "upstart," whose "father's chief badge of cognizance was the weaver's shuttle or the tailor's shears." I. M. describes this "new upstart" as "tread[ing] the streets so

stately attended, . . . so gallantly guarded," and so extravagantly attired
that he "flourish[es] [his] fair cloaks, as though he were the Prince of
Peacocks."[28] As Lawrence Stone has shown, new-made men, young men
from the yeomen or minor gentry ranks who were typically land-rich but
cash-poor, felt compelled to keep servants in a compensatory move.[29]
The pressure to consume conspicuously and maintain sumptuously attired
domestics threatened to drain the already limited resources of this group of
men who experienced the obligation to "spend generously, even lavishly,"
as de rigueur even if, paradoxically, such conspicuous consumption was
financially unwise or infeasible. As records of the wardrober, the keeper
of the closet and other household accounts indicate, after land, apparel
proved the largest investment of men's fortunes.[30] The exhibition of one's
new status was an expensive but necessary prospect, and the "land-poor
son" needed to negotiate carefully between economic and symbolic capital
since he could potentially liquidate his estate in showcasing his newfound
status.[31]

In a cultural atmosphere in which gentility was increasingly difficult to
define and the key markers of social distinction, in particular sumptuous
apparel, were becoming more widely available, distinguishing oneself took
on new urgency for new-made men and established gentlemen alike.[32]
Between 1560 and 1590, England moved from an export to an import
economy as new kinds of manufacturing ventures were encouraged and
popular imported items such as felt hats, feathers, furs, leather goods, and
a variety of "new draperies"—lightweight cottons and linens—were produced domestically. As historians have shown, the commercial economy
of this period was marked by a proliferation of goods, and innovations in
the clothing trade offered consumers access to an unprecedented array
of fabrics, dyes, and fashions. The gradual displacement of markets in expensive imports heralded the reclassification of those objects traditionally
considered "luxury" items, and those items that were once only available
to the wealthiest were increasingly found in households at every level of
society. London as a port city and the capital became the center of a new
theater of display, particularly since the proximity of the royal court to
the city resulted in many elite leaving their country estates and setting
up residence in London. The increased availability of finished textiles
and an enhanced material consciousness fueled a culture of competitive
emulation in which the accelerating rate of fashion provided the conditions

for new outlaw markets in castoffs and secondhand clothes. Brokers of used clothing enabled even the "meanest" sort to rent and purchase secondhand sumptuous apparel.[33]

In response to the increasing pressure to distinguish oneself, heads of households invested heavily in the rituals of display associated with elite status. Such investments became all the more pressing since the young men who worked as personal servants came from similar if not identical social backgrounds as the men they served. Despite the claims of contemporaries that their servants represented the "untried dregs and dross of less esteem," as opposed to the "pure and refined" gentle serving men of times past, historical evidence shows that there was only a slight drop in the number of gentle-born men entering households and corporations.[34] While the ideal of the prestigious gentle-servant was in decline, sons of the lesser gentry continued to take up positions as servants throughout the seventeenth century and participated in what was, in the eyes of some, a cruder emergent wage-based system alongside their nongentle counterparts. Significantly, the largest portion of immigrants into London at this time were not from the lower ranks, members of an oppressed peasantry expropriated from the land by the gentry, but rather the offspring of "moderately prosperous rural folk."[35] The increasingly fractured criteria for gentle status and the residual practice of primogeniture reshaped the material and social conditions of life for a large majority of gentle-born but subservient young men. The custom of primogeniture that privileged eldest sons and disenfranchised younger ones resulted in an influx of "surplus" gentle-born, young men into urban centers, where they sought employment in corporations or in households.[36]

An uneasy dividing line separating masters from their gentle servants became, at the end of the sixteenth century, a tightly policed border. While frequent complaints about servants' mercenary motives and popular depictions of domestic "upstarts" consuming too much food and apparel are typically interpreted as indicative of clashing class sensibilities within the household, representations of the rapacious servant also index the discomforting reality of a shared social background between master and domestic. While we may read masters' complaints at face value, such descriptions also functioned as rhetorical strategies deployed by those householders who attempted to distinguish themselves from their gentle-born servants by projecting acquisitive impulses onto them. Similarly, observations about servants' rampant materialism reveal awareness on the part of masters that those who served them had had similar life experiences and thus intimate knowledge of the cultural codes of their "betters."[37] Even if servants had little opportunity to obtain the economic capital that would allow them to realize themselves as elite, young male domestics from gentle backgrounds who were required by masters to dress sumptuously may have regarded expensive couture as their intrinsic right.

The fantasies of gentle-born young men who desired to take up the "easy and pleasant life of servingmen" are a persistent theme of prescriptive and imaginative literature.[38] In *A Diamond Most Precious, Worthy to be Marked,* a manual "instructing all masters and servants how they ought to live their lives," a young man fantasizes about serving in the household of a wealthy Londoner so that he can "have [his] delight as gentleman hath . . . two new coats a year, . . . suits of hose, . . . hats with feathers" and "be all in bravery."[39] Richard Climsell also depicts the enticing possibilities of domestic service in the eyes of a young man who boasts, "Why should I labor, toil, or care / since I am fed with dainty fare? / My gelding I have for to ride, / my cloak, my good sword by my side, / My boots and spurs shining like gold / like those whose names are high enrolled: / What pleasure more can any crave, / then such content as I now have?"[40] Young men's desire to be "in bravery" is also represented in the period's dramatic literature in comedies such as Chapman, Jonson, and Marston's *Eastward Ho!,* which opens with an apprentice "pump[ing] it" in the "accoutrements of a gallant."[41] The apprentice defends his sartorial extravagance by reminding his master that "though [he is] a younger brother and a prentice," (1.1.28–29), he is "a gentleman and may swear by [his] pedigree" (1.1.123–24). Throughout the play this apprentice mocks his betters, steals from his master, and runs away until he is caught and reprimanded for his "neat and garish attire" and for having "prodigally consumed much of [his] master's estate" (4.2.302–5).

While William Gouge, author of *Of Domestical Duties,* observes that servants' apparel credits their master, he also acknowledges the tensions intrinsic to a domestic situation in which gentle-born servingmen are provided with expensive clothing. He warns against attiring one's servants too extravagantly, stressing that "the apparel also which servants wear must be so fashioned and ordered, as it may declare them to be servants, and under their masters, and so it will argue a reverend respect of their masters."[42] For Gouge, one purpose of apparel is to show "a difference betwixt superiors and inferiors, persons in authority and under subjection."[43] Noting that "through too much familiarity" servants will come to "carry themselves fellow-like," Gouge observes:

Exceeding great is the fault of servants in their excess apparel. No distinction ordinarily betwixt a man's children and servants: nay none betwixt masters and their men, mistresses and their maids. It may be while men and maids are at their masters' and mistresses' finding, difference may be made: though, even then also, if they can any way get wherewithal, they will do what they can to be as brave as they can. But, if once they be at their own finding, all shall be laid out upon apparel, but they will also be as fine as master or mistresses: if not so costly, yet in show as specious and brave. New fashions are as soon got up by servants as by masters and mistresses. . . . If the Queen of Sheba were now living, she would as much wonder at the disorder of servants in these days, as then she wondered at the comely order of Solomon's servants.[44]

Similarly, I. M. writes of meeting "a fine gentleman," a justice of the peace worth two thousand marks annually whose servant wore apparel "much better than his Master's."[45] An ideology of service that linked sumptuousness with obedience represented dressing-up, a practice that according to Elizabethan clothing laws when engaged by subordinates directly challenged the foundations of the established social hierarchy, as a servant's *duty* to his master. At the same time, changes in migration patterns and commercial arrangements provided the conditions for a class of men who, according to Gouge, "being born of gentlemen" and "of good degree, . . . forget their present place and condition; or else (which is worse) . . . willfully presume above it."[46] Young gentlemen who perceived themselves as socially displaced and younger sons of yeoman and members of the merchant class who were perceived as "upstarts" negotiated the complex implications of status demotion through a range of symbolic forms that did not ultimately entail dramatic deviation from the expected codes of service.

The system of service was such that young men could "metaphorize" the dominant order by placing its codes in another register without abandoning them altogether.[47] In his exploration of the fusion of class consciousness and comic dramaturgy in *The Shrew*, Thomas Moisan discusses those moments in which inferiors appeal to a highly traditional notion of service to justify insubordination. Focusing on textual junctures marked by comic impasse, Moisan argues that exchanges characterized by "verbal misprision," in which servants "misunderstand" their masters' commands, result in inferiors interrogating and thwarting their masters' authority in the name of obedience.[48] Even if the play ultimately relegates such moments to its margins by representing subordinates as merely comical in their confusion, the anxieties and antagonisms underwriting the early modern class system, Moisan stresses, are nonetheless expressed in the dramatization of the parity borne of mutual misunderstanding.

One such "misprision" occurs between Petruchio and his servant Grumio upon their arrival at Hortensio's house. Grumio (mis)understands his master's request to "knock me here soundly" (1.2.8) as an order to knock or hit Petruchio rather than Hortensio's gate. By laying claim to the tenets of a traditional ideal of service in which the servant's duty is to absorb the knocks or hits others might visit upon his master's person, Grumio refuses to follow Petruchio's seemingly nonsensical order to "knock him." As a result, Hortensio's gate does not get knocked, Grumio is punished, and Hortensio scolds Petruchio for capriciously abusing his servant in public. In his discussion of this exchange, Moisan reads Grumio as the colonialized subject who has so thoroughly internalized his inferiority that his dutiful obeisance produces an obtuseness and rigidity that inadvertently challenges the working order of the very system that fashioned him:

Having so internalized the ideology of service and the best interests of his master, Grumio cannot compromise his principles for the mere sake of obeying his master and discharging his duty as an employee. . . . In fact, so thoroughly does he merge his identity with—or confuse it for—his master's that he even comes at one point to address Petruchio as a master would a truculent or incorrigible servant, complaining that "My master is grown quarrelsome."[49]

For Moisan, Grumio's exaggerated compliance signals his overidentification with the structures of oppression that shape him, even if that identification leads, perversely, to disobeying his master. Yet a fuller excavation of those sites where servants pay homage to the ideal of service while withholding service reveals flamboyant submissiveness to be a tactic of subversion that grows out of cross- or disidentification rather than overidentification. While Moisan's analysis highlights the momentary semantic and social disorder that results when inferiors push ideals to their limits, it does not account for the ways in which the process of assimilation is dialectical insofar as dependents appropriate that with which they identify. As Jonathan Dollimore observes, appropriation is never "mere duplication" but almost invariably involves "challenge and transformation."[50] By shifting the emphasis from the Bloomian notion of "misprision" to Henry Louis

Gates's notion of Signifyin(g), we can read Grumio's "misunderstanding" as a complex strategy whereby he evacuates the role of the dutiful servant without abandoning it.[51]

The fractured nature of the identificatory process and the destabilizing presence of partial or incomplete transformations are explored in those instances in which *The Shrew* anatomizes the material economy of service by focusing on livery, represented most broadly in the play by the transmission of clothes from master to servant. In revealing such instances of sartorial transmission as inspiring heterogeneous, scattered practices rather than serving a coherent system of social incorporation, the play documents the irreverent ways that servants wear their clothes to work through and against the cultural logic of servitude. For instance, Lucentio's plan for his servant to take his place and become the "master . . . in [his] stead," assuming his dress and "port" (1.1.194-95), showcases how a servant can wear the clothes assigned to him in the service of *disidentification* rather than as material reminder of his servitude.[52]

A loyal servant, Tranio assumes the task of suturing the breach between his master's symbolic and economic capital but, in this instance, takes this particular function of service to its extreme. Accepting his assignment to not only embody the household's magnificence, Tranio also agrees to boast of exorbitant holdings, which include, significantly, the conventional staples of established gentility: parcels of arable land, several country estates, and merchant vessels. Bianca's other suitor, Gremio, enters the competition for her hand with an offer of a house in the city "richly furnished" with plate and gold, basins and ewers, Tyrian tapestries, ivory coffers stuffed with crowns, cypress chests full of costly apparel and expensive linens, Turkish cushions embossed with pearl, gold-trimmed draperies, and pewter and brass (2.1.340-49). Tranio trumps Gremio's mere "movables" with "houses three or four as good . . . Besides two thousand ducats by the year of fruitful land" (2.1.362-63). When Gremio comes forward with a farm with more than a hundred head of cattle and sixty oxen and a merchant vessel, Tranio tops this with "three great argosies, besides two galliases, and twelve tight galleys" (2.1.371-72), obtaining Bianca's father's consent on the basis of his extravagant (fictional) fortune.

Tranio regards maintaining the fiction of luxury as his duty, and he claims that he performs his role solely in the name of devotion to Lucentio to whom he has sworn to be "serviceable" at all costs (1.1.204-9). He doffs his blue cap of service to don a new set of livery consisting of his master's "colored hat and cloak" (1.1.199) in preparation for "ply[ing] his [master's] book, welcom[ing] his friends, / visit[ing] his countrymen, and banquet[ing] them" (1.1.188–89). Despite Tranio's insistence that he assumes his master's silks and velvets in order to serve him, others do not perceive Tranio's sumptuousness as safely inscribed within the bonds of service. Biondello, a fellow servant, accuses the lavishly attired Tranio of having stolen his master's clothes (1.1.215). Nor are Biondello's doubts about Tranio's motivations assuaged by Lucentio's explanation that Tranio has "changed into Lucentio" and is in effect the new master, to which Biondello cynically replies, "The better for him. Would I were so too!" (1.2.229).

Lucentio's father Vincentio also reads Tranio's sartorial splendor as evidence that he and his son have in their youthful extravagance taken advantage of him by using their allowances to purchase and model luxurious ensembles throughout Padua. Confronted with the sight of Tranio dressed in finery and with a man in tow, Vincentio openly laments, "O immortal gods! O fine villain! A silken doublet, a velvet hose, a scarlet cloak, and a copintank [high-crowned] hat! O, I am undone, I am undone! While I play the good husband at home, my son and my servant spend all at the university" (5.1.51–54). When he discovers that Tranio has also assumed his son's name, Vicentio concludes that Tranio has murdered his master and stolen his apparel so that he may pass as a sumptuously attired gentleman (5.1.67). Tranio's obedience to Lucentio justifies maintaining the lie that he is indeed a gentleman and that Biondella is his man, and, moreover, compels him to speak imperiously to Vicentio asking (a question that echoes Jonson's saucy apprentice), "Why, sir, what 'cerns it you if I wear pearl and gold? I thank my good father, I am able to maintain it" (5.1.58–59). Tranio's insistence on his prerogative to wear luxurious apparel generates a series of misunderstandings such that Tranio orders the arrest of Vicentio on the grounds that *he* is impersonating a gentleman. Only in the final instance with the last-minute arrival of Lucentio, who reveals that he has authorized Tranio's fabulousness, does the play skirt its dangerous climax in which the sumptuously appareled servant effectively strips the elite patriarch of his authority and sends him to prison.

The various points at which onlookers accuse the sumptuously dressed Tranio of taking advantage of his master's generosity, of stealing from him, and even of murdering his master do not merely function as commentaries on the hermeneutic of suspicion employed by those who witness an elegantly attired servant. Nor does the play's disavowal of the treacherous implications of its comic subplot effectively contain the subversive scenario it develops. Despite the appearance of repair, such moments of rupture reveal the social to be "nothing more than a fragile symbolic tissue, which can be torn at any moment by the intrusion of the real."[53] When desires cannot be adequately contained within the symbolic and intrude upon the everyday, what seems most familiar suddenly becomes strange, taking an irrevocable dangerous turn. *The Shrew* reveals the familiar/familial figure of the dutiful servant as a site of rupture, a naive illusion dependent upon the master's successful repression of the elasticity of his own hegemonic ideal. Through the use of doubling, in which the seemingly harmonious Tranio and Lucentio are juxtaposed with the suspicious Biondello and Vincentio, the text simultaneously secures and removes the veil of loyalty and goodwill between master and servant.

Tranio's sartorial acting out suggests, however, that the tissue can never be repaired, and *The Shrew* charts what happens when the normative rules of livery provide the ground for subversive strategies that inflect and mutate the ideology of service from within. What these characters (and the audience) witness is not simply an extravagantly dressed Tranio but rather, as the stage directions are careful to note, a servant who enters "*brave*" (1.2.209). In other words, onlookers are stunned not simply by *what* Tranio wears (his master's luxurious apparel) but rather *how* he wears his sumptuous ensemble, apparently in a manner whereby he impudently promotes his own sense of glamour. The adverb "brave" indicates that Tranio, described by one critic as an "upstart knave," dresses ostentatiously with a confidence bordering on impertinence.[54] In the late sixteenth century, brave meant being finely dressed to a fault such that by wearing his apparel with the explicit aim of showing off, the wearer defied all expectations of sartorial propriety. A descriptor that was no doubt deployed to label men who surpassed the sartorial codes of their station as extravagant and insolent, the characterization of braving always included the charge of irreverence. Braving was also a competitive sartorial mode in which the wearer attempted to outshine someone else, for instance, by wearing his apparel in a way that enabled him to appear "more gayer" than "a lord."[55] The verb "to brave," with its connotations of to boast, to vaunt, and to swagger, was, according to the sixteenth-century usage, associated with inappropriate or combative sartorial behavior exemplified by those men

who "strut it, stout it, [and] brave it in [their] costly apparel" (*OED*, 1610).
Also used as a noun, a "brave" was in this period another term for a gallant, a
young man renowned for his "upstart bravery" and the flamboyant manner
with which he wore his finery (*OED*, 1600).[56]

The disruptive effects of servants' sartorial braving on household order
comes into full view when the verbal expression of irreverence in the
form of rhetorical braving is also considered. An early form of ritualized
insult anticipating contemporary subcultural signifying practices such as
the dozens, reading, shading, or dissing, "braving" in the early modern
period entailed the demonstration of verbal bravado that combined insult
with wit. When engaged in braving, each participant was pressed to devise
a progressively more cutting comment in order to top his opponent, and, in
this respect, braving provided a mechanism whereby subordinates could
release their resentment and assert their verbal panache without deviating
too far from established codes of repartee. Just as sartorial braving allowed
the wearer to showcase his sense of style through his ability to manipulate
and embellish items of apparel, verbal braving enabled the speaker to
perform his linguistic agility. Braving was a mode of signification that
referenced the *way* its practitioner signified rather than a specific trope
or rhetorical figure. The enunciative potency of braving resided in the
speaker's ability to outwit his opponent not by *what* he said but rather by
how he said.

In the only scene in *The Shrew* in which sartorial style is addressed
explicitly, Petruchio's servant Grumio and the tailor engage in an extended
verbal battle over who actually commissioned the design of Kate's gown.
Petruchio objects to the gown's overly ornate style, exemplified by its
"curiously cut" sleeves (4.3.137). Although the literal definition of *curious*
was "careful, skillful, or well-done," in early modern usage the word described a style marked by perverse extravagance, and Petruchio chastises
Grumio for presumptuously ordering a design bearing the mark of his
curious sensibility.[57] Insult is added to injury when Grumio resorts to a
highly stylized rhetorical mode to deflect blame from himself. Denying
that he authorized the "note of fashion" (4.3.125), Grumio engages the
tailor in an exchange marked by the flamboyant unpacking of the surplus
meanings of words, a mode of symbolic insurgency reminiscent of Tranio's
irreverent sartorial manner whereby he maximizes the luxurious copia
of each item that he wears. Insisting that in constructing the dress he
dutifully followed his master's directions, the tailor points out that his

master, in turn, faithfully adhered to Grumio's "order how it should be done" (4.3.116). Grumio, abdicating all responsibility for the cut of the dress, defends himself from *his* master's censure by denigrating the tailor and emphasizing that a tailor's job is to "fac[e] many things" or artificially dissimulate such that he is able to skillfully mask blemishes and is thus a master of fabrication (4.3.121). By mobilizing the terms "face" and "brave," words meaning "to decorate" and "to defy," Tranio highlights the elements of baiting and boasting subtending style. He warns the tailor, "Face not me. Thou hast braved many men; brave not me. I will neither be faced nor braved. I say unto thee, I bid thy master cut out the gown, but I did not bid him cut it to pieces. Ergo thou liest" (4.3.123–25). Grumio's defensive tactic is, though, itself an example of "facing" in which he engages the Signifyin(g) practice of taking an implied accusation (that he is a liar) and puts it right back in his opponent's face.[58] In addition to mocking the tailor's profession, Grumio also plays off of the early modern stereotype of tailors as lascivious and effeminate peddlers of exotic wares and foreign fashions who seduced men and women alike into economic and sexual excesses.[59] By representing the tailor as indiscriminately shifting from facing to braving, Grumio ascribes to him a suspicious bimodality, whereby he may, by implication, gain an unfair advantage over his opponent. In demonstrating the ways that braving functions as strategy to defy authority and defer punishment, *The Shrew* connects rhetorical and sartorial braving as tactics of symbolic aggression that subordinates utilize to manipulate the parameters of their situations. Through the demonstrative practice of flaunting, with words or items of apparel, domestics engaged in what was a battle over the signs of household supremacy that was played out symbolically and literally on the terrain of dress.

Since braving in its verbal and sartorial forms was in essence an end in itself, its resolution was arbitrary. Yet, as in the case of the tailor scene, braving always illuminated the stakes of insubordination for household order. In *The Shrew,* braving ultimately leads to the evocation of domestic violence, which, in turn, signals the vulnerability of household authority and lays bare the extent to which the household revolves around physical contact between men. While masters relied on physical discipline to reassert the household hierarchy, in certain contexts physical contact between master and servant (whether defined as sport or discipline) endangered the hierarchical order within the household by troubling the boundaries that prescribed intimacy between men.[60] As the debate over style between Grumio and the tailor reaches its pitch, Grumio activates a series of homonymic puns whereby he pushes the word "cut" along the signifying scale, dramatizing the slipperiness between eros and discipline within the household. As Grumio repeats the word "cut" (appearing five times over the course of thirty-five lines), Kate's gown recedes as the word's proper referent and "cut" comes to elliptically signify Kate's cut, a "conceit" that is, Grumio notes, "deeper than you think" (4.3.153).[61] By reacting with shock at Petruchio's request that the tailor "take up" or take away Kate's gown for his master's "use" (4.3.149), Grumio insists on interpreting Petruchio's directive as an order to lift Kate's dress to assist another man's erotic "use" of her.[62] Persisting in sexualizing the word "cut" and conceiving of service as the duty to erotically obey those in authority, Grumio's astonished exclamation "Take up my mistress' gown to his master's use! O, fie, fie, fie!" (4.3.154-55) is a histrionic response that at once exaggerates and illuminates his master's perversity and his own unavoidable complicity in it.

In the spirit of performative obeisance, Grumio lays out the protocol for his own penalty by declaring that if it can be determined that he ordered the curiously cut, "loose-bodied gown," then his master should dress him in it and beat him "with a bottom of brown thread" (4.3.130-31). By assuming this new livery, the gentlewoman's gown intended for Kate, Grumio takes the place of Kate as the object of Petruchio's corrective and, by implication, erotic energies. Moreover, by constituting himself as the object of pedagogical violence, Grumio's request invokes the homosocial/homoerotic milieu of the early modern grammar school in which schoolmasters disciplined their young male students with corporeal punishment that consisted of flogging them with birch rods.[63] By attending to bottoms—of the brown thread with which he is being beaten and his own where the beating is being applied—Grumio invokes his own cut, highlighting the corporeal site upon which disciplinary activity and sexual subordination converge. The ass, as Mark Thornton Burnett notes, was a particularly potent social symbol in the period since the beast of burden was the primary emblem for the dutiful servant.[64] Mario DiGangi has called our attention to the homoerotic valence of this symbol by demonstrating that the public language of male dominance and the private language of male desire coalesce around the symbol of the socially dependent and erotically available male servant.[65] Luxuriating in the semantic possibilities of the cut, Grumio flaunts the semiotic surplus of the signifier to produce a nexus, which, by connecting

sartorial style, eros, and household discipline, illuminates the economic
and erotic links that both constituted and endangered master and servant
relations in the early modern household.

Raging and Rioting

An ideology of service that encouraged domestics to exhibit a "histrionic
'self-fashioning'" created the conditions in which young men could use
the sartorial expectations of their position to impudently outshine their
masters and potentially disobey them in other matters.[66] At the same time,
those masters who based their social privilege on the sartorial splendor
of their charges could not reign in their servants without demystifying
their own claims to legitimacy. Sumptuousness required the willing sus-
pension of moderation, since the magnificent man distinguished himself
by spending "gladly and generously," for, according to the order of the day,
there was nothing more "petty" than "exact book-keeping." The gentle
householder was, thus, by definition "more deeply interested in embodying
his conception in its most beautiful and appropriate form than to ask
himself how much it will cost and the cheapest rate at which it can be
done."[67] By dressing their servants down, masters only stripped themselves
of their own signs of luxury, as well as revealed their own pecuniary
anxieties and perhaps the limited nature of their resources. By overdressing
themselves and out-dressing their superiors, domestics tacitly threatened
to expose the compensatory fiction of their masters' largess, if not exhaust
its potential altogether. Concerns about domestics' inappropriate sartorial
display represented, however, greater fears among heads of households
than how they appeared in the eyes of their peers. The servant who
braved it in his livery deeply affected perceptions of authority *within* the
household, and householders' anxieties about irreverent display and its
effects among household members suggest that there was more at stake
than the usurpation and debasement of the signs of luxury.

Servants who braved it were perceived as jeopardizing the household's
financial stability, since their sartorial upkeep and putative desire for sumptuous items threatened to wear out their master's estate. The anxiety that
one's servants could consume one's estate is addressed in *Of Civil and
Uncivil Life,* whose author complains of his servants wearing out his
household "stuff," in particular bed linens, wall hangings, and "curtains and
canopies of silk." He bemoans that "within a little time" such a "great deal

of good stuff" is spoiled such that he, "the poor master of the house," ends up with "all his linen soil[ed], all his provision eaten, and his household stuff made unsavory, and oft times torn and spoiled."[68] Householders' fears of being materially vulnerable often shaded into fears of being taken advantage of on various levels. The fear of becoming worn out or spent was also articulated in the early modern period as an anxiety about the debilitating effects of exhaustion associated with an expended postcoital state.[69] Wearing resulted in one's becoming "spent" or worn down from the incessant friction or rubbing of sexual activity that ultimately culminated in depletion.[70] While the sexual exploitation of servants was the most common abuse of power within the household,[71] the gentle domestic's appetite for household stuff was understood by his superiors as having profound implications for not only the economic but also the erotic order of the household. Mario DiGangi cites an anxious awareness within the dramatic literature of the period that the homoerotic conventions inform-ing relations of service could be manipulated not only for the master's profit but also for the servant's pleasure. A servant who took advantage of his master economically could also control him erotically, and under such conditions the orderly hierarchical arrangement around which the household was organized was transformed into a disorderly homoerotic order. Sexual intimacy between master and servant was not prohibited, DiGangi stresses, but when such intimacy occurred between a master and a putatively acquisitive servant, perceptions of this arrangement shifted dramatically since disorderly erotic behavior was both the sign and effect of other socially disruptive behaviors.[72]

The cultural preoccupation with the violation of social and sexual bound-aries between men, which interrogated the tenets of mastery and desta-bilized relations of service, provides the context for analyzing Petruchio's maxim about "wear." While the dangers of "wearing" are addressed by Petruchio in a heteroerotic context, the visual and rhetorical syntax of the wedding scene make sense only when this scene is read in light of a wider range of significations than those typically brought to bear. Writing his servant out of this scene altogether, critics interpret Petruchio's unseemly appearance as an early instance of his taming strategy whereby he publicly humiliates Kate with his sartorial misconduct.[73] This reading of Petruchio's sartorial misbehavior has dominated analyses of the wedding scene largely because Petruchio and Grumio's disruptive appearance seems singularly mysterious if not tangential to what are presented traditionally as the larger concerns of the play. A discussion of "wear" grounded in cultural anxieties about sartorially extravagant servants whose braving potentially interrupted the productive and reproductive function of the household addresses both Petruchio's disruptive behavior and his servant's flamboyant sartorial performance.

Having arrived at his wedding dressed in "unreverent robes," Petruchio is described as an "eyesore" and "shame to [his] estate." His attire registers a general state of destitution: he wears "a new hat and an old jerkin, . . . old breeches thrice turned; a pair of boots that have been candle-cases, one buckled, another laced, an old rusty sword . . . with a broken hilt, and chapeless," with the points attaching his clothes "broken."[74] His servant, Grumio, on the other hand, is not simply dressed up for the occasion, but described as "caparisoned," or decked out. He wears "a linen stock on one leg and a kersey boot-hose on the other" and, in place of a garter, a flourish of red and blue strips of cloth. His hat having "the humor of forty fancies pricked in't for a feather" is so ornate that it defies description.

As a way of explaining his scandalous apparel, Petruchio tells Kate's father Baptista that "to me [Kate's] married, not unto my clothes. / Could I repair what she will wear in me / As I can change these poor accoutrements, / 'Twere well for Kate and better for myself" (3.2.107–10). In emphasizing the "wear" Kate will effect, Petruchio refers to the favor he is performing Baptista by marrying Kate, since once she is married off she and, as a result, her sister will no longer wear away or consume their father's resources. As critics have suggested, Petruchio's comment about wear references a persistent concern expressed in late sixteenth-century conduct books, household manuals, and sermons that women drive their fathers and husbands to ruin by their habits of excessive expenditure and, more particularly, by their sartorial extravagance.[75] In the ballad *The Cruel Shrew*, for instance, the speaker describes a typical day for his wife: "As soon as she is out of bed / her looking-glass she takes, / (So vainly is she daily led); / her morning's work she makes / In putting on her brave attire, / that fine and costly be, / Whilst I work hard in dirt and mire. / Alack! What remedy?"[76] Since the primary goal of the household was the maintenance of order, the spendthrift wife challenged the sovereignty of her husband by her refusal to be a productive domestic and by her putative exhaustion of his estate. A compensatory fantasy disavowing the social dependency of those men, such as Petruchio, who sought to avoid work and to elevate their station by marrying wealthy women, this ballad depicts the wife as threatening to undo her husband's gentle status and reducing him to manual toil.[77]

As Nastasha Korda has shown, *The Shrew* participates in the period's changing perceptions of the housewife as women moved away from performing the duties expected of domestic laborers (agricultural chores or tasks associated with home-based industry) and assumed a new managerial position as the overseer of household stuff purchased outside the home.[78] An analysis of the wedding scene that de-centers Kate, however, and considers the cultural significance of this ritual for the groom allows for an examination of the fluidity of household dynamics beyond the marital dyad. As an emergent affective ideology of marriage was only gradually beginning to reshape the assumptions underwriting a traditional dynastic ideology of marriage, marriage continued to serve as the primary means by which men realized themselves as patriarchs.[79] In a period in which the phrase "a man's house is his castle" became proverbial, the household was not yet realized as a "separate sphere," analogous yet distinct from the public arena.[80] Whether primarily a site of production, in which its members were expected to work together performing chores and producing goods, or a site of consumption, a space defined by leisure and display, the household was above all the primary unit of social control in early modern England. The wedding was the communal ritual that conferred upon men their role as the head of what was considered "the foremost disciplinary site in the period," and the wedding ceremony inaugurated the groom into his new status, which was grounded in his authority to supervise men who served under him.[81] As the crucial site where patriarchal norms became ritually inscribed within relations of production, the early modern marriage ceremony did not merely serve to initiate the reproductive heterosexual couple. A "political event in the life of the community," the wedding was a public ritual in keeping with other key cultural ceremonies of investiture by which corporate entities were constituted.[82]

While *The Shrew* lends itself to a critical focus on Kate and Petruchio's relationship, the consistent privileging of their dynamic has served a "presentist" perspective that permits the critic to read early modern domesticity through the lens of contemporary assumptions about the family.[83] The anachronistic focus on the heterosexual pair has blinded critics to this play's representation of the domestic as a space shaped by various sets of superiors and subordinates, husband and wife being but one. Recent historiography suggests that the household in this era was comprised of a broad kinship network and not characterized by a nuclear family consisting of a man, woman, and child. Rather, a hybrid notion of "family" that extended beyond marital or blood ties, which was marked by the traffic of the extrafamilial men and women, informed this nebulous entity that was poised between residual and emergent notions of the public and the private. De-emphasizing the marital dyad allows us to see the early modern household more clearly as a site of mobile social and erotic relations that were not organized solely around gender difference and as a space that enabled same-sex intimacy. Although feminist critics in particular have gained much purchase from historicizing gender inequity and from grounding the institution of marriage in broader cultural and social formations, critical readings of *The Shrew* that fail to interrogate ahistorical perceptions of the family buttress a conception of heterosexuality as a historical given. The bias that presumes heterosexuality is evident in the tendency to read *The Shrew* through an analytic framework that privileges either gender or class but never sexuality, a category that drops out of the discussion altogether. In *The Shrew,* though, the reproductive household is constituted and challenged by the erotic, which serves as the overdetermined site of gendered discourses and class processes.

Scholarship on the homoerotic bonds that underwrote the institution of service in this period has been particularly important in demonstrating the degree to which on both symbolic and material levels the daily life of the household revolved around the shared intimacies of men. Like the guild or the university, the household was an environment in which the most important positions of domestic responsibility were awarded to single men. As a socially sanctioned space where men worked together, studied together, played together, ate together, and, as Bruce Smith emphasizes, "like everybody else in the sixteenth century, slept together two to a bed," the household provided the conditions for an exclusively male subculture expressed through and based on bonds of service.[84]

Patriarchal privilege, as *The Shrew* demonstrates, meant that marriage did not signal the curtailment of homosocial bonds or the homoerotic relations they implied.[85] Rather, in the absence of a distinct ideology of affective heterosexuality, the installation of the household signaled the continuation of physical and emotional closeness between and among men. An understanding of the wedding scene as centering on the solidification and continuation of male community requires a reanimation of the familial, erotic, and economic connections among men that are usually repressed by readings of the play that focus exclusively on marital dynamics. *The Shrew* shows men coming together in financial and emotional support of one another as they pursue wealthy women and as their respective courtships, in turn, provide the pretexts for further solidifying male bonds.[86] Much stage time is devoted to charting the elaborate arrangements in which men aid each other in negotiating Baptista's rule that makes access to the younger, more appealing Bianca contingent on the nuptial fate of the older Kate. Early on, Bianca's suitors openly acknowledge that Baptista's "bar in law makes [them] friends" (1.1.130), and they agree to "be happy rivals" as they "labor and effect one thing specially" (1.1.115–16), that being the project of finding her older sister a husband. This homosocial network in which men's pecuniary ties to one another underwrite their erotic bonds to women revolves around their mutual "labor," in which they work together aiding each other in achieving higher social positions by marrying up. Petruchio's need for ready cash is satisfied by these male supporters who also promise to enhance their initial subsidy once he and Kate are married (1.2.264).[87] Petruchio's visual pairing of himself with another man, his servant, rather than with his bride, at his wedding amplifies the significance of this ceremony as a public rite that bonded men.

A reading of this scene that emphasizes the primacy of male relations locates Petruchio and Grumio's sartorial misconduct squarely in the context of householders' prevalent anxieties that male domestics perceived their "work" not as the labor of household chores but rather as the task of consuming their masters' goods. While Petruchio's "unreverent robes" may, as his own explanation suggests, simply allude to the "wear" his wife will effect, a reading that takes Grumio's ensemble into account must ultimately place Petruchio's sartorial behavior in dialogue with his servant's. The sartorial tableau produced by Petruchio and Grumio lays bare the anxious underpinnings of the master-servant dynamic in which the servant flaunts it out in elaborate apparel while his shabbily attired master appears stripped of his stature. Their visual performance satirizes those masters who depend too much on the sartorial signs of entitlement and thus become vulnerable to their sartorially rapacious servants who may abuse this signifying system. Tranio (Lucentio's servant who braves it in his master's sumptuous attire) is, significantly, the only onlooker who claims to make sense of the sartorial spectacle before him, announcing to the bewildered crowd that "[Petruchio] hath some meaning in his mad attire" (3.2.114). As a servant with firsthand experience with the intricate workings of braving, Tranio demonstrates a keen understanding of the relationship between sartorial display and social power, which informs his "perverse reading" of their sartorial performance.[88] Thus, on the occasion of Petruchio's inauguration into his new role of householder, Tranio parses the meaning of the visual pun that belies the solemnity of the occasion.

The emotional affinity between and among men that underwrote invisible networks of credit and profit in the period ensured a continuation of a system of mutual obligation among households. At the same time, the intimacy among men that was instrumental to the formation of a working order within the household also potentially led to the blurring of boundaries and the straining of those hierarchical distinctions around which the household was organized. Despite its ideal as a central unit of social control, the everyday practices of household life belied the rigid tenets of a strict social hierarchy. Subordinates were at once confidants and companions and as such served as potent flash points for the contradictions that inhered in domestic arrangements, since they were, as Frances Dolan notes, "dependent yet depended upon, familiar yet not wholly known or controlled, a class and yet not one."[89] While the social identity of the servant was variously categorized, the figure of the male domestic exceeded prevalent social taxonomies. As David Evett emphasizes in his discussion of the various representations of master-servant relationships in Elizabethan drama, a residual social mythology that conceived of servants as surrogate family members coexisted with an increasing cultural need to ascribe subjects a clearly defined place within the traditional social hierarchy. There were multiple, often competing, definitions of service, which were only further confused by attempts to narrow the category.[90] The notion that a servant was someone who, most broadly, worked for others and that a domestic was anyone who lived-in did not succeed in clearly demarcating who was and who was not a servant. By the end of the sixteenth century, the majority of young men spent some part of their lives in service, and service was considered as much a developmental phase in a man's life as a permanent social status. Conduct manuals focused on household sartorial politics because apparel was "the sign" of "the wisdom of the master . . . in well-governing [his] servants," and they recommended rigid prescriptions for comportment between masters and servants as the means by which to manage the ambiguity that informed relations among men within domestic settings.[91]

As Mark Thornton Burnett notes, even though the inordinate dress of servants and apprentices had been a typical preoccupation of early modern householders, in the late sixteenth and early seventeenth centuries official complaints about domestics' dress and comportment "assumed a particularity and an intensity unrivalled in previous decades."[92] Complaints by authorities of "wayward" young men who were associated with sartorial excess and pride dominated popular and legal tracts in this period, and, as Griffiths stresses, "the matter of apparel" among male youth "prompted gloomy forecasts about respect for social order" as well as a perception of immorality and criminality that came to be associated with the servant class.[93] In 1572, the lord mayor of London warned of "servants and apprentices within [the] city [who] are by indulgence and lack of convenient severity grown to great disorder in excess of apparel and fashions" and appear "uncomely for their callings."[94] Apprentices are described by local ordinances as having abandoned their traditional uniform of a flat cap, close-cut hair, narrow falling bands, russet coat, and cloth hose for the "idol of fashion."[95] I. M. censures those servants who are not content with standard livery but must be dressed in "apparel of the newest fashion," since, as he notes, stylish items sell more quickly at the secondhand markets on Birchin Lane.[96] A series of laws was issued in the last decade of the sixteenth century by city authorities, the lord mayor, the Corporations, the Court of Aldermen, and the Common Council in conjunction with the royal administration attempting to regulate the apparel of servants and apprentices. These laws made heads of households responsible for the sartorial propriety of their charges by fining them for their subordinate's sartorial misconduct.[97]

Householders interpreted their domestics' sartorial extravagance as an inherent sign of a disorderly sensibility and connected what they described as an excessive appetite for clothes, food, and money with the propensity to "riot." Servants who "rioted it," as the early modern usage of the word suggested, exhibited behavior marked by a complete lack of restraint and engaged in any number of outlaw activities distinguished by an unbridled excess that disregarded all legal and moral limits.[98] At a stage of life that, according to sixteenth-century medical discourse, young men were understood to be particularly vulnerable to unrestrained indulgence, whether manifested as wasteful expenditure or sexual debauchery, male youth were characterized by physicians' reports, sermons, legislative tracts, and household manuals as prone to riot.[99] Accused of general "wantonnesse, . . .

wastefulness, [and] prodigality," which included engaging in "filthy and detestable loves, horrible lusts, incest, and buggery,"[100] the rioting of servants in this period resulted in the incarceration of a disproportionate number of young men at Bridewell prison and Bedlam hospital.[101] A 1595 pamphlet criticizing masters for overindulging their domestics warns that subordinates who are treated "too proudly, too wantonly with excess of both of meat and apparel," inevitably practice "rioting," participate in a range of "lewd" practices, and are led to "whor[ing]."[102] As one Ben Jonson character aptly observes, "of riot comes whoring" (*EH*, 4.2.367–69), and the conflation of rioting and whoring demonstrated the extent to which erotic and economic transgression were intertwined in the eyes of authorities. Domestics, it was assumed, exhausted household funds either by spending their wages on prostitutes or by whoring themselves, whereby they wore their sumptuous livery bravely to attract customers whose payments enabled them to purchase more clothes. By disrupting the proper channels of expenditure that structured the domestic economy, the domestic's "lewd" activities halted the productive and reproductive function of the household.[103]

Conduct manuals are dominated by representations of young male domestics as "lewd [in] government" and "riotous" and "prodigal."[104] There are also numerous accounts of young men's communal "rioting" at various urban locales, including the ordinary, St. Paul's, the Royal Exchange, and the playhouse, where they are described as "acquaint[ing] themselves too much with the licentious customs of the city: as with quarreling, dicing, dancing, deceiving, lusting, braving, and indebting."[105] These young men, as I have discussed elsewhere, were regularly censured for "rioting" and "raging" of apparel both within and without the household, by which they articulated a shared distinctive sartorial style marked by a flagrant disregard of social and aesthetic norms, one that authorities deemed "monstrous."[106] In the minds of householders', the licentious nature of riot, in which servants reveled in various practices associated with loose living, inspired a range of related dissident activities connected to insubordination more broadly, such as creating disorder within the household, instigating violence on the streets, and even fomenting organized rebellion.[107]

Masters were ultimately held accountable for the behavior of their charges, and the character and behavior of the master of the house set the tone for the entire household.[108] While much attention was focused on subordinates' comportment, household manuals also prescribed sartorial rules for householders instructing them to maintain sartorial propriety in front of their domestics. *A Godly Form of Household Government* contends that the proper government of the family resides in the "comeliness" or the seemliness of its governor as well as in the proper comportment of those governed.[109] Sartorial disarray that signaled insolence among subordinates indicated the loss of mastery in their "betters," since there was "nothing more unseemly in a civil gentleman, than his apparel out of repair, torn, or broken."[110] The inability to "order [one's] own person" indexed, according to the instructional literature, the inability to "rule [one's] own house" and, by extension, properly govern the commonwealth.[111] Sartorial indecency is specifically associated with "unmeet" household government marked by "familiarity" with those under governance.[112] I. M. warns masters against "riotous spending [of] their patrimony in gay clothes" and practicing "lascivious lewdness."[113] Similarly, William Gouge in his *Of Domestical Duties* advises masters to comport themselves always in ways that are "worthy of their place and worthy of that honor which is due to them."[114] Gouge, emphasizing the importance of maintaining proper carriage in front of one's servants, contends that when masters "carry themselves basely and abjectly before their servants, being light in their behavior, foolish in their carriage, given to . . . uncleanness . . . and other vices," they have abdicated their authority.[115] He instructs masters to refrain from "suffer[ing] their servants to be their companions, playing, drinking, [and] reveling with them," and from addressing them by saying "hail fellows met."[116]

Many late sixteenth-century advice manuals do not chastise heads of households for deploying overly strict measures in exacting deference but rather censure householders for being too lenient or familiar with their dependents and thus inspiring them to "take libert[ies]."[117] Masters who treat their servants "too delicately" cause them to "forget [their] place, scorn to be as a servant, [and] aspire to be [their] master's child, which is next to [their] master's mate."[118] In *A Godly Form of Household Government* (1598), Robert Cleaver uses the anarchic city as an analogue for domestic disorder, since the city, like the disordered household, was a space marked by the promiscuous intermingling of those who, despite their shared environs, were not of the same station. Cleaver warns:

For as in a city there is nothing more unequal than that every man should be like equal, so it is not convenient that in one house every man should be like and equal together. There is no equality in that city where the private man is equal with the magistrate, the people with the senate, or the servant with the master, but rather a confusion of all offices and authority.[119]

Householders in this period were advised of the importance of maintaining a proper distance from their domestics and of not mistaking their subordinates for "fit companions," since "when masters are over-ruled by their servants, . . . servants soon prove [to be] masters."[120]

The desires and fears associated with the dangerous proximity between masters and their domestics are played out in the counterfactual social order of *The Shrew*'s induction, in which a drunken tinker who lays claims to a gentle pedigree is temporarily elevated to the status of a lord. While this world-upside-down scenario may have functioned as a socially sanctioned occasion for lower-rank audience members to safely vent their resentment, the promotion of the "monstrous" Sly (Ind.1.30) does not simply function as a moment of social containment.[121] As James Scott suggests, "the argument that off-stage or veiled forms of aggression offer a harmless catharsis that helps preserve the status quo assumes that we are examining a rather abstract debate in which one side is handicapped rather than a concrete material struggle."[122] The stage action of the induction highlights the ways in which the process of domestic domination is firmly anchored in material practices, and the play details the crucial role of objects such as rings, costly suits, sack, and conserves in the confirmation of status. Accordingly, the induction also dramatizes Sly's ability to use objects as sources of pleasure and thus appropriate the situation as an occasion to luxuriate in "stuff."

Sly's profession as a tinker, one who repairs household objects, recommends him as one who is able to render the household a productive space of mobile identifications rather than simply a site of discipline. The lord's experiment, designed to determine whether or not the drunken Sly will forget himself once conveyed to bed and "wrapped in sweet clothes" (Ind.1.33–34), provides a fictive test case for prevalent fears that sumptuously liveried servants did indeed "forget themselves." On the face of it, the Sly episode seems to confirm the essential nature of class difference since the converted Sly requests ale and not the more gentle sack and, moreover, is repeatedly admonished for lapsing back into his former identity. Yet, by pressing on the parameters of the disciplinary constraints that structure his experience, Sly performatively luxuriates in the "sweet clothes," "delicious banquet," and "brave attendants" bestowed upon him, enthusiastically declaring, "I smell sweet savors, and I feel soft things" (Ind.2.66).

Sly also, though, stands in for those masters who, like Petruchio of yeoman status, attempt to repress their own ambiguous pedigree by wrapping themselves in sweet clothes and surrounding themselves with brave attendants. The induction shows that by performing the role of the submissive domestic, members of the lord's train are able to confer authority upon Sly. In order to create the desired effect, the lord instructs his servants to carry Sly gently and:

> Balm his foul head in warm distilled waters,
> . . . .
> And if he chance to speak, be ready straight,
> And with a low submissive reverence
> Say "What is it your honor will command?"
> Let one attend him with a silver basin
> Full of rosewater and bestrewed with flowers;
> Another bear the ewer, the third a diaper,
> And say "Will 't please your lordship cool your hands?"
> Someone be ready with a costly suit,
> And ask him what apparel he will wear;
> Another tell him of his hounds and horse,
> . . . .
> This do, and do it kindly, gentle sirs.
>
> (Ind.1.44–62)

The lord's followers guarantee that they "will play [their] part" so well that Sly will be convinced by their performance of "true diligence" to the point that "he is no less than what we say he is" (Ind.1.65–67). It is, however, at the juncture at which Sly attempts to disrobe the cross-dressed page in order to have sex with him/her (Ind.2.109) that the dreamlike quality of the scene threatens to disintegrate. As the text takes great pains to show, Sly has not fully internalized his new station; he repeatedly requests "a pot o' the smallest ale" and periodically calls out for his tavern friends Cicely Hacket, Stephen Sly, old John Naps of Greet, Peter Turf, and Henry Pimpernel (Ind.2.84–89). Along similar lines, there is little reason to believe that Sly is convinced that the cross-dressed page before him is his "lady." Rather than perpetuating the fictive nature of this scenario, Sly's desire for the page/lady remains in keeping with the very real early modern perception of the page as an erotically available figure whose social and sexual dependence typically conferred and yet also, under certain circumstances, challenged his master's authority.

The potential of the household erotics to disrupt household order is implied in the induction by the "wanton pictures" furnishing Sly's bed-chamber (Ind.1.43). Representations of Venus's seduction of Adonis, Jove's ravishment of Io, and Apollo's pursuit of Daphne capture the precipitous moment at which unbridled sexual desire evolves into absolute chaos. Ovidian representations of rape, as Leonard Barkan suggests, narrate the forcible union of things that should be kept separate. While the moment of consummation produces ecstatic pleasure, this transgressive union initiates an irreversible transformation.[123] Linking disorderly desire with metamorphosis, "an experience that breaks all previously accepted rules," the pictures adorning Sly's chamber associate eros with instability as they allude to the pleasures made available by an antiauthoritarian atmosphere of flux in which the operative categories organizing traditional, patriarchal order are skewed and overturned.[124]

The absent-presence of the "best known myth of homoerotic desire in early modern England," that of Jupiter's seduction of his page Ganymede, is reinserted into the pantheon as Sly assumes the role of Jupiter by command-ing his page/lady to disrobe and lie with him.[125] This myth, which connects unbridled passion with the upheaval of domestic organization, exemplifies what Lynn Enterline describes as "the polymorphic exuberance of the poem's ever-changing desires [that] pull against Ovid's metarhetorical and heteronormative story of rape."[126] Sly's order to his page "undress you and come now to bed" (Ind.2.109) and his page's request for a "pardon" for "a night or two" (Ind.2.111) reproduce the Ovidian moment at which differ-entiated bodies marked by the distinctions of gender and class hover on the cusp of dissolution and reconstitution. The realization of Sly's request promises to metamorphose a "woman" into a boy and a "lord" into a beggar. Sly's reenactment of the Jupiter/Ganymede myth also anticipates the play's larger concerns with the expression of eros between master and servant and how the realization of this passion threatens to dissolve the seemingly rigid categories that order relations between men. Sly's passion destabilizes the precarious tenets of his own authority, since once he removes his "sweet clothes," he strips himself of not merely the trappings of his elite status but, in this case, the very materials that constitute it. Once divested, Sly reoccupies the space of the dispossessed tinker, and his desire for the page reveals his social inferiority to this gentle servant, whose obeisance is, like Sly's elevated status, revealed to be an elaborate fiction.

To Serve, Love, and Obey

Petruchio's "rough" wooing of Kate (2.1.133) and vexed relations with his servants provide the entertainment that effectively defers Sly's consummation with his servant. The play performed for Sly and his lady/page significantly presents a domestic arrangement that undercuts rather than buttresses the regulatory function of the ideal early modern household. Before meeting Kate, Petruchio envisions a disorderly domestic economy infused with the dynamics of mutual expenditure and exhaustion rather than a household constituted by a stable hierarchy of clearly demarcated gender and class roles. Predicting that he and Kate will come together like two raging fires that "do consume the thing that feeds their fury," Petruchio constructs the domestic as an arena where equally matched, uncontainable appetites—unhinged even from human form—range free and merge. Describing himself submitting to Kate as she "yield[s] to [him]" (2.1.132–36), Petruchio's fantasy of erotic role reversal and sexual subservience invokes the disorderly outcome of wearing, whereby the head of the household "give[s] [his] servants power over [his] body" as well as the impression that they will be "maintained and bolstered up by the master . . . whom they have known."[127] This potentially anarchic arrangement whereby masters enable their subordinates to erotically dominate, sexually exhaust, and materially consume them could be contained only by a domestic ideology that constructed the household in terms of gendered spheres of influence.

In her final speech, Kate also describes the household as revolving around its members' appetites, but by detailing the benefits of lying "warm at home, secure and safe," while her "lord" and "keeper" "commits his body to painful labor" (5.2.156, 152–53), Kate articulates a vision of household order in which the master's/husband's duty is to travel abroad and procure household stuff for the wife to enjoy.[128] As Natasha Korda has argued, *The Shrew* distinguishes itself from previous shrew-taming narratives by its interest in a shift in modes of production such that the very terms through which domestic economy was conceived were, in this period, becoming radically altered. An emergent conception of the home as a sphere of consumption rather than production was, at the beginning of the seventeenth century, borne of the transformations brought on by a movement away from household production and toward nascent capitalist industries. Most significantly, as men and women purchased what they once produced, skilled labor moved outside the home into the market and the menial duties of domestic upkeep were increasingly assigned to servants. As the "cultural valuation" of housework changed, however, so also did the material form and cultural function of service.[129]

Kate's description of her domestic duty as the enjoyment of the rewards of her husband's labor, significantly represented as merchant adventurism rather than manual toil (5.1.153), signaled the emergence of the housewife as the manager of household stuff, but it also heralded the demise of the lavishly attired male servant whose primary function was to appear comely. The steep drop in numbers of servants employed within elite households, such that the percentage of live-in servants made up less than 10 percent of the population by the early 1700s, speaks to the gradual dissolution of the household that revolved around its decorative male domestics.[130] *The Shrew* would thus seem to explore the dynamics of the master-servant household, only in the final instance to instantiate the master-mistress household by identifying marriage as a regulatory apparatus that secured a new gendered division of production and consumption. In this respect, *The Shrew* inaugurates the private realm by excising the non(re)productive male consumer and designating the household as the wife/woman's sphere, where now the mistress will "entertain[ ] all comers, conduct[ ] their guests to their chambers, care[ ] [for] their breakfasts, keep[ ] them company at cards" and perform "many more complements of this nature."[131] In accordance with this new gendered ideology of household management, which was subsequently explicated and promoted in early seventeenth-century economic treatises, conduct manuals, and theatrical representations, men who consume household stuff outside of the context of matrimony register as effeminate and excessive. These young men come to be associated with "unruly" expenditure or waste. Ironically, the conspicuous consumption of the young unmarried man is cited as the *cause* of the demise of traditional service, exemplified by descriptions of city gallants stripping their servants of their liveries and discharging them so that the gallants can have more money to spend on sumptuous apparel and urban pleasures such as the theater.[132]

The Shrew, though, addresses the de-skilling of domestic labor and denigration of service not by erasing the effects of this trend but rather by staging its implications. As Kate is progressively interpellated into her new role as domestic consumer, the margins of the text become increasingly populated by reluctant and seemingly incompetent male servants. Petruchio arrives home to "no attendance," "no regard," and "no duty"

(4.1.95). His grooms are "unpolished" (4.1.94) and in a general state of sartorial disarray, as Grumio reports:

> Nathaniel's coat, sir, was not fully made,
> And Gabriel's pumps were all unpinked i' the heel.
> There was no link to color Peter's hat,
> And Walter's dagger was not come from sheathing.
> There were none fine but Adam, Ralph, and Gregory.
> The rest were ragged, old, and beggarly.
>
>   (4.1.101-6)

The sartorial impudence of his servants is matched only by their seditious behavior in which one servant "plucks" Petruchio's "foot awry" in removing his boots (4.1.116), another spills water on him, and yet another serves him burnt meat. As Kate's rebelliousness subsides, insubordinate behavior becomes exclusively associated with male servants, whom Petruchio seems only able to discipline through recourse to violence. In this respect, *The Shrew* maps out not only the ideological separation of feminine and masculine spheres of domestic labor but also suggests the ways in which changes in the perceptions and practices of housework impacted the culture's changing fantasies about the role of male domestics.

Throughout my discussion I have focused on those instances in which *The Shrew* compels us to perceive characters as moving in and out of various familial and erotic roles. My emphasis on positions and modalities rather than on stable representations or fixed identities grows out of a desire to pry open the term "shrew" in order to obtain the various ways in which "shrewness" is embodied throughout the play. "Shrew," like the words "harlot," "punk," or "scold," was a term of denigration that referred to both men and women until it underwent a semantic shift in the late sixteenth century.[133] Even as the gender valence of "shrew" changed, the word remained haunted by associations with male class revolt or riot. As David Underdown points out, scolding was predominantly a juridical offense ascribed to lower-rank women, but a scold or a shrew was a social outcast or newcomer to the community of either gender who was perceived as disturbing civic order.[134] Like the "skimmington," a violator of community norms as well as, more generally, "something or someone undesirable," "shrewness" in this period described a range of behaviors that were perceived first and foremost as challenges to authority.[135] These behaviors included flouting gender norms and exhibiting erotic unruliness as well as instigating local disturbances and even organizing popular rebellion.[136] Reactivating the bi-gender, politicized valence of the term "shrew" brings into relief those sites in Shakespeare's play where "shrewness" is deployed such that it exceeds the context of marital relations.

The play promotes "shrew," I am suggesting, as a mobile term that references various instances of material and linguistic excess rather than a stable descriptor attached to a specific character or gender. Shrewness functions as a *mode* of insurgency, one that is manifest at those moments when the links among the familial, the erotic, and the economic are exposed. In revealing the household to be a volatile space, where its members' unruly desires and identifications are promoted as much as contained, *The Shrew* should not be read as a text that either asserts the triumph of mastery or celebrates the spirit of rebellion. Rather than an anatomy of transgression that ultimately legitimates the *heimlich,* the play charts how those who occupy an ambivalent relationship to dominant culture work with and through exclusionary practices by transforming them for their own purposes. A testament to the *unheimlich,* or the antithetical that inheres within, *The Shrew*'s focus on livery, broadly construed, identifies household stuff or clothing as the symbolic and material terrain for such transformative practices. More specifically, I have attempted to show that by engaging in braving, servants inserted themselves into the dominant structure of livery. By using those very objects that were culturally coded to effect their incorporation in the service of spectacle, gentle-born domestics demonstrated that the conditions of their servitude enabled their reworking of its tenets. By revealing the contradictory components inherent in their position, for instance by letting the seams show, servants who braved it performed their servitude with an unseemly over-the-topness. How they embodied their clothes called attention to the processes by which dominant culture attempted to inscribe them as well as to their own abilities to use the clothes assigned to them as the raw material of a dissident style.

Notes

1. According to Ann Kussmaul, in *Servants in Husbandry in Early Modern England* (Cambridge: Cambridge University Press, 1981), approximately 60 percent of the population in early modern England was employed in some form of service (3). Alan Macfarlane, in *The Origins of English Individualism: Family, Property, and Social Transition* (Oxford: Basil Blackwell, 1978), estimates that somewhere between a quarter and one half of the population

worked in service at one time or another and that perhaps one quarter to one third of the families in early modern England had servants (79). On early modern England as a "service society," see Paul Griffiths, Adam Fox, and Steve Hindle, eds., *The Experience of Authority in Early Modern England* (London: Basingstoke, 1996). On service as a component of the early modern life-cycle, see Peter Laslett and Richard Wall, eds., *Household and Family in Past Time* (Cambridge: Cambridge University Press, 1972); Lawrence Stone, *Family, Sex, and Marriage in England, 1500-1800,* abr. ed. (New York: Harper and Row, 1979); Anthony Fletcher, *Sex, Gender, and Subordination in England, 1500-1800* (New Haven: Yale University Press, 1995); Susan Dwyer Amussen, *An Ordered Society: Gender and Class in Early Modern England* (London: Basil Blackwell, 1988); Alice Clark, *Working Life of Women in the Seventeenth Century* (1919; reprint, London: Routledge, 1982).

2. I will use the terms "servant" and "domestic" interchangeably throughout. As Ann Kussmaul argues, in the sixteenth century there was no clear distinction between "productive servants" and "idle" or "unproductive" servants. Moreover, the differences among "day-laborers," "menials," "domestics," and "servants" were not fully articulated until the nineteenth century. The meaning of the term "servant" in this period extended to all of those who worked for others, and domestics were, most broadly, those servants who lived-in (Kussmaul, *Servants in Husbandry,* 5-7).

3. I. M. refers to the "Blew coates" of service in *A Health to the Gentlemanly Profession of Servingmen: or, The Servingman's Comfort* (London, 1598), in W. C. Hazlitt, ed., *Inedited Tracts: Illustrating the Manner, Opinions, and Occupations of Englishmen during the Sixteenth and Seventeenth Centuries* (London: The Roxburghe Collection, 1868), 107. Hereafter referred to as *Servingman's Comfort.*

4. Peter Stallybrass emphasizes that livery in a household signified servitude whereas livery in a guild signaled freedom. For a fuller discussion of the term "livery," a word whose etymology suggests both delivery and distribution as well as deliverance, liberation, and release, see his "Worn Worlds: Clothes and Identity on the Renaissance Stage," in *Subject and Object in Renaissance Culture,* ed. Peter Stallybrass, Margreta de Grazia, et al. (Cambridge: Cambridge University Press, 1996), 289-320. On badges and household emblems, see David Starkey, "The Age of the Household," in *The Later Middle Ages,* ed. Stephen Medcalf (New York: Holmes and Meier, 1981), 246-47 and 264-76. For a discussion of the body's inscription into the social more generally, see de Michel de Certeau, *The Practice of Everyday Life,* trans. Steven Rendall (1984; reprint, Berkeley: University of California Press, 1988), 139-42 and 148-49.

5. Ann Rosalind Jones and Peter Stallybrass, *Renaissance Clothing and the Materials of Memory* (Cambridge: Cambridge University Press, 2000), 21.

6. Ibid., 26-32.

7. William Shakespeare, *The Taming of the Shrew: Texts and Contexts,* ed. Frances E. Dolan (New York: St. Martin's Press, 1996), Ind.2.132 and Ind.2.131. Hereafter referred to in the text as *The Shrew* and cited parenthetically by act, scene, and line number.

8. Andrew Clark argues that the genre of "domestic drama" should not be restricted to a particular type or theme but rather should serve as a broad categorization that applies to plays concerned with domestic doctrine and conduct; Andrew Clark, *A Survey of the Origins, Antecedents, and Nature of the Domestic Play in England: Volume 1, Domestic*

Drama (Salzburg: University of Salzburg, 1975). See also Viviana Comensoli, *"Household Business": Domestic Plays of Early Modern England* (Toronto: University of Toronto Press, 1996), 6-7. For a discussion of the distinctions and intersections between domestic drama and city comedy, see Alexander Leggatt, *Citizen Comedy in the Age of Shakespeare* (Toronto: University of Toronto Press, 1973), and Comensoli, *"Household Business,"* 3-27.

9. Lisa Jardine, *Reading Shakespeare Historically* (London: Routledge, 1996), suggests that in the early modern period dependency may have been a socially defining category that was more symbolically compelling than gender, since subordinates of both genders were positioned as socially and sexually available within the household order (70). While Jardine may overstate her claim, certainly gender difference was not irrelevant; her point that gender was not necessarily the overarching organizational category in the period is well taken. Jean Howard also emphasizes that boys and women occupied similar hierarchical positions in regard to adult men and that, in this period, social status was of equal if not greater significance in sexual relations than similarity or difference of anatomy. See Jean E. Howard, "Sex and Social Conflict: The Erotics of *The Roaring Girl*," in *Erotic Politics: Desire on the Renaissance Stage,* ed. Susan Zimmerman (New York: Routledge, 1992), 170-91. On the significance of dependency as a preeminent social logic in the period, see Kussmaul, *Servants in Husbandry,* 8-10; Peter Laslett, *The World We Have Lost: Further Explored,* 3d ed. (London: Methuen, 1983), 5; and, more generally, Lawrence Stone, *Family, Sex, and Marriage;* Ian Archer, *The Pursuit of Stability: Social Relations in Elizabethan London* (Cambridge: Cambridge University Press, 1991); Keith Wrightson, *English Society, 1580-1680* (New Jersey: Rutgers, 1982); and John Fletcher and Anthony Stevenson, eds., *Order and Disorder in Early Modern England* (Cambridge: Cambridge University Press, 1985).

10. Michael Neill, *Putting History to the Question: Power, Politics, and Society in English Renaissance Drama* (New York: Columbia University Press, 2000), 22.

11. Notably, Natasha Korda, *Shakespeare's Domestic Economies: Gender and Property in Early Modern England* (Philadelphia: University of Pennsylvania Press, 2002), esp. 52-76; Lynda E. Boose, *"The Taming of the Shrew,* Good Husbandry, and Enclosure," in *Shakespeare Reread: The Texts in New Contexts,* ed. Russ McDonald (Ithaca, N.Y.: Cornell University Press, 1994), 193-226; and Carol F. Heffernan, *"The Taming of the Shrew*: The Bourgeoisie in Love," *Essays in Literature* 12 (1985): 3-15.

12. I am implicitly invoking Bourdieu's notion of habitus, an embodied disposition that is acquired both informally and formally. While on the one hand habitus is the objective outcome of social conditions, on the other hand it is a lived practice and, as such, is, as Bourdieu emphasizes, a structuring structure. In other words, habitus is the site where durable and transposable dispositions are mediated and reshaped by the particular constraints of social contexts in the moment of their articulation. See Pierre Bourdieu, *Distinction: A Social Critique of the Judgement of Taste,* trans. Richard Nice (Cambridge: Harvard University Press, 1984); see also, Judith Butler *Excitable Speech: A Politics of the Performative* (New York: Routledge, 1997).

13. An example of this approach is Frank Whigham, *Ambition and Privilege: The Social Tropes of Elizabethan Courtesy Theory* (Berkeley: University of California Press, 1984).

14. Christopher Pye, *The Vanishing: Shakespeare, the Subject, and Early Modern Culture* (Durham: Duke University Press, 2000), 36. Pye writes that subjectivity appears at "the knotted limit of an entire array of discursive formations" (36).

15. Karl Marx, *Capital, Volume One,* trans. Ben Fowkes (New York: Vintage Books, 1977), 125. I am not suggesting a return to the notion of the individual, a concept that has been successfully challenged and historicized for the past two decades in the field of early modern studies as well as, more generally, in the fields of sociology, anthropology, and poststructuralist rereadings of psychoanalysis. I use the term "subject" with an implicit understanding that subjects are incoherent and often contradictory loci of the various social relations that shape them. My primary interest is the modes of operation or tactics that men and women use rather than the subjects who are their agents. For a discussion that focuses on modes of operating, see Michel de Certeau, *Practice of Everyday Life,* xi–xxiv.

16. David Evett, "'Surprising Confrontations'—Ideologies of Service in Shakespeare's England," in *Renaissance Papers,* ed. Dale B. J. Randall and Joseph A. Porter (Papers Published for the Southeastern Renaissance Conference, 1990), 68.

17. As Kate Mertes notes, it wasn't until the later half of the seventeenth century that women became part of the household domestic staff. As long as service was considered a position of some prestige and an avenue for social and economic advancement, women were largely discouraged from pursuing domestic positions. The proliferation of women servants after 1700 accompanies the household's decline and the denigration of service as a profession. See Kate Mertes, *The English Noble Household, 1250–1600: Good Governance and Politic Rule* (London: Basil Blackwell, 1988), 57–58. On the rise of the female domestic, see also Felicity Heal, *Hospitality in Early Modern England* (Oxford: Clarendon Press, 1990), and Mark Thornton Burnett, *Masters and Servants in English Renaissance Drama and Culture: Authority and Obedience* (New York: St. Martin's Press, 1997).

18. I. M., *Servingman's Comfort,* 139. On the shift from a militaristic ideology of service, which emphasized safety, to a notion of service that tied domestic service to household luxury, see Dorothy Marshall, *The English Domestic Servant in History* (London: The Historical Association, 1949).

19. Henry Wotton, *The Elements of Architecture By Sir Henry Wotton: A Facsimile Reprint of the First Edition* (London, 1624), as in Comensoli, *"Household Business,"* 72.

20. Heal, *Hospitality,* 7.

21. Neill, *Putting History to the Question,* 29. David Starkey discusses the early modern concept of magnificence and emphasizes that while it could be expressed in various ways, the "supreme and chosen vehicle" for magnificence was the household (255). As I argue below, the distinction between gentlemen and nobleman was a mutable one in this period. I use the term "elite" as an overarching term to describe those who identified themselves as "noble," "aristocratic," or "gentle." These particular claims to elite status functioned interchangeably in the period because the criteria of gentility were in flux.

22. Starkey, "Age of the Household," 255.

23. Mertes, *English Noble Household,* 68.

24. Starkey, "Age of the Household," 234.

25. Anonymous, *The English Courtier and the Country Gentleman, or, Of Civil and Uncivil Life* (London, 1586), in W. C. Hazlitt, ed., *Inedited Tracts: Illustrating the Manner, Opinions, and Occupations of Englishmen during the Sixteenth and Seventeenth Centuries* (London: The Roxburghe Collection, 1868), 34. Hereafter referred to as *Of Civil.*

26. *Of Civil,* 38.

27. Ibid., 43.

28. I. M., *Servingman's Comfort*, 126.

29. Even those who were not of gentle status attempted to furnish themselves with a boy or two as an accessory. I. M. writes of meeting Sir Davie Debt with six to eight "tall fellows" attending him and John Makeshift, "whose last acre lies mortgaged," also attended by six to eight fellows (125). In the *Tempest*, the "masterless" Stephano and Trinculo realize their elevated status as rulers of the island by recruiting Caliban to be their man. Similarly, the gallants in Ben Jonson's *Everyman in His Humor* hire men as a means of displaying and promoting the elevated status to which they aspire.

30. Mertes, *English Noble Household*, 45.

31. On clothing and the household finances, see Mertes, *English Noble Household*, 45, 99, and Lawrence Stone, *Family and Fortune: Studies in Aristocratic Finance in the Sixteenth and Seventeenth Centuries* (Oxford: Clarendon Press, 1973) and *An Open Elite? England, 1540-1880* (Oxford: Clarendon Press, 1984). On the costs of owning land in the period, including taxes and upkeep, see Lynda E. Boose, "The Taming of the Shrew, Good Husbandry, and Enclosure," *Shakespeare Reread: The Texts in New Contexts*, ed. Russ McDonald (Ithaca, N.Y.: Cornell University Press, 1994), 215, and Richard Lachmann, *From Manor to Market: Structural Change in England, 1536-1640* (Madison: University of Wisconsin Press, 1987).

32. On the ambiguity of gentility in the period, see William Harrison, *The Description of England* (1857; reprint, Ithaca, N.Y.: Cornell University Press for the Folger Shakespeare Library, 1968); David Cressy, "Describing the Social Order in Elizabethan and Stuart England," *Literature and History* (1976): 29-44; and Lawrence Stone, "Social Mobility in England, 1500-1700," *Past and Present* 33 (1966): 23-24.

33. On cloth production in early modern England, see Sybil M. Jack, *Trade and Industry in Tudor and Stuart England* (London: George Allen and Unwin, 1977); Norman Lowe, *The Lancashire Textile Industry in the Sixteenth Century,* (London: The Chetham Society, 3rd. ser., 20, 1972); Eric Kerridge, *Textile Manufacturers in Early Modern England* (Manchester: Manchester University Press, 1985); David Dymond and Alec Betterton, *Lavenham: 700 Years of Textile Making* (London: Woodbridge, 1982); G. D. Ramsay, *The Wiltshire Woolen Industry in the Sixteenth and Seventeenth Centuries,* 2d ed. (1943; reprint, Oxford: Oxford University Press, 1965); John T. Swain, *Industry before the Industrial Revolution: North-East Lancashire, 1500-1640* (London: Chetham Society, 3rd ser., 32, 1986); and Peter J. Bowden, *The Wool Trade in Tudor and Stuart England* (New York: St. Martin's Press, 1962). On conspicuous consumption in early modern England, see F. J. Fisher, *London and the English Economy, 1500-1700* (London: Hambledon Press, 1990), 105-18; Joan Thirsk, *Economic Policy and Projects: The Development of a Consumer Society in Early Modern England* (Oxford: Clarendon Press, 1978); Chandra Mukerji, *From Graven Images: Patterns of Modern Materialism* (New York: Columbia University Press, 1983); *Consumption and the World of Goods,* ed. John Brewer and Roy Porter (London: Routledge, 1993); Lisa Jardine, *Worldy Goods: A New History of the Renaissance* (New York: Nan A. Talese, 1996), and *Material London, ca. 1600,* ed. Lena Cowen Orlin (Philadelphia: University of Pennsylvania Press, 2000). On the secondhand clothing trade and the early modern theater, see Jones and Stallybrass, "The Circulation of Clothes and the Making of the English Theater," in *Renaissance Clothing and the Materials of Memory.*

34. I. M., *Servingman's Comfort*, 115. On the prevalence of gentle servants, see Amussen,

Ordered Society, 68, 158. Burnett discusses the growing numbers of gentry entering professional trades in general. For instance, in late sixteenth-century Shrewsbury, the Drapers Company took 20 percent of their apprentices from the local gentry, but by the middle third of the seventeenth century this figure had risen to 50 percent. The London Stationer's Company only enrolled 15 sons of gentlemen as apprentices from 1576 to 1585, but by 1630 the number of gentry enrolled had increased to 114 (Burnett, *Masters and Servants,* 41–42). For similar accounts of the rise of gentle-born apprentices and servants, see J. P. Cooper *Land, Men, and Beliefs: Studies in Early Modern History* (London: Hambledon Press, 1983), and F. H. Mares, ed., *The Memoirs of Robert Carey* (Oxford: Oxford University Press, 1972). While I am aware that personal service in this period was shifting from a patronage system based on gentleman retainers to a wage-based system employing a population from a wider class background, I believe that the significance of this claim, expressed by the now clichéd reference to "the crisis of service," has been overstated and has prevented scholars from exploring the significance of class proximity between household members. The social and economic changes in the nature of domestic service occurred in a larger, more complex socioeconomic context and took shape gradually and unevenly. Moreover, the meaning of these changes did not necessarily register coherently for those who lived through them. For a discussion of the debasing of service, see Lawrence Stone, *The Crisis of the Aristocracy, 1558-1641,* abr. ed. (London: Oxford University Press, 1967); A. L. Beier, *Masterless Men: The Vagrancy Problem in England, 1560-1640* (London: Methuen, 1985), 22–28; and Alan Bray, "Homosexuality and the Signs of Male Friendship in Elizabethan England," *Queering the Renaissance,* ed. Jonathan Goldberg (Durham: Duke University Press, 1994), 40–61.

35. Ian Archer, "Shakespeare's London," in *A Companion to Shakespeare,* ed. David Scott Kastan (London: Blackwell, 1999), 44. John Gillis, *Youth and History: Tradition and Change in European Age Relations, 1770-Present* (New York: Academic Press, 1974), refers to this group of second, third, and fourth sons as the "superfluous" or "surplus" children of the elite. He notes that in periods of population growth, such as between 1550 and 1630 (when the population of England doubled), younger sons of the elite suffered the most since demographic pressures resulted in stricter settlements on inheritance and greater competition for limited resources. Alan MacFarlane also discusses the effects of unequal inheritance in *Origins,* 154–64. For a discussion of "subordinate youth" as an age-related rather than an age-specific classification, see Paul Griffiths, *Youth and Authority: Formative Experiences in England, 1560-1640* (Oxford: Clarendon Press, 1996), 355. For a more general overview of the notion of "youth" in early modern England, see Ilana Krausman Ben-Amos, *Adolescence and Youth in Early Modern England* (New Haven: Yale University Press, 1994).

36. Gillis, *Youth and History,* 21.

37. A. L. Beier emphasizes that young men from gentle backgrounds who turned to service perceived their position as temporary, part of their "life-cycle," despite the economic realities of their lives, which indicated that a career of service would be an enduring condition (*Masterless Men,* 22–28). Mark Thornton Burnett discusses various popular texts that construct servants as consumers of commercial items not typically associated with nonelite ranks (*Masters and Servants,* 8–9).

38. I. M., *Servingman's Comfort,* 131.

39. Anonymous, *A Diamond Most Precious, Worthy to be Marked,* as in Lena Cowen

Orlin, *Elizabethan Households: An Anthology* (Washington, D.C.: The Folger Shakespeare Library, 1995), 46.

40. Richard Climsell, *A Pleasant New Dialogue: or, the Discourse between the Serving-man and the Husband-man* (London, 1626) in Fitzgeffrey's *Satyres* as in Burnett, *Masters and Servants,* 94.

41. George Chapman, Ben Jonson, and John Marston, *Eastward Ho!,* ed. R. W. Van Fossen (Manchester: Manchester University Press, 1999), 1.1.82; n.2, 69. Hereafter referred to in the text as *EH* and cited parenthetically by act, scene, and line number.

42. William Gouge, *Of Domestical Duties,* 2d ed. (London, 1626), 374, 337.

43. Ibid., 337.

44. Ibid.

45. I. M., *Servingman's Comfort,* 123.

46. Gouge, *Of Domestical Duties,* 335.

47. de Certeau, *Practice of Everyday Life,* 32.

48. Thomas Moisan, "'Knock me here soundly': Comic Misprision and Class Consciousness in Shakespeare," *Shakespeare Quarterly* 42(3) (Fall 1991): 276.

49. Ibid., 280.

50. Jonathan Dollimore, *Sexual Dissidence: Augustine to Wilde, Freud to Foucault* (Oxford: Clarendon Press, 1991), 42.

51. See Harold Bloom, *A Map of Misreading* (London: Oxford University Press, 1975). For a discussion of assimilation and appropriation, see de Certeau, *Practice of Everyday Life,* 166. My discussion of braving later in this essay is indebted to Henry Louis Gates's discussion of "Signifyin(g)." He writes that Signifyin(g) "turns on the sheer play of the signifier. It does not refer primarily to the signified; rather, it refers to the style of language. . . . Again, one does not Signify some thing; one Signifies in *some way*" (78). He also explores related modes, such as the dozens, meaning to censure in twelve or fewer statements and (as the eighteenth-century meaning of the verb "dozen" suggests) to stun, stupefy, or daze with language. *The Signifying Monkey: A Theory of African-American Literary Criticism* (Oxford: Oxford University Press, 1988), 68–88, 99–103.

52. I am using Jose Esteban Munoz's term for a mode of dealing with dominant ideology that allows one to neither assimilate to nor strictly oppose it, but rather to work on and against dominant codes by transforming their cultural logic from within. For Munoz's cogent discussion of Michel Pecheux's notion of *disidentification,* see Munoz, *Disidentifications: Queers of Color and the Performance of Politics* (Minneapolis: University of Minnesota Press, 1999), 1–34.

53. Slavoj Zizek, "The Undergrowth of Enjoyment: How Popular Culture Can Serve as an Introduction to Lacan," *New Formations* Vol. 9 (1989), as in *The Zizek Reader,* ed. Elizabeth Wright and Edmond Wright (London: Blackwell Publishers, 1999), 21.

54. Bruce Smith, *Homosexual Desire in Shakespeare's England: A Cultural Poetics* (1991; reprint, Chicago: University of Chicago Press, 1994), 54. For citations of "brave" as a stage direction in early modern drama, see Alan C. Dessen and Leslie Thomson, *A Dictionary of Stage Directions in English Drama, 1580–1642* (Cambridge: Cambridge University Press, 1999), 37.

55. *OED,* s.v. "brave." Hereafter referred to in the text as *OED* and cited parenthetically.

56. Tranio's braving in his master's sumptuous apparel is a complex phenomenon. Certainly, the extreme reactions that Tranio's appearance inspire suggest the profoundly transgressive nature of braving that carries with it the sting of parody by which a servant's exaggerated splendor reveals the ways in which authentic aristocratic style always bordered on gaudy ostentation. On another level, Tranio's flamboyant impersonation of his master also worked, reassuringly, to affirm the immutable difference between masters and those who served them by demonstrating that servants could only reproduce the sartorial splendor of their betters as garish exaggeration lacking the necessary *sprezzatura*.

57. For a discussion of the use of the word "curious" in reference to matters of style, see John Greenwood, *Shifting Perspectives and the Stylish Style: Mannerism in Shakespeare and his Jacobean Contemporaries* (Toronto: University of Toronto Press, 1988), 17. "Curiousness," as Karen Newman has shown in *Fashioning Femininity and English Renaissance Drama* (Chicago: University of Chicago Press, 1991), was also associated with an excess of significance that bespoke the effeminate decorousness of "crowded ornament" (123). Ben Jonson employed sartorial tropes to describe the improper use of language and drew explicit connections among excess of apparel, social disorder, linguistic wantonness, and sickness of mind (Newman, *Fashioning Femininity*, 125). Advocating a plain rhetorical style that he likens to dress without ornamentation, Jonson refers to those young men who are "exceedingly curious" as "always kempt'd and perfum'd; [with] the everyday smell of the tailor." Jonson declares that "too much pickedness is not manly" (Newman, *Fashioning Femininity*, 126). Exploring the connection between indecorous language and the preposterous style of the ostentatious gallant, Jonson writes:

Right and naturall language seeme to have least of the wit in it; that which is writh'd and tortur'd, is counted the most exquisite. Cloath of Bodkin, or Tissue, must be imbroidered. . . . No beauty to be had, but in wresting, and writhing our owne tongue? Nothing is fashionable, till it be deform'd; and this is to write like a *Gentleman*. All must bee as affected and preposterous as our Gallants cloathes, sweet bags, and night-dressings: in which you would think our men lay in; like *Ladies;* it is so curious.

(Jonson, *Discoveries,* in Newman, *Fashioning Femininity,* 125)

58. On "in your face" as a standard Signifyin(g) retort, see Gates, *Signifying Monkey,* 66. The more recent sense of RuPaul's "talk to the hand" applies as well.

59. Simon Shepherd, "What's So Funny about Ladies' Tailors? A Survey of Some Male (Homo)Sexual Types in the Renaissance," *Textual Practice* 6 (1) (Spring 1992): 17–31. E. A. M. Colman, *The Dramatic Use of Bawdy in Shakespeare* (London: Longman, 1974), also notes that tailors were typically represented as effeminate and lascivious, and he glosses a series of double entendres associated with the words "prick" and "yard" (224).

60. Mario DiGangi discusses the indeterminacy of the "sexual" and the importance of considering nonpenetrative and even seemingly noneerotic activities when seeking to investigate same-sex contacts that may have functioned to subvert the assumptions of reproductive patriarchal sexuality. *The Homoerotics of Early Modern Drama* (Cambridge: Cambridge University Press, 1997), 11.

61. E. A. M. Colman glosses "cut" as referring to the vulva and more generally the vagina (*Dramatic Use of Bawdy,* 190). For a discussion of the anus as a cut, see D. A. Miller, "Anal

Rope," in *Inside/Out: Lesbian Theories, Gay Theories* (New York: Routledge, 1991), 134–39. Another early modern association with the word cut is "crack," the word for an ingle or the young boy who sexually served his older patron; see Wendy Wall, *Staging Domesticity: Household Work and English Identity in Early Modern Drama* (Cambridge: Cambridge University Press, 2002), 182.

62. For "use" as a common term for sexual intercourse in the period, see James T. Henke, *Renaissance Dramatic Bawdy (Exclusive of Shakespeare): An Annotated Glossary and Critical Essays* (Salzburg: University of Salzburg, 1974).

63. The notion that what occurs at Petruchio's country house replicates the environs of an all-male grammar school is suggested by Tranio's description of Petruchio's house as a "taming school" (4.2.55). In a closed world of boys and men, pedagogical violence was seen as facilitating the rigid disciplining of the body as well as the mind and beatings were integrated even into newer humanist systems of learning. Wall notes that "the fetishized rod served as an almost ubiquitous emblem of order and knowledge" in the period (*Staging Domesticity,* 19), and Walter J. Ong argues that Latin was taught in connection with violent flogging designed to instill physical hardiness in young boys ("Latin Language Study as a Renaissance Puberty Rite," *Rhetoric, Romance, and Technology: Studies in the Interaction of Expression and Culture* [1959; reprint, Ithaca: Cornell University Press, 1971], 113–41). On pedagogical violence, see Richard Halpern, *The Poetics of Primitive Accumulation: English Renaissance Culture and the Genealogy of Capital* (Ithaca, N.Y.: Cornell University Press, 1991), 25–29. See also Smith, *Homosexual Desire,* 83–84, and Alan Stewart, *Close Readers: Humanism and Sodomy in Early Modern England* (Princeton: Princeton University Press, 1997), 84–121.

64. Mark Thornton Burnett, " 'The Trusty Servant': A Sixteenth-Century English Emblem," *Emblematica* 6(2) (1992): 1–17.

65. DiGangi, *Homoerotics,* 67–80. The sexual, sadistic, and scatological are invoked a few lines later when Grumio threatens to prove his innocence to the tailor, even if the tailor's "little finger [is] armed in a thimble." To this the tailor replies, "This is true. . . . An I had thee in a place where thou shoulds't know it." While the "it" refers to the correct version of the bill and the place a court of law, as the textual note suggests, the tailor's "it" may also ambiguously refer to his little finger ("armed" in a thimble), which, if the tailor had Grumio in another, more private, place, he, Grumio, would have the opportunity to "know it." Grumio retorts, "I am for thee straight," or I am ready, "Take thou the bill, give me thy mete-yard [a long measuring stick] and spare me not" (4.3.141–44).

66. Neill, *Putting History to the Question,* 19.

67. Aristotle, *The Ethics of Aristotle,* ed. and trans. J. A. K. Thomson, as in Starkey, "Age of the Household," 256.

68. *Of Civil,* 64. Householders' concerns about their servants wearing out household stuff were not entirely irrational, since, as Kate Mertes points out, one of the most lucrative sources of household income came from the recycling and selling of household materials, whether foodstuffs, the metals of pots and pans, or household linens and cloth (Mertes, *English Noble Household,* 98).

69. Until the eighteenth century, luxury was synonymous with lechery since both words described the sin of excessive desire, which posed a threat to both the social hierarchy and the individual soul. Margreta de Grazia discusses the connection between "lavish spending

and dissipate fornicating" in *King Lear* in "The Ideology of Superfluous Things," in *Subject and Object in Renaissance Culture,* ed. Margreta de Grazia, Maureen Quilligan, and Peter Stallybrass (Cambridge: Cambridge University Press, 1996), 28. Thomas Laqueur, in *Making Sex: Body and Gender from the Greeks to Freud* (Cambridge: Harvard University Press, 1990), notes that the word "purse" in the early modern period referred to the scrotum, since coin and seed were mutually understood to be a potent currency (63–64). In the ballad "The Lamentation of a New-Married Man," the wife scolds her husband for "spending" all "among his minions":

> You do not love me,
> To leave me all alone;
> You must goe a gadding,
> And I must bide at home,
> While you, among your minions,
> Spend more than is your owne.
> (As in DiGangi, Homoerotics, 49)

   70. *OED,* s.v. "spent." In Sonnet 129, Shakespeare uses the metaphor of expenditure to describe ejaculation. Noting that "Th' expense of spirit in a waste of shame / Is lust in action," the speaker describes an erotic economy in which the subject of the poem is spent once he wastes his "spirit" or semen in the act of lust. David Bevington, ed., *The Complete Works of Shakespeare,* 4th ed. (New York: Longman, 1997), 1690.

   71. Amussen, *Ordered Society,* 159.

   72. DiGangi, *Homoerotics,* 5. DiGangi discusses a number of early modern plays that revolve around characters attempting to achieve their erotic and social ambitions through the "homoerotics of mastery" (65), a phrase that describes the homoerotic potentiality within the master-servant power structure and recognizes the importance of homoeroticism within satire. DiGangi cogently demonstrates that the satiric texts of the late 1590s disseminated the disorderly terms and character types that Jonson, Chapman, and Middleton drew on for their comedies.

   73. Lynda Boose, "Scolding Brides and Bridling Scolds: Taming the Woman's Unruly Member," *Shakespeare Quarterly* 42(2) (1991): 192, reads Petruchio's ensemble as an attempt to make Kate the object of ridicule. By writing his servant out of the scene altogether, or assuming that Grumio merely functions as an accessory to his master, critics have argued that in creating a "spectacle" Petruchio is attempting to match or outdo Kate's "shrewness" (Newman, *Fashioning Femininity,* 41). Barbara Hodgdon, for instance, contends that this scene marks the moment when the play promotes a cross coding of shrewness onto the male body; see "Katherina Bound, or, Play(K)ating the Strictures of Everyday Life," *Publications of the Modern Language Association* 107(3) (1992): 538–53. And Valerie Wayne contends that "Petruchio tames a shrew by becoming one"; see "Refashioning the Shrew," *Shakespeare Studies* 17 (1985): 171. Joel Fineman argues that "Petruchio's lunatic behavior, even when it is itself nonverbal, is understood to be a corollary function, a derivative example, of the shrewish voice of Kate"; see "The Turn of the Shrew," *Shakespeare and the Question of Theory,* ed. Patricia Parker and Geoffrey Hartman (New York: Methuen, 1985), 142. Fineman mistakenly cites a bystander's exclamation—"A monster, a very monster in apparel"—as

a reaction to Petruchio, but this statement is Biondella's response to Petruchio's servant Grumio's appearance (3.2.60).

74. Peter F. Heaney discusses the diseased condition of Petruchio's horse in this scene and reads the horse's symptoms as anticipatory signs of Petruchio's domestic mismanagement. The horse, Heaney argues, has the symptoms of a disease of the mouth that bears an analogical relation to Petruchio's "outrageously inflated ego," which Heaney describes as "monstrous" and "all consuming." Peter F. Heaney, "Petruchio's Horse: Equine and Household Management in *The Taming of the Shrew,*" *Early Modern Literary Studies* 4(1) (May 1998): 1-12. Also available at http://purl.oclc.org/emls/04-1/heanshak.html.

75. Korda explores Petruchio's explanation in some depth, and my discussion is informed by her analysis of the word "wear." On men's anxieties about women spending money on clothing and the association of women's sartorial extravagance with excessive pride and lasciviousness, see C. Brant and D. Purkiss, *Women, Texts, and Histories, 1575-1760* (Oxford: Oxford University Press, 1992).

76. As in Dolan, *Taming of the Shrew,* Appendix, 251. For more examples of representations of spendthrift and vain women, see Linda Woodbridge, *Women and the English Renaissance: Literature and the Nature of Womankind, 1540-1620* (Urbana: University of Illinois Press, 1986). Lisa Jardine also discusses wives squandering the husband's wealth on finery in *Still Harping on Daughters: Women and Drama in the Age of Shakespeare* (New York: Columbia University Press, 1989), 151-54. As Frances Dolan notes in her introduction to *The Taming of the Shrew,* the "shrew" was not only depicted as verbally abusive but also as an impediment to the productive function of the household since she was lazy, vain, and prone to gossip.

77. As Boose notes, Petruchio is a stock character of the period, the young gentleman who has received an adequate inheritance and seeks to ascend the rank hierarchy by "wiv[ing] it wealthily" (1.2.70), and *Shrew* is one of many English Renaissance dramatic texts in which the attainment of the golden fleece/wife drives the plot, such as *The Merchant of Venice, As You Like It, Much Ado About Nothing,* and *Twelfth Night.* Petruchio averts a precarious financial future by becoming the son of a successful merchant, and, in this respect, embodies a fantasy of financial success and upward social mobility as divorced from labor. See also Carol F. Heffernan, "*Taming of the Shrew,*" 3-15. According to R. B. Outhwaite, it was not uncommon for men to pursue marriage as a route of social advancement; see his "Marriage as Business: Opinions on the Rise in Aristocratic Bridal Portions in Early Modern England," in *Business Life and Public Policy,* ed. N. McKendrick and R. B. Outhwaite (Cambridge: Cambridge University Press, 1986), 21-37. See also J. P. Cooper, "Patterns of Inheritance and Settlement by Great Landowners from the Fifteenth to the Eighteenth Centuries," in *Family and Inheritance: Rural Society in Western Europe, 1200-1800,* ed. Jack Goody, Joan Thirsk, and E. P. Thompson (Cambridge: Cambridge University Press, 1976).

78. On the changing roles of women's work inside and outside the home, see Susan Cahn, *An Industry of Devotion: The Transformation of Women's Work in England, 1550-1660* (New York: Columbia University Press, 1987), and Amy Louis Erickson, *Women and Property in Early Modern England* (New York: Routledge, 1993). For a cogently argued and innovative reading of the early modern housewife and the domestic, see Wall, *Staging Domesticity.*

79. Catherine Belsey, "Disrupting Sexual Difference: Meaning and Gender in the Come-

dies," in *Alternative Shakepeares,* ed. John Drakakis (London: Routledge, 1985), 166–91, and Mary Beth Rose, *The Expense of Spirit: Love and Sexuality in English Renaissance Drama* (Ithaca, N.Y.: Cornell University Press, 1988).

80. Lena Cowen Orlin, *Private Matters and Public Culture in Post-Reformation England* (Ithaca, N.Y.: Cornell University Press, 1994), 2. For the historical construction of the public and the private, see Orlin, *Private Matters,* and Amussen, *Ordered Society.* On the household as a liminal space, see Ann C. Christensen, "Of Household Stuff and Homes: The Stage and Social Practice in *The Taming of the Shrew," Explorations in Renaissance Culture* 22 (1996): 127–45.

81. Wall, *Staging Domesticity,* 1. See John Gillis, "From Ritual to Romance: Toward an Alternative History of Love," in *Emotion and Social Change: Toward a New Psychohistory,* ed. Carol Z. Stearns and Peter N. Stearns (New York: Holmes and Meier, 1988), 87–123. See also John R. Gillis, *For Better, for Worse: British Marriages, 1600 to the Present* (Oxford: Oxford University Press, 1985), and Alan MacFarlane, *Marriage and Love in England: Modes of Reproduction, 1300–1840* (London: Blackwell, 1986). For an overview of the early modern debates on so-called companionate marriage, see Viviana Comensoli, *"Household Business,"* 3–27, 49–65.

82. Gillis, *For Better, for Worse,* 13.

83. Wall, *Staging Domesticity,* 7.

84. Smith, *Homosexual Desire,* 84. On sharing beds, see Bray, "Homosexuality and the Signs of Male Friendship," 50–51; Kussmaul, *Servants in Husbandry,* 40; and Stewart, *Close Readers,* xv. On erotic practices among male domestics, see Alan Bray, *Homosexuality in Renaissance England* (reprint; 1982, New York: Columbia University Press, 1995), 46–51, and DiGangi, *Homoerotics,* 64–100. Kate Mertes claims that as a rule the early modern household was an institution that was "actively hostile" to the presence of women (*English Noble Household,* 57–58). On the male homoerotics of the early modern household, see Bray, *Homosexuality in Renaissance England;* Bray, "Homosexuality and the Signs of Male Friendship"; Smith, *Homosexual Desire;* Jeffrey Masten, *Textual Intercourse: Collaboration, Authorship, and Sexualities in Renaissance Drama* (Cambridge: Cambridge University Press, 1997); DiGangi, *Homoerotics;* Stewart, *Close Readers;* and Wall, *Staging Domesticity.*

85. I am using "patriarchy" here as what Rosemary Hennessy, in *Profit and Pleasure: Sexual Identities in Late Capitalism* (London: Routledge, 2000), 22–29, describes as a "struggle term" (26). She notes that patriarchy is a crucial concept for Feminist-Marxist analyses because it refers to the structuring of social life such that more social resources and value accrue to men as a group at the expense of women as a group. She also emphasizes that patriarchal structures are historically variable and complex and that they organize hegemonic meanings through the articulation of several axes of difference. For my purposes, patriarchy is a useful term because it allows me to analyze the historically specific distribution of property and power in the favor of men, which resulted in the production of gendered subjects and specific formations by which gender and sexuality were organized within the early modern household.

86. Gayle Rubin, "The Traffic in Women: Notes on the 'Political Economy' of Sex," in *Toward an Anthropology of Women,* ed. Rayna Reiter (New York: Monthly Review, 1975). Newman discusses how Katherine in *Henry V* functions as an object of exchange through a

reading that calls on Kristeva's discussion of woman as the site of male bonding (*Fashioning Femininity, 104*). For a reevaluation of Rubin's thesis see Nancy Hartsock, *Money, Sex, and Power: Toward a Feminist Historical Materialism* (Boston: Northeastern University Press, 1983); Gayle Rubin, "Thinking Sex: Notes for a Radical Theory of the Politics of Sexuality," in Carole Vance, *Pleasure and Danger: Exploring Female Sexuality* (London: Pandora Press, 1984), 267–320; Rubin, "Sexual Traffic," *Differences* 1994 (Summer–Fall): 62–100; and Hennessy, *Profit and Pleasure,* 179–89. For a discussion of Levi-Strauss's paradigm and its uses for Feminist-Marxism, see Nancy Fraser, "Heterosexism, Misrecognition, and Capitalism: A Response to Judith Butler," *New Left Review* 228 (March/April) 1998: 140–51.

87. Lynda Boose makes a similar argument to the one that I am making here, and she contends that Shakespeare's play performs the cultural work of disavowal by replacing the social reality of men's competition with one another and their economic dependency upon wealthy women with the fantasy that marriage effaces the social differences between men. She points out that in their new roles as husbands, men become vested with the authority to control their wives' access to class privilege. I find Boose's argument compelling and want to take her observation that the play constructs a world of homosociality in which men are conjoined with their rivals to the next level.

88. Eve Sedgwick discusses "perverse reading" as a mode of interpretation practiced by those whose marginal position encouraged them to read against the grain and identify dissonance rather than coherence in the text(s) before them; see *Tendencies* (Durham: Duke University Press, 1993), 1–20.

89. Frances E. Dolan, "The Subordinate(s') Plot: Petty Treason and the Forms of Domestic Rebellion," *Shakespeare Quarterly* 43(3) (1992): 324. See also Ann Kussmaul, *Servants in Husbandry,* 5–6.

90. For instance, the formulation that servants were wage earners was not particularly revealing, since in this period wages were not always compensated in the form of cash payment and the large majority of apprentices and live-in servants received valuable goods, such as clothes, as payment. Even delimiting the notion of service to those who were bound by a contract inadvertently broadened the classification, since this criterion included stage players, monks, tutors, grooms, courtiers, apprentices, journeymen, gentleman ushers, stewards, and, as one scholar notes, even the monarch (Burnett, *Masters and Servants,* 2).

91. Gouge, *Of Domestical,* 374.

92. Burnett, *Masters and Servants,* 42.

93. Ibid., 42. Paul Griffiths, *Youth and Authority,* 222–26.

94. Quoted in Ian W. Archer, "Shakespeare's London," in *A Companion to Shakespeare,* ed. David Scott Kasten (London: Blackwell, 1999), 46.

95. Christopher Brooks, "Apprenticeship, Social Mobility, and the Middling Sort, 1550–1800," in *The Middling Sort of People: Culture, Society, and Politics in England, 1550–1800,* ed. Jonathan Barry and Christopher Brooks (London: MacMillan Publishing, 1994), 80.

96. I. M., *Servingman's Comfort,* 138.

97. See Paul Griffiths, *Youth and Authority,* and Christopher Brooks, "Apprenticeship, Social Mobility, and The Middling Sort, 1550–1800." Joan Lane demonstrates that complaints about apprentices' personal appearance made up the largest and greatest variety of complaints about infringements of indenture conditions in the period; see *Apprenticeship in England,*

1600-1914 (London: University College London Press, 1996), 192-93. Some guilds legislated against apprentices keeping trunks and chests to make it more difficult for their employees to amass and store a wardrobe (208). An ordinance issued by the lord mayor in conjunction with the Corporations, the Court of Aldermen, and the Common Council in 1582 prohibited apprentices from wearing "colorful clothes" (207) and, arguing for the necessity of "conformity," also prohibited the wearing of stitching, cutting, edging, garnishing, ruffs, frills, girdles, and garters. Apprentices were instructed to wear "most plain" breeches, shirts, doublets, coats, and cloaks that were held together by "plain" strings and woolen caps provided by their masters (Griffiths, *Youth and Authority,* 226). This particular law explicitly set out to target young men who purportedly spent their days "haunting . . . inconvenient places," presumably taverns, inns, and public playhouses, where they modeled their extravagant ensembles (226). The London Curriers prohibited their apprentices from wearing "silk ruffles or any cloth enriched with gold, silver, or silk" (Lane, *Apprenticeship,* 205). Nor were they permitted to wear "embroidered pumps and slippers, [or] jewelry" (205). In 1611 the Grocer's Company legislated against "Spanish shoes with Polonia heels" and doublet collars with "point[s], whalebone, or plaits" (207). Instead, apprentices were ordered to wear breeches of cloth, kersey, fustian, sackcloth, canvas, English leather or English stuff and stockings of woolen yarn or kersey (207).

98. *OED,* s.v. "riot."

99. Sir Thomas Elyot, *The Governor,* Book 1, as in E. K. Chambers, *The Elizabethan Stage,* Vol. 4 (Oxford: Clarendon Press, 1923), 187.

100. Lemnus Lemnius, *The Touchstone of Complexions* (1576; 1581; 1633), as in Smith, *Homosexual Desire,* 86. Contemporaries concurred that men between the ages of fifteen to twenty-seven were particularly volatile; see Ralph Houlbrooke, ed., *English Family Life, 1576-1716: An Anthology from Diaries* (London: Basil Blackwell, 1989), and Keith Thomas, "Age and Authority in Early Modern England," *Proceedings of the British Academy LXII* (Oxford: Oxford University Press, 1976).

101. Beier, *Masterless Men,* notes that the records of Richard Napier's patients between 1597 and 1634 show that young men in their twenties were the most at risk of all age groups and that they appeared before Napier at more than twice the rate warranted by their numbers in the population (27). Beier also cites the unusually high incidence of imprisonment among this group (24, 44).

102. As in Burnett, *Masters and Servants,* 35.

103. For an overview of the instructive literature depicting the household as a productive economic unit, see Amussen, *Ordered Society,* 67-94.

104. Burnett, *Masters and Servant,* 5, and Dorothy Marshall, *English Domestic Servant,* 19-20.

105. *Of Civil,* 15. See also Henry Crosse, *Vertues Commonwealth* (1603), in Chambers, *Elizabethan Stage,* 4:247, and "Documents of Control," Appendix D, 259-345, for references to servants at playhouses and plays corrupting youth and inspiring "lascivious devices" (Chambers, *Elizabethan Stage,* 4:322).

106. Amanda Bailey, " 'Monstrous Manner': Style and the Early Modern Theater," *Criticism* 43(4): 269-300.

107. On youthful illicit sexual activities as a sign of the failure of household discipline,

see Fletcher and Stevenson, eds., *Order and Disorder,* 33, and S. R. Smith, "The London Apprentices as Seventeenth-Century Adolescents," *Past and Present* 61 (1973): 149–61.

108. Amussen, *Ordered Society,* 39.

109. John Dod and Robert Cleaver emphasize that both governor and governed should be comely and decent in their dress and appearance; in *A Godly Form of Household Government: For the Ordering of Private Families According to the Direction of God's Word* (London, 1621), as in Dolan, Appendix, *The Taming of the Shrew: Texts and Contexts,* 205.

110. I. M., *Servingman's Comfort,* 108.

111. As in Dolan, Appendix, *The Taming of the Shrew: Texts and Contexts,* 205.

112. Ibid.

113. I. M., *Servingman's Comfort,* 157.

114. Gouge, *Of Domestical,* 363.

115. Ibid.

116. Ibid., 364.

117. Ibid.

118. Ibid., 374.

119. Ibid., 205.

120. Ibid., 364; Obadiah Walker, *Of Education, Especially of Young Gentlemen* (1673), as in Anna Byrson, *From Courtesy to Civility: Changing Codes of Conduct in Early Modern England* (Oxford: Clarendon Press, 1998), 134.

121. On the descriptor "monstrous" and the term's significance for social anxieties about category confusion in early modern London, see Bailey, "Monstrous Manner."

122. James Scott, *Domination and the Arts of Resistance: Hidden Transcripts* (New Haven: Yale University Press, 1990), 187.

123. Leonard Barkan, *The Gods Made Flesh: Metamorphosis and the Pursuit of Paganism* (New Haven: Yale University Press, 1986).

124. Ibid., 11.

125. Smith, *Homosexual Desire,* 192. On the Jupiter-Ganymede myth and the myriad works of visual art representing this myth, see James M. Saslow, *Ganymede in the Renaissance: Homosexuality in Art and Society* (New Haven: Yale University Press, 1986); Leonard Barkan, *Transuming Passions: Ganymede and the Erotics of Humanism* (Stanford: Stanford University Press, 1991); and Robert Aldrich, *The Seduction of the Mediterranean: Writing, Art, and Homosexual Fantasy* (London: Routledge, 1993).

126. Lynn Enterline, *The Rhetoric of the Body from Ovid to Shakespeare* (Cambridge: Cambridge University Press, 2000), 140. My discussion of the disruptive erotics conveyed by these Ovidian scenarios is also indebted to DiGangi's reading of Ovidian mythology and queer erotics in *As You Like It,* 50–63. On Ovidian narrative in *The Shrew,* see Joel Fineman, "The Turn of the Shrew," in *Shakespeare and the Question of Theory,* ed. Patricia Parker and Geoffrey Hartman (London: Methuen, 1985), 141–44.

127. Gouge, *Of Domestical,* 364.

128. As critics have noted, through her evocation of service, Kate positions herself as the ideal wife who loves, serves, and obeys her husband, whom she describes as her lord, keeper, head, king, sovereign, and governor (5.2.143–51); see D. E. Underdown, "The Taming of the

Scold: The Enforcement of Patriarchal Authority in Early Modern England," in Fletcher and Stevens, *Order and Disorder,* 116–36, and see also Susan Dwyer Amussen, *Ordered Society.* The dutiful wife calling on the language of service to express her devotion would not have appeared unusual to Elizabethan audiences, since prescriptions of gender and hierarchies of class were treated in sermons and conduct books as homologous relationships in the period. The servant was idealized not only as a loyal employee but also as a family member, and the affective bonds between master and servant were, according to one contemporary, analogous to those between husband and wife (*Of Civil,* 114).

129. Korda, *Shakespeare's Domestic Economies,* 54.

130. Beier, *Masterless Men,* 23–24.

131. "Instructions by Henry Percy, 9th Earl of Northumberland, to his Son," as in Heal, *Hospitality,* 179.

132. Neill, *Putting History to the Question,* 30.

133. Boose discusses words such as "shrew," like the words "harlot," "hoyden," "scold," "baggage," "brothel," "bordello," and "bawd," that in this period underwent a semantic shift by which they were transposed from their original sense as contemptuous expressions for lower-class men into terms used to denigrate recalcitrant women ("Good Husbandry," 222).

134. Unlike "shrewness," scolding was a legal charge. David Underdown, "The Taming of the Scold: The Enforcement of Patriarchal Authority in Early Modern England," in *Order and Disorder in Early Modern England,* ed. Fletcher and Stevenson, 119–20.

135. Ibid., 132.

136. Ibid., 120. The bi-gender valence of shrewness is also reflected in its punishment. As historians have documented, women were subjected to shaming rituals such as the cucking-stool or charivari, but their husbands were also the foci of such spectacles. Literary critics who call on this historiography have underplayed the significance of men being publicly shamed for not upholding gender norms because their wives' assertive behaviors suggested that they had not been "man enough" to manage their wives and by extension their household. As Underdown notes, husbands who were perceived as feeble "threatened the entire patriarchal order" (127). Shaming rituals such as "Rough Music" involved theatrical tropes, most notably instances of cross-dressing in which a man dressed in women's clothes performed the role of the wife beating her husband.

See What Breeds about Her Heart: King Lear, *Feminism, and Performance*

PHILIPPA KELLY

I carried Cordelia on in those days . . . and she was an enormous lady. There were three ladies there when I got to the first rehearsal—two tiny ones and a big one, and I thought, I hope one of the tiny ones is Cordelia. It wasn't, it was the big one.
—Warren Mitchell, discussing his 1978 performance of *King Lear*

I T IS POSSIBLE to sum up in very few words the roles of women in *King Lear.* Mothers require almost no comment at all—both Lear and Gloucester, with varying degrees of disgust and relish, refer to them only as spawning bastards—and, as Warren Mitchell has somewhat farcically suggested, the three daughters can be deftly distinguished in fairly bald terms. (He continues unabashed, "But I nicked an idea from. . . . [t]he Georgian State Company. . . . [Lear] dragged her by the rope that was round her neck, and my poor fool is hanged.")[1] If, however, we consider Lear's daughters not as cameos but as characters who can themselves take center stage, Lear might find himself on a rather different kind of heath. Several recent productions of *King Lear* encourage innovative appraisals of the play's female characters, in the process opening up new facets for the tableau of an aged king accompanied by Cinderella and her two ugly sisters.[2] In drawing attention to approaches that favor or naturalize masculinity, feminist perspectives can add interest and controversy to standard readings and productions of the play, wresting it out of the hands of the two elderly patriarchs and their devotees, and giving it over to innovative women actors and critics. Carol Rutter suggests, for instance, that while certain dramatic moments (such as the death scenes in *King Lear*) conventionally play out gendered expectations of female subordination, these expectations can be acknowledged and complicated

137

by "smart actors" who learn how to "collaborate with [Shakespeare] to author themselves."[3]

But what *kind* of production claims to enable a "feminist" orientation for *King Lear,* and what does such an orientation entail? Does feminism assume masculinity as a natural Shakespearean default-position for "important" themes and speeches, so that attention to female roles requires challenge and subversion?[4] Does feminism have a recuperative purpose, as Jane Smiley suggests in her novel, *A Thousand Acres?* And in the interests of feminism, do writers such as Smiley *adapt* the play—assuming, in other words, a shared feminist sympathy with a dramatist who portrays the inequities of gender—or, alternatively, *appropriate* the play, ascribing to it a level of inculturated patriarchy that warrants contestation?[5]

In her study of feminist performance, Sarah Werner acknowledges the shifting contexts that redefine the nature and scope of feminism, suggesting that the term more generally refers to "those actors, directors, and performances which strive to question received assumptions of Shakespeare's depiction of and appropriateness for women."[6] In Werner's terms, then, feminist thought facilitates a rethinking, or a reopening, of established opinions and perceptions about female roles and audiences. This kind of flexibility might serve to question what is ascribed to gender in the play, highlighting, for example, Lear's description of tears as "women's weapons, water drops" (2.4.277), his allusion to emotion as the menstrual "mother" that heaves toward his heart (2.4.56), and his famous revulsion at the "sulphurous pit . . . burning, scalding, / Stench, consumption" (4.6.128–29).[7] It might also challenge assumptions that the sisters embody essential qualities,[8] that the play's "universal" questions about age, control, and suffering are implicitly masculine,[9] or, alternatively, that misogyny in *King Lear* is less the property of the play than that of gender-inflected ideas and terminologies imposed by critics.[10] And how are these various perspectives absorbed within the field of academic debate, which, as most of us are painfully aware, structures its subjects to crave the authority of institutional gongs, thus paving the way to tenure and promotion? This last question itself opens a different field of debate, and it is worth bearing in mind Phyllis Rackin's view that feminist scholarship might now speak so thoroughly to academic qualifications and credibilities that, "adopted as a conceptual tool by women and men without a serious political commitment to feminist political agendas, criticism designated as 'feminist' . . . can just as easily be used to naturalise women's oppression as to oppose it."[11]

While one can raise all these questions and possibilities as pertaining to the broad scope of "feminism," it is not so easy to see where they might lead. I would argue, however, that one of the aims of much feminist thought is to refuse conceptual thumbtacks that provide a common goal, refusing, in other words, to pin down common aims and flatten out divergences. I am not trying to put forward a reductive binary in which feminism defines itself in *contrast* to the supposed single-mindedness of "patriarchal" thought; rather, I suggest that many feminist approaches pay attention to female roles and audiences, and that this attention in itself often marks out a difference in the way these roles, or the dramatist himself, might be apprehended. Performatively, such differences might involve Regan as played with a stutter, Cordelia played as a deaf-mute, Lear played as a woman with a beard, or new contexts and settings that revisit and reorient familiar themes. It would be absurd to say that feminism alone attends to marks of difference. But what I do suggest is that feminist perspectives are mindful of, and interested in, differences—in representation, in interpretation—involving women. It is this mindfulness that I will try to illustrate in my discussion of performances of *King Lear* over recent decades, highlighting some of my descriptions against the backdrop of older productions.

Shifting Convention

"He shrinks from no dramatic obstacle, but combats all the passages which call for declamation, denunciation, or expression of pathos with skilful determination . . . he is on all occasions powerful," declaimed a reviewer of W. E. Sheridan's 1882 performance of the role of Lear in Australia; "and his terrible denunciation of his unfilial daughter Goneril was so effectively rendered as to elicit a burst of hearty applause."[12] In nineteenth-century England, George Frederick Cooke also played Lear with a passion so intense that he sometimes fell into fits and had to be carried from the stage.[13] And in a contemporaneous production of the play in America, Edwin Forrest's performance was described in similarly heroic terms:

Anguish, wrath and helplessness drove him mad. The blood made a path from his heart to his brow, and hung there, a red cloud, beneath his crown. His eyes flashed and faded and reflashed. He beat his breast as if not knowing what he did. His hands clutched wildly at the air as though struggling with something invisible. Then, sinking on his knees, with upturned look and hands straight outstretched towards his unnatural daughter, he poured out, in frenzied tones of mingled shriek and sob, his withered curse, half adjuration, half malediction. It was a terrible thing, almost too fearful to be gazed at as a work of art, yet true to the character, the words and the situation furnished by Shakespeare.[14]

For Forrest himself, moreover, "I hold that next to God, Shakespeare comprehended the mind of man."[15]

This interest in "the mind of man," and in the closed circle of old men— Lear, Shakespeare, and God (a very old man indeed)—has a quaint absurdity in light of recent decades. It also shows us how far current vocabulary has shifted along with thoughts about gender, culture, and colonialism. While many of the more recent productions of the play have emphasized Lear's domineering qualities (The Royal Shakespeare Company's 1976 London production, for instance), his childishness (Richard Eyre's 1997 London production at the Cottesloe Theatre), his headstrong wilfulness (Gale Edwards's 1988 State Theatre Company of South Australia production in Adelaide), or his unattractive irascibility (Australia's 1998 Bell Shakespeare Company production), some have used emblematic stage machinery to augment verbal challenges to the idea of an old man's poignantly heroic journey. David Hare's 1986 National Theatre production, dominated by wildly erratic costuming and by images of grizzly animal and later human carcasses suspended from the flies, prompted Kenneth Hurren to respond: "Reviewing the National Theatre's stab at *King Lear* is like trying to explain an accident."[16] In Deborah Warner's 1990 production of *King Lear* for London's National Theatre, Brian Cox, playing Lear, entered the stage in a wheelchair. Inspired by his experience in airports, where he witnessed "hale and hearty" elderly people get seated in wheelchairs that caused them to age twenty years, progressing rapidly through queues and security checks before arriving on board as "sprightly young things again," he used the wheelchair to signal the elderly king's manipulative determination to get his own way.[17] By riding the wheelchair with reckless gleefulness, Cox's Lear conveyed the stubborn selfishness with which Goneril and Regan were justifiably exasperated.

Complications to the conventional focus on "universal man" can of course be granted also by playing Regan and Goneril with a range of motive and reaction. In a Royal Shakespeare Company production in 1976, Judi Dench played Regan with a stutter, challenging stereotypical divisions between the saintly and demonic sisters. In a discussion of the performance, Dench observed that the stutter helped suggest how

Regan came to be as she was—she stuttered only in Lear's presence, and he showed impatience at her disability. The implication was that her "filial ingratitude" (3.4.14) resulted not from a monstrous nature but from parental tyranny.[18] The San Francisco Shakespeare Festival's 2001 production emphasized the older sisters' femininity as a form of resistance to this tyranny.[19] Goneril (Kay Kostopoulos) shrank away at her father's curse, clawing at her bosom as she wept silently. Her resolve literally swelled from this moment onward, as she determined to take a stand against her father. Regan (Jenny Lord), bewitchingly beautiful and fragile, used her femininity as a means of rebuking Lear, treating him as a vulgar old carouser whose bad manners affronted her.

In producing the play for the State Theatre Company of South Australia in 1988, Gale Edwards directed the older sisters as less the victims of their father's tyranny than as proactive women, eager to get on. Goneril and Regan appeared perfectly reasonable in their protestations about the behavior of Lear and his hundred knights, while it was Lear who violently overreacted. Yvonne Brewster, in her 1994 Talawa production in London, gave an extra edge to the two older sisters' cold reason, blending their common sense with a chilly devotion to personal gain. Goneril (Lolita Chakrabarti) and Regan (Cathy Tyson) were beautiful, strong-willed women intent on achieving what they felt to be their just deserts. Repeatedly licking her lips, Tyson accentuated Regan's increase in acquisitiveness as the action progressed. This suggestion of irresistible appetite, rather than innate evil, was supported by David Harewood's portrayal of a muscular, vigorous Edmund, who deserved the power he craved through sheer presence, if not through birthright.

Such performances might lend support to the argument, made by Jean Howard and R. S. White, that Lear's relationship with his daughters explores not so much "filial ingratitude" (3.4.14) as the erosion of the mythic status of kingship in the face of the many forces—England's political unrest, for instance, together with the opening of new worlds and the rise of the mercantile class—that effected social, political, and economic upheaval at the turn of the seventeenth century, irrevocably altering perceptions of what it meant to rule.[20] While the mercantilism embodied by Edmund, Regan, and Goneril is clearly a system that neither the old king nor the Earl of Gloucester understands, it could be argued that both have fostered it through their own abuses. Lear asks his daughters to vie for political power through protestations of love, encouraging the mercenary attitudes he later repudiates, and because Gloucester's sexual incontinence has meant that Edmund will receive nothing if he waits for "spherical predominance" to give him his due, he is understandably willing to gain lands "by wit" (1.2.183). In these terms, then, Lear and Gloucester are unable to understand, or to control, the disintegration of a feudal system over which they thought they had dominion, and their thankless children represent not so much fiendish aberrations (1.4.259) as the consequences of social and political change.

Richard Eyre's 1997 London production at the Cottesloe Theatre added an interesting complication to this way of rethinking the relationship between love and material interest. In Eyre's production, Lear (Ian Holm) continually poked his elder daughter (Barbara Flynn), whose pitiable neediness evoked Judy Dench's earlier (1976) performance. In contrast, Regan (Amanda Redman) was played as a high-society hostess who began by encouraging "Lear's faintly disturbing paternal passion for her, only to disintegrate into illness and death in a journey that seem[ed] to mirror that of her father from the safety of indoors."[21] Cordelia (Anne-Marie Duff) was also highly manipulative but arrogant and spoiled as well, expecting to get away with denying her father's wishes in the play's first scene and as shocked as anyone at his display of rage. Eyre's direction of Cordelia as a spoiled child drew on two notable past productions: Peter Brook's 1962 Royal Shakespeare Company production, in which Diana Rigg played her as fairly hard-boiled and truculent,[22] and Adrian Noble's 1982 Royal Shakespeare Company production, where Alice Krige played her as "all too clearly her father's daughter."[23]

The actresses in Eyre's production suggested that rather than misunderstanding the "true" daughter who refuses to put her love into base, material terms, Lear is faced with his own creation: a cherished and much-favored youngest child who is unafraid to speak freely back to her father.[24] While Lear's love for Cordelia seems indulgent in the play's first scene ("Our joy, / Although our last and least" [1.1.82–83]), it may also constitute a form of tyranny that has not yet been tested. The focus of so much love, perhaps Cordelia does not apprehend the tyranny that her sisters so clearly understand, until Lear spins around in 1.1 and banishes her for publicly humiliating him. When at the end of 1.1 Goneril says to Cordelia, "You have obedience scanted, / And well are worth the want that you have wanted" (1.1.278–79), she has a point: Cordelia has evidently "wanted" for nothing, and her long-held position of privilege renders her unable to imagine the lack of it. Her sisters, on the other hand, have missed out on the paternal favor that has gone all Cordelia's way and see her as deserving "the want that [she has] wanted."

Michael Kahn, in his 1999 production for Washington's The Shakespeare Theatre, provoked ambivalent responses to the play's family dynamics by improvising with a hearing-impaired actress. Monique Holt played Cordelia as a deaf mute, signing her words to the Fool to speak. While this was an interesting way of assigning causation to the events of 1.1 (Cordelia literally mishears her father and so cannot give him what he wants), it also robbed Cordelia of a sense of agency: the conventional misunderstood victim was replaced by a victim of the frailty of language as a mode of communication. In assigning Cordelia's inarticulacy to disablement (rather than disobedience), Kahn's production narrowed the interpretive potential of her role. Moreover, the spectacle of femininity as "lack" did little to interrupt a familiar male dialectic: because Cordelia's stage presence was mediated by two male characters in Kahn's production, the character herself was almost squeezed out of the masculine dialectic altogether.[25] The production interestingly counterpoised the three sisters, however. The measure of audience sympathy elicited by Cordelia's disability was offset by the sympathy for Goneril (Tania Hicken) and Regan (Jennifer Harmon), who played the sisters as sharing an affectionate relationship as well as a sense of their father's rejection. The catch in Goneril's voice when she observed to Regan, "He always lov'd our sister most" (1.1.290), was deeply affecting; later in the production when Lear delivered his curse to Goneril, she listened in anguish and then burst into tears at his exit (1.4.289). The effect "was to render Goneril a poignant and sympathetic figure, while Lear came across as pitiable but also narcissistic and self-indulgent, too wrapped up in his own histrionics even to perceive his eldest daughter's pain."[26] In 2001 Kahn restaged the production for The Shakespeare Theatre, using most of the same cast. Ted van Griethuysen again played Lear, a trifle less petulantly than in his 1999 performance. But Goneril and Regan (this time played by Kate Skinner) were more blatantly cold-blooded, "played as circling vultures."[27]

It seems inevitable that if the sisters are modeled on a simple good-versus-evil paradigm, no matter how irascible their father's conduct, audience sympathy will remain on his side. For example, Grigori Kozintsev's stunning 1970 film version of *King Lear,* despite its radical postholocaust vision,[28] retained the conventionally stark opposition between the daughters that left their aged father's pitiable condition intact. Goneril was smooth-faced and harsh, and Regan plump with a bovine expression. Cordelia was light and unaffected. At the end of the film Goneril and Regan were carried out alone on stretchers, their eyes disturbingly open. The 1999 Royal Shakespeare Company production, directed by Yukio Ninagawa, also presented wholly antipathetic older daughters, with Anna Chancellor, as Regan, giving a camp and petulant performance, and Sian Thomas playing Goneril as a "cheap Wicked Witch of the West."[29] Again, in the Sydney Theatre Company's 1994 production of the play, the two sisters were played with exaggeratedly formal dress, makeup, and gestures. From the very first scene they reacted to the news of the division of the kingdom with a kind of robotic amazement, which quickly congealed into steely coldness. This frigidity intensified in their interactions with Lear throughout the next two acts, so that they clearly represented the heartless villains of traditional productions. And in Chicago's Piven Theatre production in 2000, Gita Tanner played a sublimely evil Regan who showed up the vulnerability of Byrne Piven's catastrophically misguided father.

Productions that emphasize Regan and Goneril's severity through such mannerisms as those described above tend to align themselves with Lear's curse (1.4.275–89). This risks undermining all sympathy for the sisters, which often requires a special effort to realize given the poignancy of their aged father's predicament.[30] In Australia's 1984 Nimrod production, Goneril (Gillian Jones) stripped off her woman's clothing to reveal the guerilla uniform of a man, thus complementing her increasingly chilly devotion to her own agenda. In this way she visually complied with Lear's sexist representation of women whose avarice and ambition is incompatible with sexuality as they deny their "natural" roles by seeking material gain. (So unnatural does Lear believe his daughters to be, indeed, that he cries, "Let them anatomize Regan; see what breeds about her heart" [3.6.76–77]).

By rethinking the relationship between Lear and his daughters, it is possible to do more than give voice to (numerically) minor roles.[31] These roles can also provoke debate about gender; about social and political pos-sibilities for women, both in historical terms and in current contexts; and about the "universal" questions that have conventionally been accepted as fitting territory for aged men. This last effect was brought very clearly home to me by an inmate in my class at Sydney's Mullawah Prison for Women in 1997:

I love *King Lear.* In a thunderstorm you suddenly understand how insignificant you are in the scheme of things, and then you're all washed clean. When I was younger I used to like to walk up to the edge of a cliff in a storm, and I'd get a mad urge to jump over. We've all got a bit of madness, don't you think? So now when I want to do that I get down and wriggle on my tummy so the mad person won't take over.[32]

Rethroning the King

Like Goneril, Regan, and Cordelia, women directors will choose whether to diminish Lear or to permit him grandeur and royalty; they will choose whether to dethrone Lear or reenthrone him as hero; they will choose whether to destroy or nurture his tragic status.[33]

King Lear is a play written by a man about a man, but the fact that it is staged or choreographed by a woman does not, of course, automatically make it "feminist." Feminist sympathies depend largely on what differences are being marked in a production—whether it be by asking questions, disrupting stereotypes, or, perhaps, focusing on conventionally marginal characters or features—and on the way(s) in which these differences affect interpretation. I want to conclude my discussion by describing three different media in which female directors and artists have reconfigured *King Lear,* broadening its field of production and interpretation. Victoria Morgan based a ballet on the play; Jane Smiley wrote a novel (later adapted into a screenplay); and Helena Kaut-Howson and Maureen Shea took the king off the stage altogether and replaced him with a woman. (I will describe Morgan's ballet at somewhat more length than the other productions because there has been so very little written on it to date.)

In 1985 Victoria Morgan, a former ballerina with the San Francisco Ballet, choreographed a twenty-minute ballet called *Lear* as a segment of a four-part program,[34] and I will suggest that this ballet might have been more successful had its conception been self-consciously feminist. As I proposed earlier, what such feminism might entail is not a prescriptive agenda. But I will argue that a feminist approach—one that attempts to broaden and complicate the context of female representation and interpretation—would have provided substance for the ballet's score, rendering it challenging rather than merely idiosyncratic.

Morgan began by trying scores by Lizst, Stravinsky, and Bartok among others: "I listened to them over and over and tried to imagine bringing the Lear characters into that music. But it just didn't work for me."[35] Morgan "felt uncomfortable with their completeness; I didn't feel that I could chop up pieces."[36] So she commissioned Stewart Copeland, of the rock band The Police, to write an original score for the ballet. Copeland, who confessed to total ignorance about both *King Lear* and the ballet, took the project on as an unpaid challenge. At that time The Police were on indefinite hiatus after seven years together, and Copeland was making a trip to Africa to shoot a documentary film on African music. He began the composition accompanied by "the plains of Serengeti and the dancing wildebeest. It was actually damned inspiring."[37] While Morgan set the ballet in the year 2020, Copeland decided to compose the music as if it were medieval. He felt that the combination of the futuristic setting and the medieval music would level out to a "timeless" effect. In an astonishing (and, I believe, unconscious) parody of the heritage of *King Lear* in which critics such as Charles Lamb and A. C. Bradley have deemed the play more suited to the imagination than the stage,[38] Copeland designed a musical score some of which he described as "unplayable by human beings."[39] His score was written for a live orchestra accompanied by a machine playing computer-generated music. Copeland received character outlines from Morgan and then composed sections on a computer capable of re-creating the sounds of symphonic musical instruments. After his return to London from his communion with the "wildebeest," he exchanged floppy disks back-and-forth with Morgan over the next nine months. Morgan would choreograph to the music and request modifications. Taking bits and pieces of Copeland's music, she put it together like a puzzle, deciding which segment of music sounded "like" which character.

The performance itself did not receive great critical acclaim, despite the interest attracted by Copeland's involvement in the project. Morgan pared down the plot, excising the subplot altogether, to create a personal narrative that reflected "my own family situation. . . . I began to see the story as a universal situation. There are needs that human beings have, as fathers, and as daughters; and there is a set-up, a dynamic, an interaction that occurs between father and daughter." Morgan identified her own situation particularly with that of Cordelia: "Cordelia is a proud woman and very honest with herself. She knows that she wants to go beyond her little nest and discover what is inside of her that belongs only to her and not to her father."[40] She had Cordelia (Wendy Van Dyck) costumed in innocent white, while Goneril (Mimi Keith) and Regan (Edna Holmes) were dressed as punkers with spiky hairdos, overdrawn makeup, spangled leg-warmers, tight blouses, and short skirts. Their father, a rock star, divided his large crystal globe amongst his group, and Goneril and Regan did battle over it with a baton.

As the curtain rose on the five-member cast, the stage was in darkness. The daughters and the Fool (in this production called "the Foil") were lined up in front, and as they slowly lowered themselves onto the stage, the crystal globe came into vision. Lear rose from behind the globe. He turned the globe around, and behind him certain parts of the city of San Francisco were lit up, bit by bit, until the entire city lights were burning behind him. Morgan defined the globe as "a symbol of his power, a palpable object that the characters fight over. They take it apart with their hands."[41] Goneril and Regan cavorted and lurched throughout the performance, and Lear shook his graying locks at them, spinning and holding his head, in an emblematic portrayal of the play's "let me not be mad, not mad, sweet heaven" speech (1.5.46).

Morgan's interest in the "universal" dimensions of a personal heroic predominated over any concern with a feminist vision—indeed, her choreography relied on a conventional division between polarized daughters, two mercenary and one idealistic. And it was this conventional framework for the production that ultimately undermined the project itself: had Morgan tried to complicate the female roles, there might have been more substance for the musical score.[42] As it was, Copeland's "jejune noodling, blocks of rhythm . . . with virtually no melodic interest," and his amplification of his score to "the pain threshold" were seen as simply incompatible with the play's familiar thematics: that is, with the compelling representation of a tyrannical father, two scavenging sisters, and one victim who learns to find her strength. In light of this thematics, the complexity of Copeland's arrhythmical score seemed top-heavy, a burdensome encroachment upon "Shakespeare's majestic tragedy."[43]

If Morgan's focus on Cordelia as a bildungsroman figure closed down the spaces where her sisters might have had scope to evolve, Jane Smiley, in her novel *A Thousand Acres,* written the following year, attempted to open these spaces up. Smiley provided an overtly confrontational feminist perspective for *King Lear,* appropriating the play's characters and dynamics to write a parable of family abuse. *A Thousand Acres* details the relationships between two abused elder daughters who finally take a stand against their tyrannical patriarch, in the process "displacing not only the locus of masculine subjectivity but also its implicit claim to universal significance."[44] Smiley set the novel in midwestern America, choosing narrative over drama because she felt that it allowed her to communicate the disjunction between speech and feeling. In other words, narrative has room for *spaces*—and spaces are traditionally the areas more open to women.[45] It is what women don't say, their silence, that is often the locus of their power.[46]

In engaging with *King Lear* Smiley sought to express feelings of "anger" and "resentment" at women's exclusion from social and economic power, emotions that she saw as foundational to the 1970s feminism from which she drew her thoughts about gender. Unsympathetic to fathers partly because she never lived with her own, Smiley put forth several questions: Why should Lear be valorized as a paradigm for spiritual and emotional growth? Why should Cordelia be so greatly praised when she is "ungenerous and cold, a stickler for truth at the beginning, a stickler for form at the end"? Why should the older sisters be demonized? "The play seemed to be condemning them morally for the exact ways in which they expressed the womanhood that I recognized."[47] In Smiley's novel, Caroline (the Cordelia-figure) is a hard-nosed lawyer who mirrors her father's "megalomania"[48] and who opposes her father's wishes partly because she doesn't want to live on the property anyway. Unlike Caroline, the older daughters, Ginny (Goneril) and Rose (Regan), have been sexually abused by Daddy; having also acted as servants to him all their lives, they consider it their turn to claim compensation and rewards. And Smiley has Ginny and Rose live through the close of the novel so as to be able to reflect on their experiences in a way that Goneril and Regan cannot. (In Shakespeare's play "the one the other poison'd for my sake, / And after slew herself" [5.3.241–42]).

By narrating the novel in Ginny's voice, Smiley channels its events through the perspective of a character who has traditionally been rebuked for her frigidity. *A Thousand Acres* challenges many of the assumptions associated with *King Lear:* that the play is about good versus evil; that characters can be positioned in relation to these extremes; that the Lear and Gloucester figures are simply deluded old men "more sinn'd against than sinning" (3.2.60); and that the story need be "about" an old man anyway. (She says of Lear, "Even when cast low by events, he seemed to hog the stage.")[49] *A Thousand Acres* also challenges the place of the absent mother in *King Lear* and the legacy she has left her husband and daughters.

While *A Thousand Acres* has been drawn into many critical and pedagogical feminist contexts, even making its way into gender dynamics for sociology classes,[50] it could be argued that despite her aim to encourage deeper and more complex understandings of female roles in the play, Smiley wrests *King Lear*'s characters away from conventional critical preoccupations only to replace them with contemporary scenarios of domestic violence and sexual abuse (which are, in a sense, equally stereotypical). This domestic focus very much marked the 1997 cinematic version of the story, adapted in a screenplay by Laura Jones and directed by Jocelyn Moorhouse. Dominated throughout by Ginny's voice-over narrative,[51] the film's makers may have destined it for an eventual afterlife on the Lifetime channel, centering it firmly on the women and denying "even the old man's heartbreaking deathbed scene—that [scene] goes to one of the daughters."[52] In its passage through Smiley via Jones and Moorhouse, the tale of fallen royalty is thoroughly absorbed into cinematic close-ups with beautiful blonde women (Jessica Lange as Ginny and Michelle Pfeiffer as Rose, supported by Jennifer Jason Leigh as Caroline), an intense drama whose focal point is the hidden truth of sexual abuse that pervades the sisters' torment and justifies all of their latent hostility. In terms of this structure, not even Jason Robards's compellingly pent-up performance as the Larry/Lear-figure can draw sympathy toward their father:

> *A Thousand Acres* offers the tantalizing prospect of a "Lear" that justifies and makes understandable the older daughters' cruelty. That [it] winds up choosing a different direction from 'Lear' isn't the problem. The problem is the direction it chooses. Once Rose . . . drops the bomb about a family secret, the deck is stacked against ol' Larry. He becomes the villain, with no hope of redemption, or forgiveness by the audience.[53]

By participating in contemporary dialogues about recovered memory, it may be that the film *A Thousand Acres* skews its perspective so far toward its women that it has no room for sympathy toward masculinity at all (not only is Daddy irredeemable, but he remains largely unsupported by the thinly fleshed husbands, played by Keith Carradine and Kevin Anderson, with scant appearances by Colin Firth as Jess). However, while it certainly provokes arguments about the nature and effects of adaptation and appropriation, *A Thousand Acres,* in its different generic forms, makes controversial (and, in Smiley's case, innovative) contributions to the afterlife of Shakespeare's play.

King Lear has also been radically reconfigured, at least in the physical sense, by featuring women in its eponymous role. I have chosen two productions—Maureen Shea's 1996 production for The Company of Women at Wellesley College in Massachusetts, and Helena Kaut-Howson's production at London's Young Vic—because they took very different perspectives of what feminism involved and whether it was relevant to their regendering of the king. In Shea's production, Kristin Linklater played the title role, and, indeed, all the roles were played by women. In Kaut-Howson's production, Kathryn Hunter played the part of the king. Both productions sought to challenge the notion that *King Lear* necessarily involves a masculine (and implicitly universal) journey through suffering. But whereas The Company of Women belted out the play, Linklater's loud, passionate Lear giving every bit as good as "she" got, Hunter's soft-voiced, goateed Lear, together with the rest of Kaut-Howson's cast, were not interested in staging a play that self-consciously tried to outdo masculinity.

According to Kaut-Howson, she did not have a feminist agenda at all: it just happened that her mother had recently died, and that *King Lear*'s concern with age and power was thus uppermost in her mind at the time:

We live in a patriarchal society and Shakespeare referred to patriarchal society and therefore made Lear a man, but the play itself, the whole premise and the way it links with something really primeval and old and ancient in us . . . to the idea of life and those who give us life. . . . I tried to respond to that, because that's the way the play hit me . . . I had a strong sense of seeing the whole universe and my understanding of who I was, or my mother's understanding of who she was, collapsing because there was this massive changeover. It was this terrible injustice of nature, the terrible cruelty, that you can say things that are natural and yet they seem so incredibly violent and cruel.[54]

In line with Kaut-Howson's objective, Kathryn Hunter was less concerned with *replacing* a male Lear than with simply playing the role as it had always been meaningful to her. Obsessed with the play since studying it at school at the age of fourteen, Hunter had always related to Lear as an emblem of crisis rather than to Cordelia as an emblem of victimhood: "Adolescence is a kind of crisis state about your relation with the world."[55] It seemed natural to her, then, to take Lear's part above any other. She saw Lear as unable to recognize other people's needs, "because in the position of power and privilege that he sits [in], he's just known flattery."[56]

Kaut-Howson's production opened with an elderly figure sitting hunched in a nursing-home wheelchair in front of a television. At 7:30 p.m. the screen changed abruptly from *Eastenders* to Gloucester's opening speech, with Lear going into cardiac arrest. For the rest of the action Lear, dressed in a business suit, remained mostly in the wheelchair, leaving it only from time to time to hobble onto the "heath." "She" delivered most of "her" lines in a whisper that had something of the hoarse authority that Marlon Brando commanded in *The Godfather.* She was clearly a figure to whom diminished authority was insupportable.

In Kaut-Howson's production, Marcello Magni played the Fool, carrying a candy-colored broom and dressed in tartan. His European accent intensified the enigmatic quality of the Fool's speeches. Hayley Carmichael doubled as Cordelia and as a knight. But beside the figure of the female Lear, whose quiet presence arrested all attention, all of the other characters were comparatively pale cameos. Little thought was given to revising the relationships between the three daughters and their father:

The impression is that Kaut-Howson has approached the production largely from the angle of practical problem-solving, firstly in finding a dramatic basis for a cross-cast Lear and then in dealing with the resultant ramifications of the device she uses. Structure takes primacy over either individual performances or a distinctive collective tone, leaving Hunter, Magni and occasionally one or two others swaying uncertainly at the summit of an unsteady edifice of performance.[57]

As with Kaut-Howson's production, Maureen Shea's was praised for the strength of its eponymous role and criticized for a flawed overall conception. Indeed, the irony of this production was that while it trumpeted the histrionic magnificence of its Lear (every bit as good as a man!), the production replicated the fundamental patriarchal assumption that the three daughters, unlike their father, need only be sketched out as victims or villains. Cordelia, played by Renee Whitfield, was a still point in a chaotic universe, complying completely with her father's fondly tyrannical view that "Her voice was ever soft, / Gentle, and low, an excellent thing in woman" (5.3.273–74). Regan (Patrice Johnson) dressed and behaved like a manipulative whore, while Goneril (Adriana Inchaustegui) stalked around in a business suit, busily cracking deals and running the kingdom. In its failure to expand and complicate the daughters' roles, this production didn't live up to its aim of challenging masculinist interpretations of *King Lear* and, indeed, did much to trivialize the performance of conventionally gendered roles by women.

Whatever the criticisms of the productions of *King Lear* directed by Kaut-Howson and Shea, both served to focus attention very keenly on the possibilities generated by the interplay between Shakespeare's *King Lear* and where, how, and by whom it is staged. Whether or not a woman director sees the role of Lear as inherently masculine, the staging of a *female* Lear was nonetheless in both cases the public talking-point of the production. Conversely, in approaching *King Lear* other female directors may see themselves as pioneers in gendered territory, while the production itself may be talked about for other reasons; however, as Elizabeth Schafer has pointed out, if a woman feels like a pioneer in a masculinist tradition, then she experiences all the challenges felt *by* a pioneer.[58] And this, I think, is important to acknowledge when wondering about whether, and how, a production is feminist, because feminism is as much about diversity in interpretation as it is about diverse possibilities for representation.

Finally, it remains to be observed that by considering the productions directed by Kaut-Howson and Shea, as well as the feminist questions, interpretations, and interventions drawn into the discussion as a whole, I have sought to do three things: to ask what "makes" a feminist production or dramatic moment, to bring this question to various aspects of the play's critical and performance history, and to record some of the motives and insights that have charged and sustained feminist perspectives of this huge, anarchic play. By thinking about performance in light of feminism and what it means in various contexts, we can question our own preoccupations and biases. And such questioning makes it possible to reshape our understandings of *King Lear*'s critical heritage and of our own capacity to intervene in it. Ideas and priorities about the play may still in many forums be "givens," but they need not remain pleasurably—or, indeed, unthinkingly—received.

Notes

The epigraph is from "King Lear: Love, Tyranny and Madness—An Actors View: Warren Mitchell," BBC interview, available at http://www.bbc.co.uk/education/bookcase/lear/mitchell.shtml.

1. "King Lear: Love, Tyranny and Madness—An Actors View: Warren Mitchell," http://www.bbc.co.uk/education/bookcase/lear/mitchell.shtml. The production in which Mitchell played Lear was generally praised for its focus on "the man, made wise by affliction and redeemed by love." See Don Batchelor, "QTC Has Spoken with the Voice of Shakespeare," *Theatre Australia* (July 1978): 29.

2. The polarization of the sisters is epitomized by James Calderwood, who alludes to Cordelia's "gentle conquest" in the play's fourth act. James Calderwood, "Creative Uncreation in *King Lear*," *Shakespeare Quarterly* 37 (1986): 5-19. Calderwood pushes Goneril and Regan to an opposite extreme, mocking their actions in 1.1: "The ladies have become spacious in

the possession of dirt" (6). As Katherine McLuskie observes, to rebuke this kind of viewpoint with a feminist "thumbs up" to Goneril and Regan would be to imply the kind of dualism that equates feminism with atavistic selfishness. Katherine McLuskie, "The Patriarchal Bard: Feminist Criticism and Shakespeare: *King Lear* and *Measure for Measure*," in *Political Shakespeare,* ed. Jonathan Dollimore and Alan Sinfield (Ithaca, N.Y.: Cornell University Press, 1985), 88–108.

3. Carol Rutter, *Enter the Body: Women and Representation on Shakespeare's Stage* (London and New York: Routledge, 2001), 26, 140.

4. Several critics have discussed (necessarily abstracted) early modern contexts for understanding gendered performance. Lisa Jardine argues that women in Shakespeare's plays are purely the effect of masculinity, with boy actors playing the woman's part for "a male audience's appreciation." Lisa Jardine, "Boy Actors, Female Roles, and Elizabethan Eroticism," in *Staging the Renaissance: Reinterpretation of Elizabethan and Jacobean Drama,* ed. David Scott Kastan and Peter Stallybrass (London and New York: Routledge, 1991), 57–67. Dympna Callaghan observes, "A representational schema that understands sexual difference completely within the parameters of masculinity does not require women: it occurs entirely within a material economy of males," leaving "woman" as a body that is defined in masculinist terms. Dympna Callaghan, *Shakespeare without Women: Performing Race and Gender on the Renaissance Stage* (London and New York: Routledge, 2000), 51. Valerie Traub is similarly concerned by tendencies to naturalize masculinity, seeing the price of redemption as at times "a complete capitulation to masculine terms as well as the resurrection of the faulty structure of sexual dualism." She goes on to resist the staunch position taken by such critics as Jardine who believe that there are no women in Shakespeare (i.e., only boys who play women). In contrast, Traub reads Shakespeare's plays as a site where sexual orientations can be played out with unusual fluidity, with women able to identify with male, female, and transvestite roles in Shakespeare. Valerie Traub, "Jewels, Statues and Corpses: Containment of Female Erotic Power in Shakespeare's Plays," in *Shakespeare and Gender: A History,* ed. Deborah Parker and Ivo Kamps (London: Verso, 1995), 120–41.

5. Thomas Cartelli defines *A Thousand Acres* as an appropriation, which "serves, and works in, the interests of the writer or group doing the appropriating, but usually works *against* the avowed or assigned interest of the writer whose work is appropriated." *Repositioning Shakespeare,* (London and New York: Routledge, 1999), 15.

6. Sarah Werner, *Shakespeare and Feminist Performance,* Accents on Shakespeare Series (London and New York: Routledge, 2001), 107n.

7. Elizabeth Schafer, for instance, points out *King Lear's* "vividly expressed and poetically effective misogyny, much of it voiced by Lear himself." Noting that Lear's tirade against women is positioned late in the play when sympathy for the elderly king is riding high, she says, "Negotiating this moment without endorsing . . . Lear's deep-seated loathing of women's sexuality presents a serious challenge." Elizabeth Schafer, *MsDirecting Shakespeare* (London: Women's Press, 1998), 128. In Coppélia Kahn's terms, Lear's misogyny gives way in the course of the play to a revelation of his "hidden dependence on mothering." Coppélia Kahn, "Magic of Bounty: *Timon of Athens,* Jacobean Patronage, and Maternal Power," in *Shakespearean Tragedy and Gender,* ed. Shirley Nelson Garner and Madelon Sprengnether (Bloomington: Indiana University Press, 1996), 135–67; quotation above is from p. 138.

8. Graham Bradshaw offers a case in point: "nothing that happens in *King Lear* makes us doubt that there is an essential difference between Cordelia's nature and that of her sisters." *Misrepresentations: Shakespeare and the Materialists* (Ithaca, N.Y.: Cornell University Press, 1993), 216. Feminists might usefully see such flatly stated essentialisms as critical complicity with Lear's misogyny.

9. The valorization of Lear as universal man was most famously expressed early in the last century by A. C. Bradley, who referred to a

feeling which haunts us in *King Lear,* as though we were witnessing something universal, a conflict not so much of particular persons as of the powers of good and evil in the world.
—A. C. Bradley, *Shakespearean Tragedy* (London: Macmillan, 1905), 262.

Harley Granville-Barker wrote likewise of a "larger synthesis" that suggests a universal relevance to Lear's moral progress. Harley Granville-Barker, "King Lear," in *Shakespeare Criticism, 1919–35,* ed. Anne Ridler (London: Oxford University Press, 1936), 293. John Middleton Murray, in the 1950s, saw the "positive theme" of the play as "no less than the Self and the birth of Divine Love. That comes to pass in Lear, through absolute isolation, through his becoming 'the thing itself', through 'madness.'" John Middleton Murry, *Shakespeare* (London: Jonathan Cape, 1956), 338. This view is still reflected by many contemporary directors, such as Lech Mackiewicz, who says: "Shakespeare is the Earth's heritage, not England's, and we should not limit the production to a historical setting because the fundamentals of Lear's predicament are still relevant today." Lech Mackiewicz, quoted in Nikki Jecks, Review of *King Lear,* Playbox Theatre, *Western Review,* Perth, February 1996.

10. Ann Jennalie Cook argues for Shakespeare's "quicksilver elusiveness" and aversion to the "orthodoxies of his time" (*Making a Match: Courtship in Shakespeare and His Society* [New Jersey, Princeton University Press, 1991], 261–63), while Juliet Dusinberre argues, in contrast, that the period in which Shakespeare lived was itself far more protofeminist than is conventionally perceived by feminists. She sees feminist thought in the period as a Puritan reaction to King James' misogyny. Juliet Dusinberre, *Shakespeare and the Nature of Women,* 2d ed. (New York: St Martin's Press, 1996), esp. 2–19.

11. Phyllis Rackin, "Misogyny Is Everywhere," in *A Feminist Companion to Shakespeare,* ed. Dympna Callaghan (Oxford: Blackwell, 2000), 47.

12. Anon., "Queen's Theatre: Amusements," *Sydney Morning Herald,* 24 July 1882. For more detail on the history of Australian productions of *King Lear,* see Philippa Kelly, ed., *The Bell Shakespeare "King Lear"* (Sydney: Halstead, 2002).

13. Quoted in Jacky Bratton, *"King Lear:* A Stage History," *The Cambridge "King Lear" CD-ROM,* ed. Jacky Bratton and Christie Carson (Cambridge: Cambridge University Press, 2000).

14. William Rounsenville Alger, *Life of Edwin Forrest: The American Tragedian* (1877), 782, quoted in Christie Carson, "King Lear in America," *The Cambridge "King Lear" CD-ROM,* ed. Jacky Bratton and Christie Carson (Cambridge: Cambridge University Press, 2000).

15. Alger, *Life of Edwin Forrest,* 797, quoted in Carson, *The Cambridge "King Lear" CD-ROM.*

16. Quoted in Bratton, *"King Lear:* A Stage History," *The Cambridge "King Lear" CD-ROM.*

17. Brian Cox, *The Lear Diaries: The Story of the Royal National Theatre's Productions of Shakespeare's "Richard III" and "King Lear"* (London: Methuen, 1992), 15.

18. See Stanley Wells, *Shakespeare: A Dramatic Life* (London: Sinclair-Stevenson, 1994), 26.

19. San Francisco Shakespeare Festival, Gershwin Hall, San Francisco, September 2001.

20. Jean Howard has convincingly read Shakespeare's tragedies in terms of the implosion of the monarchy at the turn of the seventeenth century. See Jean Howard, "The Geographies of the Early Modern Stage," in *Theater of a City: Social Change and Generic Innovation on the Early Modern Stage* (forthcoming), presented as a paper at the Humanities Research Centre, Australian National University, July 2000. R. S. White provides a context for, and analysis of, the meaning of hierarchy and anarchy in relation to character development in *King Lear.* R. S. White. *"King Lear* and Philosophical Anarchism," *English* 37 (1988): 181-200.

21. Sheridan Morley, "Ian Holm's Incomparable Lear," *International Herald Tribune,* 2 April 1997, p. 9.

22. See Alexander Leggatt, *King Lear* (Manchester: Manchester University Press, 1991), 73.

23. Ibid.

24. In discussing his production, Eyre suggests that Shakespeare "present[s] sympathy even-handedly. And although you don't get descriptions of their childhood . . . the evidence you do have is that Goneril . . . has been, as it were, bullied from birth, it's clear that Regan, like many middle children, has had a kind of manipulative relationship with her father, and that he has bestowed all his unqualified and unexamined love on the third daughter. . . . [P]arenthood is a form of tyranny." BBC interview available at http://www.bbc.co.uk/education/bookcase/lear/eyre.shtml.

25. To use Judith Butler's terms, in such dialectics "the masculine constitutes the closed circle of signifier and signified." *Gender Trouble: Feminism and the Subversion of Identity* (London and New York: Routledge, 1990), 11.

26. Miranda Johnson-Haddad, "The Shakespeare Theatre at the Folger, 1990–1991," *Shakespeare Quarterly* 42(6) (Winter 1991): 48.

27. Nelson Pressley, "*King Lear,* Rating Sin with Gold," *Washington Post,* 4 June 2001.

28. Grigori Kozintsev drew on Granville Barker's redemptive line. Granville Barker had as the turning point in his production the moment when Lear turns his attention from his own woes to those of others and kneels down to pray for the "poor naked wretches." In Granville Barker's production, Lear's death was more personal than public: the play ended not only with death, but with the joy of self-renewal. Kozintsev saw Lear's development "as a thawing. Grief warms him. Disaster melts the ice; his heart quickens and begins to beat." Unlike the intimate ending of Granville Barker's production, however, Kozintsev's film brought the redemptive interpretation to a different conclusion. The final scene presented aurally, but not visually, Lear crying, "Howl" over Cordelia's body and showed the pair at the very end only through a crowd of soldiers. The camera moved into the ordinary world, where women picked up their daily lives and the Fool was kicked by a soldier. The scene focused not on the personal moment of Lear's expression in death, but rather on the social context—the hardships of everyday life—to which Lear had been awakened by his redemptive experience. In tracing Lear's moral redemption, Kozintsev had him change from an irascible old character to a sober one who recognized the power of goodness.

29. Alastair Macaulay, "King Lear on a Grand Scale," *Financial Times,* 1 November 1999.

30. For more on this point, see Leggatt, *King Lear,* 13.

31. In contrast to Lear's voluminous speeches (he has 166 lines in the Folio's first scene alone), Regan has only 182 lines in the entire (Folio) play, Goneril 149, and Cordelia 107.

32. Harriet C., inmate, Mullawah Maximum Security Correctional Facility for Women, Sydney, 1997.

33. Schafer, *MsDirecting Shakespeare,* 128.

34. The other three pieces were *Romeo and Juliet, Allegro Brillante,* and *Variations de Ballet,* choreographed by Michael Smuin, George Balanchine, and Lew Christensen, respectively.

35. Quoted in Lisa Buchanan, Review of Morgan's *King Lear* Ballet, *City Affair,* April issue, 1985.

36. Quoted in Ben Fong-Torres, "A Rocker Drums Up Some High-Brow Stuff," *San Francisco Chronicle,* 14 April 1985, p. 33.

37. Ibid.

38. Bradley suggests, for example, that "the wider or universal significance of the spectacle presented to the inward eye" is, in performance, challenged by the dissipation of "poetic atmosphere," by the "half-realised" meanings of words, and by "the tyranny of the eye" by which "we conceive the characters as mere particular men and women" (*Shakespeare Tragedy,* 269).

39. Quoted in Fong-Torres, "Rocker Drums Up."

40. Buchanan, Review, 1985.

41. Quoted in Buchanan, Review, 1985.

42. Allan Ulrich, Review of Morgan's *King Lear* Ballet, *San Francisco Examiner,* 17 April 1985.

43. Ulrich, Review, 1985. I would suggest that some evocation of pain and dissonance might indeed be in keeping with the interpretive dissonance pertaining to "Shakespeare's majestic tragedy" and that the reviewer's own assumptions about the nature and quality of *King Lear*'s universal appeal form something of a block to his appreciation of Morgan's concept.

44. Madelon Sprengnether, "The Gendered Subject of Shakespearean Tragedy," in *Shakespearean Tragedy and Gender,* ed. Shirley Nelson Garner and Madelon Sprengnether (Bloomington: Indiana University Press, 1996), 1.

45. Jane Smiley, "Shakespeare in Iceland," *Shakespeare and the Twentieth Century: The Selected Proceedings of the International Shakespeare Association World Congress, Los Angeles, 1996.* ed. Jonathan Bate et al. (Newark: University of Delaware Press, 1998), 41–59, 44–45.

46. Many interesting studies have now been made of Smiley's novel. Some of the more useful are Susan Strehe, "The Daughter's Subversion in Jane Smiley's *A Thousand Acres,*" *Studies in Contemporary Fiction* 41(3) (Spring 2000): 211–26; Catherine Cakebread, "Remembering *King Lear* in Jane Smiley's *A Thousand Acres,*" in *Shakespeare and Appropriation,* ed. Christy Desmet and Robert Sawyer (London and New York: Routledge, 1999); and James Schiff, "Contemporary Retellings: *A Thousand Acres* as the Latest *Lear,*" *Studies in Contemporary Fiction* 39(4) (1998): 367–81.

47. Smiley, *A Thousand Acres,* 43.

48. This term was used by Smiley in her plenary lecture "Shakespeare in Iceland" at the Sixth World Shakespeare Congress, Los Angeles, 7 April 1996.

49. Smiley, *A Thousand Acres,* 43.

50. In an article on the pedagogy of sociology, Kelley J. Hall interprets Ginny and Rose in terms of "traditionally feminine" roles and the men in the novel as "traditionally masculine." Kelley J. Hall, "Putting the Pieces Together: Using Jane Smiley's *A Thousand Acres* in Sociology of Families," *Teaching Sociology* 28(4) (2000): 372. She sees Ginny as learning "to speak her mind" as the novel progresses (372).

51. James Berardinelli referred to the voice-over as an unwelcome "burden." Review available at movie-reviews.colossus.net.

52. Roger Ebert, Review of *A Thousand Acres, Chicago Sun-Times,* 9 September 1997. Sy Becker adds: "*A Thousand Acres* will fill the theater with the sounds of blowing noses and muffled sniffling. And it's not just a woman's picture either. I got all choked up eavesdropping on the problems of these tormented sisters," Review of *A Thousand Acres,* 29 September 1997, http://www.wwlp.com/news/segments/sybersy/thsndacres.html.

53. Mick LaSalle, Review of *A Thousand Acres, San Francisco Chronicle,* 19 September 1997.

54. For this and all other quotes by Kaut-Howson, see http://www.bbc.cok.uk/education/bookcase/lear/helena/shtml.

55. See http://www.bbc.co.uk/education/bookcase/lear/hunter.shtml.

56. Ibid.

57. Ian Shuttleworth, Review of Kaut-Howson's *King Lear, Financial Times,* 26 February 1997.

58. "[I]f a woman director feels that she is a pioneer, it is almost irrelevant whether or not she *is* a pioneer. If she feels the pressures of pioneering, then these pressures are real and will affect her work—whether positively or negatively" (Schafer, *MsDirecting Shakespeare,* 191).

Shakespeare's Empty Plot:
The Epicenotaph in Timon of Athens

ROBERT DARCY

*T*IMON OF ATHENS has long been considered an unfinished play and felt to be partly unreadable in its state of incompletion. It has often been dismissed as the working draft of a collaborative effort never brought to its final conclusion in the professional industry of the London theaters. The play's marginal place in the Shakespeare canon and its historically lukewarm reception by readers and audiences alike have been understood principally as the result of flaws that are more craft-related than bound up with the thematic implications of the play itself or with anything particularly revealing about its fantasy or its vision. Yet the play's experiment in representational misanthropy is historically important to investigations of the English Renaissance for the way it dramatizes a radical and disturbing form of uncompromising subjectivity at a time when early modern intellectual communities in Europe, broadly speaking, were growing increasingly interested in characterizing and disseminating notions of subjectivity that would facilitate the way individuals might bond to their cultures, particularly as those cultures were changing in response to the new economic pressures of a burgeoning merchant and industrial capitalism. If readers have found *Timon of Athens* raw and creatively abortive in its effects, they respond much differently to a companion work that to my mind is no less radical in its conception of a world-alienating subjectivity but that impressively charts an alternative path toward "anthrophilic" recovery and harmony rather than disappearing into the misanthrope's deserted wild. The work I mean is Descartes's *Discourse on Method,* which tells the biographical story behind his *Meditations on First Philosophy* and is remarkable in the way it embraces skeptical annihilation and relates that to a rejection of a populated world. Famously alone in the wintry room, with no voices or other human distraction and only an enclosed stove to draw his eye, Descartes begins (at the beginning of his second discourse) an intellectual process of dismantling the knowledge of the world around him until all that remains is the distilled, irreducible cogito, with its first-person assertion of self—itself a claim of novel discovery—serving as the final magical ward against his own intellectual annihilation.[1] Armed with the fantasy of first-authority embedded in his cogito, Descartes returns to the world he nearly destroyed armed with a new claim to cultural worthiness and to the economic security it seemed ready to compel.

   Timon of Athens does not tell the same story. To understand how deeply connected Descartes was to an unspoken, psychological version of what has emerged more recently and more overtly as a pragmatic negotiation of social life—as a "willingness to center [one's] hopes on the future of the race, on the unpredictable successes of [one's] descendents," (as Richard Rorty has characterized Francis Bacon with demonstrating, a figure who for Rorty, but not for me, is the counterpoint to Descartes)[2]—is simultaneously to recognize how troubling *Timon* is as a record of what might have remained in the first decade of the seventeenth century of an embattled psychological and intellectual commitment to metaphysics when that institution bore the signs of a beleaguered struggle to preserve, against swelling resistance, a noneconomic basis for social relations. In refusing to confront *Timon of Athens* in a serious way through these particular modes of inquiry, modern critics may be understood as shying away from the record of a loss that is fundamental to discussions of subjectivity, a record of loss that, in its connection to a tradition of metaphysical inquiry, has been routinely mistaken as a triumph of discovery. If the early modern moment under investigation here has been credited with developing a modern sense of inwardness and a routine awakening into subjectivity, *Timon of Athens* may suggest something radically contrary to that narrative in locating the death of subjectivity at precisely the time when its absent presence—its residual imprint—was insistently made to seem, perhaps in unwilling confirmation of its loss, like the real thing emerging as though for the first time. Unlike the Cartesian fantasies embedded in the metaphysics of the cogito, *Timon of Athens* allows for no such illusory trace as the misanthrope's body, which, having been propelled away from the social centers that earlier posed so serious a threat to its own subjective condition, is missing from the play's conclusion and never seen again. In what follows, I elaborate on this potential reading of the play and try to theorize the basis for modernity as historically punctuated by the logic not of an important discovery or birth of Western conceptions of subjectivity, as Descartes has claimed, but of a difficult and surprising death, whose after-image is the fleeting trace of the body of the misanthrope.

Cartesian Proofs

In response to the painter's platitude about the world in the opening scene of *Timon of Athens,* the poet's declaration, "Ay, that's well known" (1.1.3), binds the two speakers in a collegial bond as it confirms their shared wisdom and common speech.[3] Yet for the play's English audience, at a time when questions about early modern subjectivity would shortly coalesce in Descartes's revolutionary cogito, the poet's comment may also carry the tinge of critique as the painter's response only confirms what is already widely known. If Descartes, in his *Discourse* and *Meditations,* models through his ingenious cogitation a process for securing cultural authority in proportion to the surprise of one's original intellectual contribution, the poet may register (with Cartesian foresight and through a comparative measure of what is "new" against what is "known") a critique of the painter for failing to think beyond the limits of what the two already hold in common between them.[4] While the brief, opening exchange between these two professional acquaintances ends quickly and unremarkably, its mundane mechanism is no less integral to understanding the crisis of acquaintance and friendship that this play will fully dramatize. Through their dialogue, the poet and painter confirm the way in which social banter—those highly conventional tags of social conversation that make up the bulk of daily speech—crucially establishes knowledge held in common between two speakers, effectively bonding them in a social kinship. Yet their exchange cannot help but beg the question of cultural value, introducing a latent disappointment in the apparent dependence of social cohesion on repetition and cliché, or even on what has been well documented as Renaissance imitation, despite its plagiaristic tinge.[5] This disappointment is latent in that its emergence depends on the discriminating listening patterns of any given participant. Only some listeners will hear a cliché with distaste while others will not hear it at all, accepting it uncritically as a direct—even original—form of expression.

The opening scene of *Timon* seems deliberately to excite this latent critical discrimination in its audience. When the painter describes his painting and when the poet recites a few lines from his freshest work, the failure of either to achieve an original vision is made patently clear. Each has failed in trying to perform what would shortly be understood as a Cartesian claim to subjectivity, though neither is apparently aware of or encumbered by that failure. Timon, on the other hand, with both his prodigious generosity and eventual misanthropy, can be understood as having undertaken a worthy process of subjectivity but having failed to win a permanent assurance of privilege from the social realm that alone can grant it. From Timon's perspective, the social logic by which he has earned his position in Athenian society, if it has been secured through something resembling a Cartesian process, must attach not merely to accidents of wealth and service, which other accidents might see reversed, but to intellectual justifications for privilege and authority that are impervious to contingencies of time and space.[6] Reflecting Timon's own expectations about the special rights reserved for him, Alcibiades similarly appeals to the senators for the perquisites of earned subjectivity. Seeking a pardon on behalf of a friend who, goaded into a fight, murdered his adversary, the general reveals his anticipation of results based on precisely this cultural economy of privilege:

> It pleases time and fortune to lie heavy
> Upon a friend of mine, who in hot blood
> Hath stepp'd into the law, which is past depth
> To those that, without heed, do plunge into't.
> He is a man, setting his fate aside,
> Of comely virtues;
> Nor did he soil the fact with cowardice
> (An honour in him which buys out his fault)
> But with a noble fury and fair spirit,
> Seeing his reputation touch'd to death,
> He did oppose his foe;
> And with such sober and unnoted passion
> He did behove his anger, ere 'twas spent,
> As if he had but prov'd an argument.
>   (3.5.7-23)

Alcibiades seeks to counteract fluctuations of "time and fortune," ministers of accident that have landed a worthy soldier and friend before the sentence of the law. The law, here figured as a dangerous body of water "past depth, / To those that, without heed, do plunge into't," drowns its foolhardy swimmers as a passive mechanism of capital punishment that redirects responsibility for such serious punitive consequence back onto the sentenced party. In calling on the senators to prevent his friend's certain death, Alcibiades seeks to rescue him by means of a human-operated form of deus ex machina. Alcibiades reminds the senators of their power to step into a position of divine first-authority, to alter the mechanism of the law, and to save a worthy citizen on the basis of his merit, here relayed as a store of virtue that "buys out his fault," balancing the debt of his crime. Although Alcibiades clearly expects his own record of meritorious service to Athens to influence the senators in granting his appeal, he does not miss the chance to analogize his friend as a philosopher, or accomplished cultural thinker: the passion of the homicide and the ensuing calm resembled the mere proving of "an argument," settled here by unorthodox but, Alcibiades proposes, forensically defensible means.

The senators are not so easily persuaded by Alcibiades' case about his friend's argumentative style and the judicial latitude they might award its use. They do not satisfy his pleas any more than they agree to forgive Timon's debt, and the play will see them learning to regret deeply their unwillingness to grant special privileges to those cultural members who have contracted through a performance of subjectivity the right to stand beyond the arm of the law. The senators regret their unwillingness precisely because they learn that Alcibiades can repeat his performance: he returns to conquer Athens, again solving arguments and proving his worth through homicidal acts. The problem for Timon, however, different from that facing Alcibiades, is that he discovers that his own grand act of subjective performance, that is, of transforming culture through boundless generosity—a dream of nostalgia, a dream of first authority—is an empty act. Timon's banquet is an empty feast, and his wealth an illusion. Unlike Alcibiades, Timon does not retain through his experiences a sustained belief in his own subjective powers. He is not merely interested in securing the privilege that comes with performances of subjectivity: he has believed profoundly in the legitimacy of that subjectivity, too, and the play's audience watches as he is transformed by its irrevocable hollowness into the shape of someone who has been defrauded by his own subjective claims.

Timon's Cenotaph

If Timon's demonstration of first authority is ultimately fraudulent, if his cogito can be reduced in substance to an empty utterance, then misanthropy is his response to those weighty deprivations. The play offers a way for understanding this sequence, leading as it does to a social void figured ultimately as a tombstone and grave. The notion that Timon's grave may actually be a cenotaph—the potential for imagining the failure of this hero to die and therein to be unable to inhabit the monument of his death— inserts a new fiction into *Timon of Athens,* with a deliberate rewriting of the generally accepted story. In this play—this play called a "life" in its first and only print appearance during the monarchical English Renaissance (and only later dubbed a "tragedy")—the hero, who boasts, "I am *Misanthropos,* and hate mankind" (4.3.54), is generally believed to die alone in his hermetic retreat, thereby escaping in a final way the plague of visitors frustrating his bitter wish for solitude. The soldier who discovers Timon's death, however, does not discover Timon—that is, he does not discover a corpse: he finds instead, when he arrives on orders to search the Athenian out, a burial mound and an epitaph on a tombstone atop this mound. Timon is apparently dead, and from this fictionally unchallenged look of things, modern editors often position this play with their classificatory nomenclature as a failed *Lear,* a somewhat botched and peculiarly anemic strain of bloodless tragedy.[7]

By evoking the cenotaph, however, or empty tomb to the dead, of which art historians talk when surveying the tombs of quattrocento Italy, one strips the play of its tragic pretense. The cenotaph invests this burial mound with a hollowness, an absence in death matching Timon's failure in life to fill an appropriate space back within Athenian society. In entertaining the possibility of the cenotaph, one can acknowledge that regardless of a general readerly lack of faith in this play's logical integrity—inherited from editors who are bothered by inconsistencies in monetary units and character names throughout[8]—a person nevertheless cannot effect his own burial or position an epitaph atop his own tomb, at least not easily. And Timon in particular has both dramatic and metaphysical motive to stage his own death and thereby end the public pursuit of his private person. If one can accept the reasonableness of the premise that Timon may never actually die in this play—no one sees him die, after all—then one is charged with trying to figure out what to do with this new infusion of dramatic irony. If Timon's tomb does not contain him, what does it—or could it—in point of fact contain?

The answer circulating here is "nothing," and "nothing" is no welcome sort of answer—neither for its nihilism nor for its absenting foreclosure of more practical discoveries. But the nothing-filled cenotaph would nonetheless figure into a collection of similar dramatic props at work throughout the play. When Lucullus, anticipating a gift rather than an appeal for money, asks Timon's servant what he carries under his robe, the servant tells him, "Nothing but an empty box, sir, which, in my lord's behalf, I come to entreat your honor to supply" (3.1.15-16). And having been denied the aid of his friends and welcoming them to a false feast set before them on "covered dishes" concealing not food as promised but bowls of warm water, Timon offers an ironic prayer of thanks: "For these my present friends, as they are to me nothing, so in nothing bless them, and to nothing are they welcome" (3.6.79-81). "Nothing" is both the offending content of Timon's empty box and the substance of the misanthrope's revenging feast as he fills his guests' bowls with that which will fail to fill their hungry stomachs.[9]

Losing for the play its watery claim to tragedy, the seaside cenotaph should become readable instead as a set design with metatheatrical implications—a staged scene (staged, that is, within the world of the fiction) that the anonymous soldier, the unquestioning discoverer of Timon's tomb, is too dim to suspect as a form of theater. His inability to read the epitaph is a further clue as he makes for more learned eyes a wax imprint of the chiseled words "whose soft impression," he says, "[i]nterprets for my poor ignorance" (5.4.68-69). The soldier is indeed ignorant, a poor witness to those who would rely on his report because, like the wax he carries with him, he is shaped too easily to the scene. In less than ten lines, he will have come and gone, turning in so brief a space into an overly hasty messenger of death. Another Timon, from Lucian's source dialogue for the play, focuses the point:

To leave generalities and illustrate from my own case—I have raised any number of Athenians to high position, I have turned poor men into rich, I have assisted every one that was in want, nay, flung my wealth broadcast in the service of my friends, and now that profusion has brought me to beggary, they do not so much as know me; I cannot get a glance from the men who cringed and worshipped and hung upon my nod. If I meet one of them in the street, he passes me by as he might pass the tombstone of one long dead; it has fallen face upwards, loosened by time, but he wastes no moment deciphering it.[10]

Like the lack of regard Lucian's Timon receives in his luckless state, comparable to a tombstone whose inscription is left unread because it is worn and inscrutable to the passing eye, consideration of the tombstone of this play seems prohibitively brief. The decipherability of the play's final scenes has perhaps not been measured with sufficient care. Editorial emendations of the play as a whole but in particular of these final scenes are a record of impatience: the Oxford text omits two problematic lines entirely from the soldier's scene,[11] and the Riverside and Arden editors explain the presence of two seemingly contradictory epitaphs dutifully recorded on the soldier's wax tablet as a sign that the playwright himself had been conscious of writing only a draft and had not yet decided which he would ultimately use.[12]

Despite what may appear to be hasty editorial decisions and conjecture, one cannot blame the editors completely. Compared to other plays, *Timon of Athens* is notoriously hard to read, and the long-standing notion that the play is not as finished as others appearing in Shakespeare's Folio is hard to dismiss.[13] But it is important for a sustained participation in the play on its own terms to consider ways of absorbing what are presented as editorial anomalies into a reasonably meaningful understanding of the fiction. Why, for example, should one insist that the soldier's wax tablet be clearly intelligible? Why is it acceptable only that the soldier should need an interpreter but not that the play's general audience should be limited by the same necessity? Despite Alcibiades' confidence in reading aloud the wax letters and in summarizing Timon's final status, not only as dead but as worthy of a culture's forgiveness and respect, the crux-generating double epitaph nevertheless embeds its own interpretive challenges:

> Here lies a wretched corse, of wretched soul bereft:
> Seek not my name. A plague consume you, wicked caitiffs left!
> Here lie I, Timon, who, alive, all living men did hate.
> Pass by and curse thy fill, but pass and stay not here thy gait.
>   (5.4.70-74)

"Seek not my name" the epitaph instructs before making Timon's name the center of relevance. If this four-line epitaph is really separable into two unrelated couplets[14]—as indeed Plutarch's source material definitively separates them[15]—their presence together in the play has suggested to some that one was an alternate, a substitute or replacement for the other which would not have survived into a fair copy had the play been brought to the stage and adjusted for performance.[16] Yet if one ignores textual issues that have nothing to do with the play's internal story, the two verses may instead represent a choice Timon had failed to make between drafts of his own epitaph, rather than only pointing to a metafictional lapse of the playwright. The failure of puzzling out these four lines into separate drafts should perhaps best be borne by the general Alcibiades, who at the end of the play, despite proving to be the illiterate soldier's idea of a gifted interpreter, is nevertheless ready to prove his argument with his sword in a manner that may detract from his status as a sensitive reader. Indeed, the general may have a dramatic interest at this point in accepting Timon's death on its face, in ignoring the gaps in the soldier's story or the anomalies in the wax imprint. And his acceptance, I suggest, should not necessarily govern our own. From the tombstone identified by the soldier, Timon vacillates widely between suppressing his name and declaring it outright. Rather than the playwright, it is Timon who seems not to have made up his mind: Timon is the one who has been working out a draft.

The notion, dramatic or not, that a person should labor over the production of her or his own commemorative epigraph, even under desperately trying circumstances as those apparently facing Timon, is worth some further meditation. Erving Goffman, a sociologist conducting his fieldwork in resort hotels during the 1950s—not, however, without a disturbing set of prejudices—observed a phenomenon strikingly reminiscent of Timon's double epitaph. He reported that hotel security learned to anticipate, after a series of isolated incidents, to find in the room of a suicide discarded drafts of the note that was ultimately meant to be found. Crumpled up in the wastebasket, its lines crossed out and words adjusted, one note read:

Darling—
　By the time you get this I will be where nothing you can do will hurt me—
　By the time you read this, nothing you can do will be able to hurt.[17]

The selection and hesitation between drafts are signs of the seriousness afforded the performance, but they are also surprising given the extremity of the context, which would seem to leave not much room for preparation or a preoccupation with details: "The final feelings of a desperately uncompromising person," Goffman writes, were here proven "somewhat rehearsed in order to strike just the right note and in any case were not final."[18] The climactic finality of a life brought suddenly to its desperate conclusion is revealed to be a staged event, by evidence of the discarded draft.

Writing one's suicide note or else one's epitaph, imagining as it does a posthumous readerly moment from a premortem writerly condition, showcases a peculiarity of writing that becomes a major theme in certain kinds of literature and will dominate my interpretation of the ending of this play. As a thoroughly exhausted literary theme, the open-ended capacity of a literary work to exist beyond the death of its author and its readers had clear implications for Shakespeare's sonneteer, for example, who in Sonnet 81 could promise immortality to the addressed youth even after introducing the eventuality of the young man's epitaph. "Such virtue hath my pen," the sonneteer could boast, waving the instrument of his craft like a magus waving a Virgilian wand. The peculiarity here, of course, is that the claim about the pen's power to extend one's presence beyond death is surely accurate from a particular point of view, as my quotation from a dead man's sonnet and conjuration of the youth therein addressed may help to illustrate. In claiming to have the power to revive a memory that will call the dead back into presence, the sonnet is a near example of what Freud has called a "permanent memory-trace," the memory of a thing preserved in a reliable, static record distinct from the human brain and its vulnerability to neurological and bodily decay.[19] Yet, as Derrida has suggested in consideration of Freud's unfolding metaphor for the unconscious mind, one cannot be sure that literature serves merely as a metaphor, or that writing is merely the trace of something that has prior existence, as though merely the trace, say, of the human hand.[20] The Mystic Writing Pad upon which Freud imagines one to write and rewrite as part of a subconscious pattern of memory and repression is, troublingly, a metaphor communicable only in terms of the material stylus and wax, physical implements of writing whose presence overwhelms the concepts they would merely pretend to represent.

Derrida's famous critique of Western logocentrism—as vulnerable to deconstruction given its dissemination in written, rather than oral, forms—suggests that Freud's privileging of neurological memory over writing further begs the question of writing's potential supremacy, not mere utility, in the process of generating human consciousness, or at any rate of making that consciousness available to discursive investigation.[21] As Derrida suggests, writing overwhelms the scene that attempts to stage something else. If for Freud this "something else" is a psychological process nowhere visible except in the field of metaphorical language, the "something else" for the audience of *Timon of Athens'* final scene is the misanthropic body, which is present only through the discursive assertion of the epitaph: "Here lies a wretched corse." The corpse is present during this final scene only as a written and spoken word, attached to a deictic of location, although the "here" of Timon's corpse has been further displaced by the soldier's movement away from the site of the tomb. Characters such as Alcibiades—but clearly also generations of audiences and readers of the play who have been uncommunicative about the displacement enacted in this final scene—have remained unbothered by this displacement, that is, not only of the epitaphs, which have been transported from their fixed location by virtue of the soldier's wax, but also of Timon's body. The question of Timon's actual location at the end of the play is absorbed into the rhetorically created space of the epitaph rather than being answered definitively by the material site of his tomb and an exhumation, if necessary, of his purportedly buried corpse. This ability of language to dematerialize physical presence by absorbing it referentially into rhetorical space is also at work in Descartes's interrogation of presence in his *Meditations,* when he suggests that "there is the fact that leads Descartes to say, I am here, seated by the fire, attired in a dressing gown, having this paper in my hands and other similar matters."[22] Of this Cartesian presence, now firmly text-based, Judith Butler, in her essay whose title "How Can I Deny That These Hands and This Body Are Mine?" quotes Descartes, observes:

[T]he "I" is "here," "ici," because this term in this sentence is a deictic one, and it is a shifter, pointing to a "here" that could be any here, but that seems to be the term that helps to anchor the spatial ground of its indubitability. When Descartes writes "here," he appears to refer to the place where he is, but this is a term that could refer to any "here" and so fails to anchor Descartes to his place in the way that we might expect it to. What does the writing of his place do to the indubitable referentiality of that "here"? Clearly, it is not here; the "here" works as an indexical that refers only by remaining indifferent to its occasion. Thus the word, precisely because it can refer promiscuously, introduces an equivocalness and, indeed, a dubitability that makes it quite impossible to say whether or not his being "here" is a fact as he claims that it is. Indeed, the very use of such an equivocal term makes it seem possibly untrue.[23]

Butler objects that "[t]he written status of the 'I' splits the narrator from the very self he seeks to know and *not* to doubt."[24] But in an unexpected way, Descartes is "here" accomplishing precisely what he set out to accomplish, if indeed he is telling the truth in claiming to demonstrate through his novel discovery that "this *I* that is thinking is *an immaterial substance* with no bodily element."[25] "Thus, an 'I' emerges," Butler observes, "narratively, at a distance from its former opinions, shearing off its historicity, and inspecting and adjudicating its beliefs from a carefree position."[26]

If Cartesian subjectivity is accomplished by generating an "I" which is a floating signifier that is "carefree" in its reference to "no bodily element," then Cartesian subjectivity is approached whenever one writes in the first-person and abandons all expectation of being named by the pronouns operating therein. Timon's narcissistic wounding by his fellow Athenians could have been spared him, this new formulation suggests, had he managed to separate his ego from the discursivity of the act and the utterance that generated his cultural prominence in the first place—had he, in other words, understood more fully the terms of subjectivity as performance. His double epitaph is a confusing negotiation of these lessons, bearing a reluctance in the first draft (the first two lines) to reveal the cultic identity inhabiting the "my" of the author's command, "Seek not my name," while relenting on this point in the second draft, on the other hand, yoking the first-person pronoun with the name which the earlier draft jealously concealed: "Here lie I, Timon." The yielding of the name in the second draft, contrary to working as an assignation and reassertion of stable identity, may in fact reveal an abandonment of identity and of any notion of an ideal correspondence of the written first-person and proper name to any stable bodily element.

Unlike Descartes, who performs the separation of himself from his "I" with aplomb, and taps into the economy by which the discursive "I" might generate the means of subsistence for his bodily self, Timon finally performs such a separation only through the epitaph. Achieving the early terms of Cartesian subjectivity may, after all, constitute a dying act if it involves abandoning one's hope of generating authentic subjective presence in one's own bodily person.

Alcibiades' Glove

The hand that discovers Timon's epitaph is almost as mysterious in its motivation as the one that chisels it into the headstone. This discovering hand is the soldier's, of course, who is himself but a hired appendage of

Alcibiades, general and figural head of an incorporated army. But it is a surprise that this soldier is equipped well enough with wax and therefore capable of taking an imprint of the lettering on the stone. His inability to read the epitaph may suggest illiteracy, but so may it suggest merely that the language of the inscription is foreign to the soldier, just as the language of monuments recorded by Renaissance antiquarians would have been, in Latin or Greek, unreadable to anyone trained for little more than soldierly service.[27] The soldier says:

> What's on this tomb
> I cannot read. The character I'll take with wax;
> Our captain hath in every figure skill,
> An ag'd interpreter, though young in days.
> Before proud Athens he's set down by this,
> Whose fall the mark of his ambition is.
>
> (5.3.5–10)

Like the epitaph, the soldier's final sentence requires an expert's gloss. For his own part, the Arden editor knots and then unravels a syntax by which the soldier merely locates his general in space, as "set down," or camped, before the city of Athens, "whose fall" is his militaristic ambition. But in this interpretation, the agency of Alcibiades being set down "by this," cannot, except through an awkward redundancy (by what is he set down—by Athens?), be resolved. If on the other hand the soldier adheres to a more natural syntax, his words more sensitively predict that Alcibiades will be "set down," or made glum, by this bad news about his friend, even as he stands with all military might before the city he would defeat. The fall, then, is not of Athens; rather, "this" inscription in which Alcibiades will read the epitaphic name of his friend is the fall that forecasts the general's own inevitable end, the soldier suggests, in the sense that all ambitions necessarily lead to death, tombs, and epitaphs as the ultimate markers of their extrapolated trajectory.

The soldier is perhaps more thoughtful than I originally credited him with being as he plays Cyriacus to this stone,[28] recording its figure as on a Mystic Writing Pad, in a permanent memory-trace that will be legible to more learned, more authorized eyes.[29] If his own eyes cannot read, his hands at least can record the figure and leave that record so that others may puzzle out the meaning. Yet the play will not produce a sensitive interpreter, despite the soldier's confidence in his general's interpretive powers. The memory is preserved through the wax impression, but only as a literary device. Alcibiades addresses his friend after he reads (backwards and in wax relief) the substance of the epitaphic drafts:

> These well express in thee thy latter spirits.
> Though thou abhorr'dst in us our human griefs,
> Scorn'dst our brains' flow and those our droplets which
> From niggard nature fall, yet rich conceit
> Taught thee to make vast Neptune weep for aye
> On thy low grave, on faults forgiven. Dead
> Is noble Timon, of whose memory
> Hereafter more.
>
> $\qquad\qquad\qquad\qquad\qquad$ (5.4.74–81)

The instant forgiveness Alcibiades imagines for Timon's "faults" is transparently a grant made possible by the misanthrope's death, which allows the general to begin reclaiming the friend, who cursed and spit at the world, in terms that will satisfy him personally just as it will, more generally, satisfy the polis, which must continually produce narratives of nobility to authorize its larger, historical presence.[30]

The problem with Alcibiades' production of memory, of which "hereafter more," is that it places the activity of remembrance unsettlingly though rather accurately into future time. Memorializing friends no less than cultural heroes is by definition an act not of true remembrance—that is, of recreating the past—but of invention, of replacing the missing body with narratives that can only serve as representational traces. Appropriately enough, in correspondence with his reclamation of Timon's memory, Alcibiades has just agreed to terms of peace with Athens that will similarly transport control of his own memory into narratives of history that will ultimately subsume him, a literary eclipse of his own corporeal presence. Alcibiades participates in his own hollowing out when he first allows the senators to characterize his intent and then capitulates to their terms of agreement. The first offer that the senators make to the general at their gates is one Alcibiades rejects, not because he is hard at bargaining but because the offer is harrowing in its randomizing terms of justice. The senators claim that the ones responsible for Alcibiades' anger, for rejecting his appeal for clemency on behalf of a friend, are now dead: "Nor are they living / Who were the motives that you first went out" (5.4.26–27). In lieu of these throats, the senators offer others:

> By decimation and a tithed death,
> If thy revenges hunger for that food
> Which nature loathes, take thou the destin'd tenth,
> And by the hazard of the spotted die
> Let die the spotted.
>
> (5.4.30-33)

Let die by the die, the senators suggest, every tenth person in Athens, designated by lottery to satisfy Alcibiades' militaristic hunger for revenge.[31] As proof of his intention not to kill everyone in the city and of his agreement only to slaughter "those kin / Which in the bluster of thy wrath must fall / With those that have offended" (5.4.40-42), the senators ask the general to "Throw thy glove" as a "token of thine honour" (5.4.49-50). Prepared in any case to reject the premise of random slaughter in Athens, Alcibiades capitulates: "Then there's my glove" (5.4.54). And he attempts to exorcise the specter of the spotted die, calling once again on the ghost of a friend to strengthen his claim: "Those enemies of Timon's and mine own / Whom you yourselves shall set out for reproof / Fall, and no more" (5.4.56-58). But in the interest of demonstrating "honour," a term deeply discursive despite its felt association with action, Alcibiades generates the play's final container, filled here again—in the absence of his hand—with nothing. Alcibiades' glove authorizes the hazard, in the dual sense of danger and randomness, that the senators propose and that the general would ultimately make a move to deny. These events are not his to control once they enter into the air as language disembodied, as terms of diplomacy and culture. Alcibiades' glove hits the ground as the trace of a hand no longer present, the shape of a body unfleshed, and he invokes Timon's name— prior to receiving the news from the soldier and his delivery of the wax which filled the empty space of the letters on Timon's chiseled stone— as though they were commorientes, kin who stood to inherit from one another but instead, by the hazard of circumstance, died at approximately the same time.

The play *Timon of Athens* seems to chronicle occasions for discovering a fundamental emptiness, in institutions of friendship, in economic communities, in the theater, and in performances of subjectivity—institutions whose monuments are elaborate but may house little or nothing underneath. The epitaph is always potentially an "epicenotaph," then, an inscription over an empty tomb. Katherine Duncan-Jones hears an echo of Timon's epitaph in the one that eventually graced Shakespeare's headstone:

"Blessed be the man that spares these stones, / And cursed be he that moves my bones."[32] That the revered bones are, in fact, removable, or indeed that they may never get properly buried there in the first place engenders a cynicism of misanthropic proportions, jeopardizing what would become Cartesian assurances of metaphysical presence and subjective performance. That the inscription of Shakespeare's tomb should implicate its own potential failure to be more than an epicenotaph is the impressively inelegant, "final" bequest of bardic wisdom (by virtue of its inscription over W. S.'s enduringly silent tomb) and the unattractive assertion of the play. But if, in finding this play unattractive, one dismisses it as an unfinished draft that contains and can tell nothing—about *Lear,* say, about cultural misanthropy, or about the hollowness of monuments from the past and of the present—then perhaps one should feel ready to desist from reading Renaissance texts as a serious effort, rather than a mere rehearsal, of digging for bones.

Notes

Earlier versions of this article were delivered in paper form at the annual meeting of the Group for Early Modern Cultural Studies in Philadelphia in 2001, and at Utica College as part of its Nexus faculty seminar series in 2003. A written version of the paper benefited from the attention of members of a seminar on *Timon of Athens* at the Shakespeare Association of America annual meeting in 2002 in Minneapolis. For their helpful feedback and insight for improving this work, I wish to thank the audience members and participants at those events, especially Madhavi Menon, Alexander Leggatt, Jonathan Gil Harris, Henry Turner, Ayanna Thompson, Daniel Vitkus, Jeremy Lopez, Mary Anne Hutchinson, Frank Bergmann, Mary Ann Janda, and Robert Halliday.

1. For this scene in a translation that my paraphrase echoes, see the opening of the second discourse, *Discourse on Method and the Meditations,* trans. F. E. Sutcliffe (New York: Penguin, 1968), 35.

2. Lars Engle quotes Rorty in his *Shakespearean Pragmatism: Market of His Time* (Chicago: University of Chicago Press, 1993), 10. Rorty's quotation is from his essay, "Habermas and Lyotard on Postmodernity," *Essays on Heidegger and Others: Philosophical Papers,* vol. 2 (Cambridge: Cambridge University Press, 1991), 172. I don't place Bacon and Descartes in contradistinction to one another as Rorty does, largely because I see Descartes engaged in the same preoccupations as those that Rorty credits exclusively to Bacon. Rorty claims to dislike Descartes's foundational philosophy, which he discredits, but I distinguish between what are really only pretended foundations in Cartesian thought, which yield multiple pragmatic benefits, and those theoretical foundations that elude and forever lose for us the misanthropes who make no tacit compromise toward pragmatic social life.

3. All references to *Timon of Athens* are from the Arden edition, ed. H. J. Oliver (London: Methuen, 1959; Croatia: Thomas Nelson and Sons, 1997).

4. In the only book-length study of the play, Rolf Soellner reads this exchange as having a similarly negative inflection, calling it "casually ominous." But while Soellner is invested in seeing the aging of the world as the carrier of threat here, I think he may also be responding implicitly to the tension between originality and cliché as a key obstacle to establishing cultural value. *Timon of Athens: Shakespeare's Pessimistic Tragedy* (Columbus: Ohio State University Press, 1979), 3.

5. See Thomas M. Greene, *The Light in Troy: Imitation and Discovery in Renaissance Poetry*, Elizabethan Club Series, no. 7 (New Haven: Yale University Press, 1982); and Harold Ogden White, *Plagiarism and Imitation during the English Renaissance: A Study in Critical Distinctions*, Harvard Studies in English, no. 12 (New York: Octagon Press, 1975).

6. For Ken Jackson, this removal of contingent factors might be expressed as a rejection of "exchange" and its concomitant dynamism in favor of the irreversible moment in which Timon's "gift" can be given absolutely. Ken Jackson, "'One Wish' or the Possibility of the Impossible: Derrida, the Gift, and God in *Timon of Athens*," *Shakespeare Quarterly* 52 (2001): 34–66. While I admire and have learned much from Jackson's article, almost none of our terms overlap: what he sees as a deeply religious core desire in Timon I interpret much less charitably as Timon's delusions about secular subjectivity, fueled by a wish not for God, or "the infinite," as G. Wilson Knight has argued (in an essay pivotal for Jackson), but for terrestrial authority. See Knight's "The Pilgrimage of Hate: An Essay on *Timon of Athens*," in *The Wheel of Fire: Interpretations of Shakespearean Tragedy* (Oxford: Oxford University Press, 1930; London: Routledge, 2001), 235–72.

7. The *Riverside Shakespeare* is conspicuous in advancing this view (ed. G. Blakemore Evans, 2d ed. [Boston: Houghton Mifflin, 1997]), but Arden editor H. J. Oliver, in a revealing defense of the play as "not merely an inferior *King Lear*" (xli), also brings this resonance home. Maurice Charney traces this traditional comparison to Coleridge, who found *Timon* to be "a *Lear* of the satirical drama, a *Lear* of domestic or ordinary life . . . a *Lear*, therefore, without its soul-scorching flashes, its ear-cleaving thunder claps, its meteoric splendours." Charney's reception history of the play, chronicling the numerous efforts by a variety of critics to contradict the dismissal of *Timon* as unfinished or artistically inferior, is testament to the entrenched status of the original detraction; "Coriolanus and Timon of Athens," in *Shakespeare: A Bibliographical Guide*, ed. Stanley Wells (Oxford: Clarendon Press, 1990), 306.

8. See Oliver's section "Inconsistencies and Loose Ends" in his introduction to the play (xiv–xvi). Frank Kermode, in his own introduction, also notes that "Shakespeare had clearly not made up his mind about the value of the Athenian talent. He uses different values inconsistently" (*Riverside Shakespeare*, 1490).

9. Much has been made of metaphors of eating in the play, and the method by which Timon himself is eaten. See Michael Chorost, "Biological Finance in Shakespeare's *Timon of Athens*," *English Literary Renaissance* 21 (1991): 349–70; Ruth Morse, "Unfit for Human Consumption: Shakespeare's Unnatural Food," *Shakespeare Jahrbuch* 119 (1983): 125–49; and Daniel Ross, "'What a Number of Men Eats Timon,': Consumption in *Timon of Athens*," *Iowa State Journal of Research* 59 (1985): 273–84. For a remarkable analysis of eating as a sexual metaphor in the play, see also Jody Greene, "'You must eat men': The Sodomitic Economy of Renaissance Patronage," *GLQ* 1 (1994): 163–97.

10. Lucian, *The Works of Lucian of Samosata,* trans. H. W. Fowler and F. G. Fowler (Oxford: Clarendon Press, 1905), 32–33. This English translation of Lucian is quoted in Appendix C of the Arden edition of the play. No English translation of the dialogue is known to have existed until Thomas Heywood's "Misanthropos, or the Man-Hater," written in heroic couplets and published in a hefty volume with translations of other Lucian dialogues as well as dialogues by Textor and Erasmus, short dramas, forty-six emblems, speeches, funeral elegies, epitaphs, and translations of Italian and Latin epigrams; *Pleasant Dialogves and Dramma's* (London, 1637).

11. The two lines cut from the Oxford text (and therefore also from the Norton), which some have construed to be a third epitaph, written in a language the soldier can read, are, "Timon is dead, who hath outstretch'd his span: / Some beast read this, there does not live a man" (5.3.3–4). For a consideration of the lines' potential as a third epitaph, see Oliver's note in the Arden edition.

12. Frank Kermode, in the Riverside introduction to the play, noting the contradiction of the two epitaphs, suggests that Shakespeare "would have cancelled one in making a final version" (1490), and Arden's editor concurs: "There seems little doubt that Shakespeare copied down from North's *Plutarch* two epitaphs, each in a couplet, meaning to omit one or the other (probably the first) in revision" (139–40).

13. As is widely known, *Timon of Athens* was apparently a late addition to the First Folio, taking the original place of *Troilus and Cressida* in the Folio's print run when that play's copyright came under last-minute arbitration. The Arden editor recites the history and a sufficient bibliography for the issue on p. xiii and in the first note of his Introduction. For a more recent meditation on *Troilus and Cressida*'s murky printing history as it relates to *Timon*'s appearance in the First Folio, see Phebe Jensen, "The Textual Politics of *Troilus and Cressida,*" *Shakespeare Quarterly* 46 (1995): 414–23.

14. And indeed, epigrammatic verses that might be chiseled on tombstones were, in Jacobean England, generally limited to two lines, both to spare funerary expense in preparing the stones with their limited surface area and as part of the poetic challenge and aesthetic appeal of the form. For an excellent introduction to the English epitaph as a historical, political, and theoretical literary form of the later Renaissance, surviving into the nineteenth century, see Joshua Scodel, *The English Poetic Epitaph: Commemoration and Conflict from Jonson to Wordsworth* (Ithaca, N.Y.: Cornell University Press, 1991).

15. In his "Life of Marcus Antonius," Plutarch attributes the first two lines to Timon himself and the second to an apparently more familiar epitaph attributed to the poet Callimachus; see Sir Thomas North's translation of *Plutarch's Lives,* ed. Roland Baughman, 8 vols. (New York: Limited Editions, 1941), 7:169.

16. Though I am generally arguing in this chapter for finding ways to incorporate the play's inconsistencies into a harmonious understanding of its larger fiction, the possibility for treating this play as a single- or dual-author draft that had not yet been polished through the process of stage production offers a tentative glimpse at the rough state in which a primary author's material—his "foul papers"—might have arrived into the hands of a theater company before being worked collaboratively into a more polished work. This approach, which I do not pursue here as it runs contrary to my present interests, would hold fascinating implications for the cult of the single author that some recent work has labored

to question; see especially Jeffrey Masten, *Textual Intercourse: Collaboration, Authorship, and Sexualities in Renaissance Drama* (Cambridge: Cambridge University Press, 1997). On the other hand, for a recent suggestion that *Timon* was both written and performed publicly at least early enough to be parodied in Marston's *Jack Drum's Entertainment,* see Sandra Billington, "Was *Timon of Athens* Performed before 1604?" *Notes and Queries,* n.s., 45 (1998): 351–53. Billington argues, as John Jowett has, for Middleton's coauthorship based on both topical and circumstantial evidence. Jowett's argument was made at the Shakespeare Association of America in Miami, 12–14 April 2001, in his paper "Middleton and Debt in *Timon of Athens,*" for the paper session "Middleton: Men, Women, and Money."

17. Erving Goffman, *The Presentation of Self in Everyday Life* (Garden City, N.Y.: Doubleday, 1959), 56.

18. Ibid.

19. Sigmund Freud, "A Note upon the 'Mystic Writing Pad,'" *The Standard Edition of the Complete Works of Sigmund Freud,* vol. 19, trans. James Strachey (London: Hogarth Press, 1961), 227.

20. Jacques Derrida, "Freud and the Scene of Writing," in *Writing and Difference,* trans. Alan Bass (Chicago: University of Chicago Press, 1978), 196–231.

21. In "Freud and the Scene of Writing," Derrida writes, "Freud first considers writing as a technique subservient to memory, an external, auxiliary technique of psychical memory which is not memory itself" (221). For the major work establishing Derrida's critique of Western logocentrism, see his earlier *Of Grammatology,* trans. Gayatri Chakravorty Spivak (Baltimore: Johns Hopkins University Press, 1974).

22. This passage is from a translation of Descartes's *Meditations* quoted by Judith Butler in "How Can I Deny That These Hands and This Body Are Mine?" *Qui Parle* 11(1) (1997): 1–20, repr. in *Material Events: Paul de Man and the Afterlife of Theory,* ed. Tom Cohen et al. (Minneapolis: University of Minnesota Press, 2001), 254–73. For a further, deeper discussion of this Cartesian passage, see Jacques Lezra, *Unspeakable Subjects: The Genealogy of the Event in Early Modern Europe* (Stanford: Stanford University Press, 1997), 102–13.

23. Butler, "How Can I Deny," 260.

24. Ibid.

25. This quotation from Descartes's correspondence is found in Jean-Luc Marion, *On Descartes' Metaphysical Prism: The Constitution and the Limits of Onto-theo-logy in Cartesian Thought,* trans. Jeffrey L. Kosky (Chicago: University of Chicago Press, 1990), 131; originally published as *Sur le prisme métaphysique de Descartes: constitution et limites de l'onto-théo-logie dans la pensée cartésienne* (Paris: Presses Universitaires de France, 1986).

26. Butler, "How Can I Deny," 259.

27. Indeed, antiquarians themselves were frequently at a loss to read the inscriptions they happened to find. In his journal later selectively published in Samuel Purchas's *Purchas His Pilgrimes* (London, 1625), Thomas Coryate, the early seventeenth-century world traveler from Odcombe, England, recorded such an experience at what he believed were the ruins of Troy: "In our iourney to the Pallace, wee found certaine faire peeces of stone, as curiously carued and wrought with exquisite borders and workes as euer I saw. In one great peece, but broken, I found an inscription, which what it ment I could not deuise, it was written in Latine characters, *viz.* the word *Numinid:* likewise after I found a stately peece of white Marble

of some foure foot long, and two foot broad, on the which was a very ancient inscription in Latine words written with capitall Letters, but they are such exoticke characters, and so worne out with antiquitie, that neither I my selfe, nor any else of my whole Company could perfectly read it" (1815). Elsewhere in the same record, Coryate humorously demonstrates that conclusions can be drawn despite such limitations: "It grieued me to the heart that I could not learne either by inscriptions, or any other meanes, whose Monuments these were: for it is vaine to be induced by coniectures, to say they were these or these mans; onely I hope no man will taxe me of a rash opinion, if I beleeue one of them might just be the Monument of King *Ilus,* the enlarger of the Citie of *Troy*" (1813-14). For a history of English travelers to Greece and the Levant, and for the commentary they generated, see Warner G. Rice, "Early English Travelers to Greece and the Levant," *Essays and Studies in English and Comparative Literature,* vol. 10 (Ann Arbor: University of Michigan Press, 1933), 205-60.

28. Cyriacus of Ancona, an Italian merchant who lived from roughly 1391 to 1455, is famously one of the first collectors of Greek and Latin inscriptions off monuments and reliefs, which he would sketch and record in the notebooks from his travels. For a critical edition of a single year's material from Cyriacus's collected "commentaria" (in untranslated Latin and Greek), including reproductions of twenty-four of his sketches and inscriptions, see Edward W. Bodnar and Charles Mitchell, *Cyriacus of Ancona's Journeys in the Propontis and the Northern Aegean: 1444-1445,* Memoirs of the American Philosophical Society, no. 112 (Philadelphia: American Philosophical Society, 1976). For evidence of English antiquarianism in the period of the sort that would have included sketches or descriptions of Greek and Roman sarcophagi and memorials, see Rice, "Early English Travelers," and for a historical survey of British voyages to Crete and the development of antiquarian methods, see Davina Huxley, *Cretan Quests: British Explorers, Excavators and Historians* (London: British School at Athens, 2000). In related work, Henry Turner has analyzed the novel aspects of antiquarianism and chorography occurring about and within English borders during this period, pitting its tinge of dilettantism against satirical treatments of it and also against more conservative traditions of chronicling national history; see his "Nashe's Red Herring: Epistemologies of the Commodity in *Lenten Stuffe* (1599)," *English Literary History* 68 (2001): 529-61.

29. The child's toy that fascinated Freud is actually a modern variation of an implement that has a long history in classical and medieval pedagogy and record keeping. Because its surface could be smoothed clean with a thumb or heated stylus, the wax tablet, when not employed for school exercises or as a notebook, was primarily intended for first compositions, or drafts, of legal documents, for example, or poetic verse, which could then after inspection be carefully copied onto more expensive and more permanent writing surfaces such as papyrus or vellum. See Michelle P. Brown, "The Role of the Wax Tablet in Medieval Literacy: A Reconsideration in Light of a Recent Find from York," *British Library Journal* 20 (1994): 1-16; and Richard and Mary Rouse's two essays, "Wax Tablets," *Language and Communication* 9 (1989): 175-91, and "The Vocabulary of Wax Tablets," *Harvard Library Bulletin,* n.s., 1(3) (1990): 12-19.

30. Amanda Collins has written about Venice's wish during the sixteenth century to secure its place as the "daughter of Rome" by means of epigraphic evidence, though its hopes were dashed by a diligent scholar and Florentine, Vincenzo Borghini. The city of Viterbo in contrast reveled in the falsified epigraphic scholarship connecting it to Egyptian origins.

Annius, the Dominican friar responsible for fabricating these origins, used a technique that connected cities to historical personages based on likenesses in their names—a technique interestingly called *aequivocatio.* See Amanda Collins, "Renaissance Epigraphy and Its Legitimating Potential: Annius of Viterbo, Etruscan Inscriptions, and the Origins of Civilization," in *The Afterlife of Inscriptions: Reusing, Rediscovering, Reinventing and Revitalizing Ancient Inscriptions,* ed. Alison Cooley, Bulletin of the Institute of Classical Studies Supplement, no. 75 (London: Institute of Classical Studies, 2000), esp. 59–61. As note 10 of Collins's article cites, Christopher Ligota analyzes the concept of *aequivocatio* as a factor in epigraphic analysis; see his "Annius of Viterbo and Historical Method," *Journal of the Warburg and Courtauld Institutes* 50 (1987): 44–56.

31. The playwright could have learned this ancient Roman practice, as punishment for a defeated or humiliated army or populace, from its description in Plutarch's *Life of Crassus,* in which Crassus punishes his own army with decimation for their cowardice: "Hereupon Crassus was grievously offended with Mummius [who had acted against his orders], and receiving his soldiers that fled [and, in fleeing, abandoned their equipment], gave them other armor and weapons, but yet upon sureties that they should keep them better thenceforth than they had before done. Now Crassus of the five hundred that were in the first ranks, and that first fled, them he divided into fifty times ten, and out of every one of those he put one of them to death as the lot fell out, renewing again the ancient discipline of the Romans to punish cowardly soldiers, which of long time before had not been put in use" (*Plutarch's Lives,* 4:405).

32. "Shakespeare, Scrooge of Stratford," *New Statesman,* 26 March 2001, 30–31.

Marston, Collaboration, *and* Eastward Ho!

SUZANNE GOSSETT

*E*ASTWARD *Ho!* WAS published three times in 1605 with apparently thorough external evidence of its circumstances of production on the title page: "As It was playd in the *Black-friers. By* The Children of her Maiesties Reuels. *Made by* Geo: Chapman. Ben: Ionson. Ion: Marston" (Quarto 1, 1605). The triple authorship of this play has never been questioned, and I do not intend to question it here, yet a number of factors suggest that Marston's role was anomalous. First, despite Drummond's report that Jonson said "he was delated by Sr James Murray to the King for writting something against the Scots jn a play Eastward hoe and voluntarily Imprissonned himself w^t Chapman and Marston, who had written it amongst y^m," Marston seems not to have been imprisoned along with Jonson and Chapman, and the personal consequences of his participation are unclear.[1] Albert Tricomi proposes that Anthony Nixon's reference in *The Black Year* (1606) to Marston being "sent away *Westward* for carping both at Court, Cittie and countrie" may mean he was "detained or imprisoned, albeit elsewhere."[2] Yet we have no letters from him or any documents referring specifically to his imprisonment or, for that matter, to his participation. Jonson and Chapman's letters from prison to the king and to Salisbury refer by name only to each other, although Chapman assures the king that the "chiefe offences are but two Clawses, and both of them not our owne."[3] By July 1606, whatever had happened to him in the intervening months, Marston was restored to favor and writing a city pageant. Next, attempts to break down the authorship of the play have come to widely varied conclusions about the extent of Marston's participation, some critics finding Marston only in the first act, others detecting his hand intermittently throughout the play. Finally, recent scholarship has problematized the issue of collaboration in other parts of the Marston canon and, indirectly, the likelihood of his participating willingly in a three-man production. In fact, it seems entirely possible that Marston had no effective experience of collaboration before he took part in the production of *Eastward Ho!*

By contrast, the early career of Ben Jonson forms a progression from a kind of apprenticeship spent writing with other men to preponderantly individual authorship. Whether or not Jonson was already writing plays by himself—possibly *The Case is Altered* was composed early for Pembroke's Men—by 1597 he had written *The Isle of Dogs* with Nashe, and, once out of prison for that offense, had begun working for Henslowe, who paid, for example, for *Hot Anger Soon Cold* by Porter, Chettle, and Jonson in 1598 and *Page of Plymouth* by Jonson and Dekker in 1599. That same year Henslowe also paid Jonson, Dekker, Chettle, and an "other Jentellman" for *Robert the Second, the King of Scots Tragedy.*[4] Jonson gained attention as the single author of *Every Man in His Humour* in 1598 and *Every Man Out of His Humour* in 1599, yet even as late as 1603, when he was an established if controversial figure, a "second pen" had a "good share" in his *Sejanus.* This pattern was not uncommon among early modern dramatists: Thomas Middleton, for instance, began by working with Dekker, Drayton, Munday, and Webster on *Caesar's Fall; or, Two Shapes* in the spring of 1602 before writing his first solo drama, *The Chester Tragedy,* later that year. He then proceeded to alternate solo writing and collaboration throughout his career.[5]

The second pen of *Sejanus* is often thought to have been Chapman. Perhaps his relationship with Jonson went back to 1597, when Chapman was paid by Henslowe for his "play book and two acts of a tragedy of Benjamin's plot."[6] Chapman may or may not have actively collaborated with Jonson on that unnamed play, but in his later dramatic career he, like Jonson, wrote alone. In one particularly intense period, fourteen months in 1598 and 1599, Chapman worked on seven plays, including the tragedy on Benjamin's plot, and David Kay suggests that he "ventured into playwriting periodically to support his translation of Homer."[7]

John Marston, whose father was a reader at the Middle Temple, certainly did not need to write for money early in his life, although the consequences of his break with his father are sometimes assumed to account for his appearance in Henslowe's diary. (W. Reavley Gair states that "What evidence there is suggests that Marston became a private theatre playwright in order to avoid debtors' prison," but Philip Finkelpearl considers it "fair to assume that Reader Marston's only son and heir was relatively wealthy after his father's death in 1599."[8]) In what has been a standard view of Marston's early career, Chambers assumes that the form his early work took was largely collaborative, either from need or from inexperience in writing for the theater. Chambers opines that an entry in Henslowe's diary for 28 September 1599, in which Henslowe paid two pounds to "Mr Maxton the new poete" on behalf of the Admiral's Men, "was meant to make up a complete sum of £6 10s. for *The King of Scots* and that Marston was the 'other Jentellman' who collaborated with Chettle, Dekker, and Jonson on that lost play." However, "The setting up of the Paul's boys in 1599 saved Marston from Henslowe. For them he successively revised *Histriomastix*, wrote *Antonio and Mellida* and *Jack Drum's Entertainment*, helped Dekker with *Satiromastix*, and wrote *What You Will*."[9]

All of the collaboration implied here has, bit by bit, been reconsidered and challenged since 1923. First, there is no evidence that Marston was the "other Jentellman" of *The King of Scots;* Chambers himself noted that Greg proposed Porter for that position. In 1958 Gustav Cross suggested that Marston may instead have been working on *Lust's Dominion* or *The Spanish Moor's Tragedy,* for which Henslowe paid Dekker, Haughton, and Day in February 1600; based on elements of Marston's style and vocabulary visible in that play, this assignment has been generally accepted.[10] Calling Marston "but an exotic bird of passage in Henslowe's drab world," Cyrus Hoy argued that in September 1599 the dramatist worked on revising *Lust's Dominion,* originally a play of the early 1590s, but abandoned Henslowe and the play for the newly established company at Paul's. Henslowe then called upon his trio of regulars, Dekker, Haughton, and Day, to finish the job. Thus, although a few scenes contain linguistic signs of both Dekker and Marston, this results from Dekker "reworking some of the scenes that Marston had previously retouched" rather than from simultaneous collaboration.[11] Recently Charles Cathcart has reexamined the authorship, date, and revisions of *Lust's Dominion* and concluded that the play, which was only printed in 1657 and then attributed to Marlowe only in the second issue, "may be accounted for by the revision by Dekker and his colleagues of an unfinished play by Marston without the necessity of positing an earlier version."[12] In either case, whether Marston the "new poet" was working on another man's material or had begun and then abandoned a play of his own, he was still working alone.

Similarly, *Histriomastix* may not have been a collaboration. Scholars have been divided between the older view of E. K. Chambers and Anthony Caputi, who assume Marston revised an old play; the view of those such as Finkelpearl and Albert Kernan, who believe Marston wrote the play alone, probably for an Inns of Court performance in 1598; and those such as David Lake, who believe it was a product of two hands. (Significantly, editing Marston with Michael Neill, MacDonald P. Jackson, the dean of attribution studies, takes no stand on whether Marston was the sole author of *Histriomastix* or working in collaboration.[13]) Using traditional methods of attribution that have been increasingly refined in studies of Middleton and Shakespeare, Lake does a careful analysis of the play's "style," by which he means primarily vocabulary, turns of phrase, and passages parallel to other Marston writing, and its "linguistic features," by which he means the presence or absence of colloquialisms such as *I'd* or *'em,* elisions, alternate verbal forms such as *does* or *doth,* favored exclamations such as *pish* or *tush,* and consistent preferences between word forms such as *while/whilst* and *among/amongst.*[14] Such linguistic features are presumed to be largely unconscious and thus particularly good indicators of authorship. Lake concludes that "the fact that non-Marstonian linguistic features overlie speeches very Marstonian in style proves that Marston was not merely revising some old play; he was being revised himself. At least, his is not the last hand in these portions of the play." Lake hypothesizes that the other author "was one of Marston's friends at the Middle Temple" who began and completed the play.[15] Thus Lake's scenario of dual authorship, like revision of an old play, would again not require Marston to have been actively engaged with another writer.

Roslyn Knutson has recently denied Marston's hand in *Histriomastix* altogether.[16] James Bednarz's reexamination confirms Marston's presence in the authorship by showing how Jonson, in *Every Man Out of His Humour,* mocked Marston's language in the play and in *The Scourge of Villanie* together, as he did in *Poetaster.* But Bednarz further complicates any vision of the play as a collaboration. Noting that the extant version contains material that could not have been written before 1604/5, that is, a reference to the very popular Sir Petronel Flash from *Eastward Ho!,* Bednarz concludes that *Histriomastix* must have been altered after it was parodied in *Every Man Out,* which was published in 1600. *Histriomastix* was first published in a quarto of 1610, and we do not know how different the printed text was from "from the script of the controversial play." It thus remains possible that the play "either began or ended its life at the Inns of Court."[17] If it was altered for the academic milieu *after* it was acted at Paul's, the theories of Bednarz and Lake may converge—that is, we may return to the "friend" in the Middle Temple whom Lake imagined as the last hand in the text. But in any case, once again Marston was not actively engaged with another dramatist in the period in which he either created or adapted the play.

Satiromastix, too, has ceased to be considered a compositional collaboration, at least on the verbal level that traditionally obtains in attribution studies. Hoy explains, "The plans for it as anticipated in *Poetaster* call for two authors, and Dekker's plural 'Poetasters' in his prefatory address 'To the World' . . . has led to a general assumption that Marston aided him in the play. This is possible so far as a contribution to the dramatic portraiture and the satiric strategies are concerned, but Marston had nothing to do with the actual writing of the play."[18] Bednarz agrees: "Playing his assigned role, Dekker refers to himself in the quarto's dedication as a collaborator even though he was not."[19]

And finally, to anticipate, Marston's last dramatic endeavor, *The Insatiate Countess,* published first as by John Marston (Quarto 1, 1613), next as by "Lewis Machin and William Bacster" (Quarto 1, second issue), and finally as by "William Barksteed" (Quarto 3, substitute title page, 1631), is, as Giorgio Melchiori argues in his Revels edition, most probably a play Marston began alone but abandoned when he gave up his theatrical career, probably more or less at the time, 8 June 1608, when he was imprisoned for his play against the Scots.[20] Perhaps symbolically, in some copies of this "diachronic collaboration," such as the one in the Bodleian Library, Marston's name has been "physically cut out," apparently a temporary measure before the printing of a substitute title page could give credit to Machin and Bacster. The final shape of the play, as Lucy Munro shows, was much affected by its staging at the Whitefriars Theatre, which she treats as another collaborator in its construction. But as Marston never wrote for this theatre and "possibly never visited it," he was once again not a participant in the collaborative elements of this creation.[21]

This survey of Marston's career highlights how atypical was his work on *Eastward Ho!* He was temporarily reconciled with his once and future enemy Ben Jonson—notoriously, Jonson would later report to Drummond that "he had many quarrels with Marston beat him & took his Pistol from him, wrote his *Poetaster* [1601] on him."[22] Marston was instead writing in response to and in competition with Thomas Dekker, coauthor of *Westward Ho!* but also the author with whom Jonson, in *Every Man Out of His Humour, Poetaster,* and possibly *Cynthia's Revels,* had repeatedly associated Marston. More importantly, Marston was apparently engaged in simultaneous joint composition, rather than revision or independent work.

Heather Hirschfeld has recently argued that the very fact of collaboration in this case was parodic and angry: "In *Eastward Hoe,* collaborative work signifies the complicated and vexed response of private theater playwrights to the democratic mode and mood of their public theater counterparts."[23] By writing collaboratively for the boys, Hirschfeld believes, Webster and Dekker had imported "into the private theater milieu a form of writing associated almost exclusively with the public amphitheaters" and invited parody not just of their content but of their production method.[24]

It is true that *Westward Ho!* introduced a new form of authorship to Paul's. However, the children's companies that reopened after 1599 were quite unlike their 1580s forebears for whom John Lyly wrote. For one thing, they were clearly commercial operations rather than choir schools. More importantly, the new companies of "boys" at Paul's and at the Blackfriars themselves differed strikingly. Gair estimates that at Paul's the boys "ranged in age from six to fourteen or fifteen. At Blackfriars . . . the actors were 'youths' of seventeen or eighteen or older." It is thus less surprising that once he moved from Paul's to Blackfriars, "Marston, the innovator of children's drama, seems to be drawing closer at Blackfriars to the more common stage techniques of the Globe and the adult companies."[25] There is plenty of parody in *Eastward Ho!,* but there is no need to assume it was the sullying of the private theaters with collaborative writing that stimulated it, or that drove Marston to change his writing habits.

By arguing that the collaborating authors of *Eastward Ho!* indulge in a "rhetorical strategy of stylistic erasure designed to eliminate, and thereby protect, the writers' individual signatures from the play," Hirschfeld would appear to bar the possibility of specific authorial assignment for parts of the comedy.[26] This seems unlikely to stop research on the topic, even given increased theoretical diffidence about "the author." Yet her argument—like Hoy's description of Henslowe's "drab world," which discounts Henslowe's involvement with plays by Marlowe and Kyd—is a particularly clear example of the way in which attitudes toward collaboration affect interpretation of evidence. Her very words seem chosen to suggest that to collaborate is to be diminished: she claims that "the narrative and rhetorical structures of *Eastward* are . . . designed to blunt the *anxieties* attendant on *sacrificing* individual dramatic voice to a joint text. In this play Chapman, Jonson and Marston deliberately *eliminate the stylistic self-expression* that, in other venues, they champion." Instead, "they saturate their play with common places to preempt *threats to their personal and professional status.*"[27] Implicitly, then, despite her attention to the influence of the constraining conditions of production, Hirschfeld accepts a view of authorship as primarily individualistic and of collaboration as a sign of inferiority.

The long career of the well-connected, if impecunious, Beaumont and Fletcher, which began immediately after *Eastward Ho!,* demonstrates that collaboration, per se, could not have been uniformly regarded as threatening, down-market, or unfit for the private theatres. (Finkelpearl assigns *The Woman Hater* to 1606 and treats it as a collaboration; it was produced at Paul's.[28]) In contrast, Jonson's elimination of the "second hand" in *Sejanus* anticipates the romantic championing of the individual author as solitary genius. Thus, to borrow Hirschfeld's terms but modify her conclusions, the "practice of joint writing" is not only "historically embedded" but "personally inflected"; it certainly represented something different to Dekker than it did to Jonson. And the interpretation of "joint writing" is also historically embedded, as repeated attempts to deconstruct the composition of *Eastward Ho!* have shown.[29]

Eastward Ho!'s authorship has been analyzed both impressionistically and by means of linguistic evidence. Apparently substantial agreement about the ascription of much of the play has gradually emerged, but some scenes (e.g., 2.1) have at times been assigned to each of the three authors. I will shortly turn to the drawbacks and complications of the various techniques employed, but it is important to realize that underlying disagreements about specific assignments is a more fundamental divergence of opinion about the methods and possibilities of collaborative authorship. The tendency has been to exaggerate and simplify two extreme positions. On the basis of evidence from Henslowe's diary and contemporary lawsuits, G. E. Bentley determined that "Separate composition of individual acts is a division of labor which was quite common from 1590 to 1642."[30] Those who imagine that authors must have worked largely alone and that collaborators did not, even could not, write jointly, consequently slide quickly over the fact that many scenes of *Eastward Ho!* bear indications of more than one hand. Lake concludes that "the three authors wrote compact allotments of work: Chapman had the largest share (1461 lines), followed by Jonson (974 lines) and then Marston (328 lines)."[31] Parrott implies work based on a different structural division by assigning Chapman the subplot of Sir Petronel, Security, and Winifred.[32] On the other hand, accepting Schoenbaum's suggestion that some dramatists preferred "to work in intimate association, going over one another's drafts, revising, deleting, and interpolating" (a form of joint authorship that Bentley identi- fied with the modern theater, although in a lawsuit Dekker explained that for *Keep the Widow Waking* he wrote not only "two sheets containing the first act" but also a speech for the last scene), Van Fossen, the Revels editor, is comfortable finding "overwhelming" evidence in 4.1 for the hands of all three authors.[33] Earlier Simpson, without explaining the method of production, divvied up some scenes (e.g., 2.1, 4.1) into as many as four parts. Proceeding impressionistically, he found in 3.2, for example, Marston's hand in "the quick movement of the action" and the "vulgar indecency of Gertrude's reference to her old relations with Quicksilver" but "Jonson's manner" in the "firmer" style and "steadier" action later in the scene.[34]

Accumulated scholarship on *Eastward Ho!* has seen the bulk of the comedy as composed sequentially by Marston, Chapman, and lastly Jonson. Even Van Fossen concludes that Marston "was assigned the opening, Act I and Act II, scene i. . . . Chapman's stint ran from II.ii to III.iv. . . . To Jonson was assigned the *dénouement,* from the opening of IV.ii . . . to the closing scene. . . . The three segments thus assigned to individual authors are each tight-knit, almost self-contained." Van Fossen treats IV.i as an exception; only this scene "must have been reserved for the kind of close collaboration suggested by Schoenbaum."[35] However, editing the play for the Cambridge Jonson, David Kay and I have found evidence that many scenes, at least by the time they reached their final form, had been touched, or touched up, by more than one author. Some, such as 3.2, appear from linguistic and stylistic markers to combine sections by different authors. These hypotheses are not irreconcilable: assuming that the men planned the play together (or perhaps agreed to work from one of "Benjamin's" plots) and each then made a preliminary draft of his assigned sections, they might nevertheless have had meetings at which they improved and enlarged each others' work. For example, Marstonian elements and echoes in the acts presumably by Chapman and Jonson run the gamut from a paradoxical praise of usury similar to the praise of bawds in *The Dutch Courtesan* (but also recalling the paradoxes in Chapman's *All Fools*), description of the stages in a rake's progress structured like the cyclic progression from Peace to Plenty, Pride, Envy and War in *Histriomastix,* to favorite words, proverbs, and Shakespearean echoes. Equally significant, the staging of the prison scenes (5.3 and 5.5), in which Security, heard but not seen, tells Bramble that his case "is stone walls, and iron grates," seems to be based on Marston's *Antonio's Revenge,* where Mellida, imprisoned, "goes from the grate."[36] Marston, who had "virtually disappeared from sight for three years" after being attacked in *Poetaster* (1601),[37] and had actually been fined and expelled from his rooms in the Middle Temple in October 1601,[38] had resurfaced or returned by 1604, when he wrote *The Malcontent.* So all three writers were—until Marston fled again—in London. The *Eastward Ho!* collaboration was probably more like those of Beaumont and Fletcher than like the one that produced *The Two Noble Kinsmen,* which Lois Potter suggests was intentionally structured so that it could be completed by two authors who did not expect to see each other frequently.[39]

Turning now to specific attributions, we glimpse the weakness of much earlier analysis as soon as we ask a basic question: who conceived *Eastward Ho!*? Most modern editors follow Herford and Simpson in assuming "the idea of the play to have originated with Marston." But why? Simpson's only explanation is that Touchstone and Sindefy "reflect two contrasted types which strongly appealed to him."[40] In light of the contrasting character types, including citizens and women of dubious virtue, who appear throughout Jonson's canon, this does not bear responding to, especially since the opposed apprentices seem more basic to the structure. Parrott, too, "fancies" that the "initiative for this collaboration" came from Marston. As already noted, he believes that Chapman's work was "limited to the underplot"; to confirm Jonson's "slight connexion with the work" he invokes Jonson's claim that Chapman and Marston "had written it amongst them" and his failure to include *Eastward Ho!* in his *Works.*[41] While biographical and bibliographical evidence is stronger than mere impressionism, neither of Parrott's explanations is self-substantiating. Jonson carefully excluded collaborative work from his *Works,* and his allegations regarding Chapman and Marston seventeen years later sound merely exculpatory of himself. Caputi's argument that Marston learned how to construct *The Dutch Courtesan* from working with Jonson on *Eastward Ho!* (both are dated

1605, and arguments about priority continue) could instead suggest that Jonson was the motivator and model for the collaborated play.[42] In fact, all the claimed parallels to *The Dutch Courtesan,* including the paradoxes and the similarities between Gertrude's song in 5.1 and Francescina's song in 2.2 pointed out long ago by Parrott, demonstrate the weakness of this method. Given that in all likelihood the two plays were being written simultaneously, the order of influence could go in either direction.

Stronger support for a Marston initiative might be found in commercial rivalry. It was Marston who owned a one-sixth share in the Blackfriars,[43] and, despite the prologue's disclaimer of envy or imitation of Paul's *Westward Ho!,* it is possible that he saw an opportunity for the company to profit by showing "that eastward westwards still exceeds" (Prologue, 9). If Marston undertook to write the play in collaboration, it could have been the economic incentive, along with the need to complete and stage this provocative satire before the king's return from his progress, that drove him to work unusually closely with other men.[44]

Almost all analysis of *Eastward Ho!*'s authorship has been distorted by dependence on unexamined attitudes toward collaboration among early modern playwrights. In searching the text for clues, various scholars at various times have assumed that the author changed when the play shifted from prose to verse, for example, in 3.2 (Simpson); assumed that the collaborators allocated the plots, so that the significant shift in 3.2 is to the subplot, the verse being incidental (Parrott); worked from presumptions about which author was more likely to use bawdy (Swinburne) or alchemical language (Parrott); depended on selectively noted parallels of words, sentence structure, or character (Simpson); invoked compositorial variation (C. G. Petter thinks the compositors worked at least in part with the separate foul papers of each author[45]); and treated spellings and the use of Latin in stage directions as indicators (Parrott). Almost invariably, however, they have assumed that they were searching for one author at a time, in what Jeffrey Masten calls "an anachronistic attempt to divine the singular author of each scene, phrase, and word."[46]

A good example of the division of opinion concerns the Prologue. This is assigned by Parrott and Simpson to Jonson, largely on grounds of the scornful tone. Petter assigns it to Marston, claiming that two appearances of "de" for "ed" indicate that it could not be Jonson's. Petter also comments that Marston's connection to the Queen's Revels Company makes the ascription "most plausible."[47] Disregarding ed/de, Lake finds "no linguistic evidence" for the authorship of the Prologue or Epilogue.[48] No one has assigned the Prologue to Chapman since Sykes in 1915, who pointed out its similarity to the Prologue to the second quarto of *Bussy D'Ambois*. That, however, was printed late—1641—and its Prologue is presumed to be a contemporary addition. However, the citation from Plutarch in line 10 of *Eastward Ho!*'s Prologue, "Honour the sun's fair rising, not his setting," occurs in both Plutarch's *Life of Pompey* and his *Morals*, both drawn on by Chapman shortly before in *Caesar and Pompey* (1604-05). For the ironic tone of the first ten lines, where, as Hirschfeld comments, "the second clauses undercut the first ones, confusing or revoking the praise,"[49] Kay invokes the mocking comparison of wits and poets in the Prologue to Chapman's *All Fools*. We thus will suggest that Chapman is at least as likely an author for the introductory poem as either of the other collaborators—or, perhaps, the prominently placed Prologue was itself the result of collaboration.

Insistence on uninterrupted and "compact" divisions weakens the most careful examination of the question, David Lake's. Lake uses "contrastive linguistic features" from a large corpus of other plays of the three authors, including interjections, word forms, elisions (e.g., *y'are, i'th*), and variant Latin and English speech prefixes as the basis for a thorough analysis that expands and corrects earlier work along these lines by Petter. Yet Lake pushes his evidence. For instance, he admits that for 3.1 there is "little linguistic evidence. The 6 instances of *them* without a single *'(h)em* might suggest Marston," but as these instances occur in two "clumps," Lake concludes that they are not really independent of each other and therefore, "When evidence is so weak, it is best to hold to the simplest hypothesis. Chapman wrote the preceding and . . . the following scene, and therefore I assign III.i also to Chapman."[50] This conclusion ignores the more obvious possibility suggested by the clumping, namely that Marston inserted two sentences into a Chapman draft. Similarly, a desire to avoid interrupting a hypothesized "Chapman section" underlies Lake's unwillingness to assign the five lines of 3.5, which climax in a parody of *Richard III*—"a boat, a boat, a boat, a full hundred marks for a boat"—to Marston, who had written a similar parody three other times. Lake concludes, "There is no linguistic evidence, but I would give the scene to Chapman on the principle of simplicity."[51] This is simplicity in violation of probability.

A further complication to linguistic analysis is the likelihood that these playwrights picked up expressions, phrases, and ideas from each other, either in conscious imitation or because the theatrical world they worked in was so small and intimate. (This is what Sheldon Zitner calls "mutual contagion of style as a result of close association."[52]) The result is that, for example, in act 1, which all analysts assign to Marston, there are a number of conspicuous parallels to plays of Chapman and Jonson. For example, Gertrude at 1.1.70 must be "attired just to the court-cut and long-tail." For conflation of the phrase "cut and long tail" (i.e., dogs of all kinds) with the court "cut" or "fashion," along with sexual allusions in "cut" and "tail," compare Chapman's *All Fools,* 5.2.189–90, "As for your mother, she was wise . . . and could set out her tail with as good grace as any she in Florence, come cut and long-tail." Again, at 1.1.111 Golding calls Quicksilver a "common shot-clog," that is, a fool or dupe invited along as company to a tavern only to pay the "shot" or bill, but otherwise regarded as a "clog" or "drag" on the festivities. The word is a Jonsonian coinage (see *OED*), first found in *Every Man Out* (1599) 5.9.47 and again in *Poetaster* (1601) 1.2.15–17. Is its use in *Eastward Ho!* an imitation, or has Jonson intruded into "Marston's" scene? As a final example, at 2.1.90— another scene normally assigned to Marston, though Lake proposes that its linguistic pattern is Chapman's and Simpson gives bits to Jonson—among other play-ends the drunken Quicksilver quotes, "Who cries on murder? Lady was it you?" The line is from Chapman's *Blind Beggar of Alexandria* (1596); it had already been quoted by Jonson in *Poetaster.* Any one of the authors might be responsible for its presence here.[53]

Lake's method assumes that the diction of all characters will uniformly express an author's unconscious preferences, unmodified by speaker or situation. In 2.1, Lake objects to Petter's citing "the extended form 'you are' (twice)" as pointing to Marston; Lake himself considers the presence of "y'are" in the scene a Chapman indicator.[54] However, "y'are" appears five times, in Touchstone's speeches usually to Quicksilver but once to Golding; "you are" appears three times, twice in Golding's speeches to Mildred and Quicksilver, once in Touchstone to Quicksilver. Touchstone's greater use of elided forms could be part of his characterization, just as Golding's formality of speech reflects his priggishness. The combination of forms suggests that the choice might have as much to do with the speaker and situation as with the author.

This review of the literature, coupled with close study of the play, leads toward agnosticism rather than to the certainty for which an editor always strives. The uniformity of style for which *Eastward Ho!* is famous might have been achieved by close work by all three authors on the final draft. Alternatively, Van Fossen points out that Jonson's characteristic abbreviation *'hem* appears seventy-five times in the play and in all but four scenes, so perhaps after the last of the collaborators' meetings Jonson went over the whole making improvements and changes, or at least copied out that final draft. Such a scenario could imply that Marston was removed from the situation and might even have already left town. However, Van Fossen notes as unexplained and "perhaps inexplicable" that *'hem* appears only four times in the last four scenes of Act 5, scenes usually attributed to Jonson.[55] Perhaps, then, the presence of *'hem* only indicates that the manuscript, or all but the final scenes, was copied by a scribe who favored that form, which Lake treats as "mere alternative spelling of the linguistic form *'em.*"[56]

We may never know how many individuals collaborated in creating *Eastward Ho!* As the last example shows yet again on the level of the letter, "the production of texts is a social process."[57] G. E. Bentley's statistics on the wide extent of early modern dramatic collaboration are more than thirty years old, but there is still much we don't understand about how this social process operated in the period before e-mailed file attachments. Ben Jonson's ambiguous phrase, "had written it amongst them," has most often been analyzed for its frustratingly opaque clues to precise responsibility for the prison-worthy elements of *Eastward Ho!* But it is equally impenetrable as a description of methodology. *How* did they write it, or any other collaborated play, amongst them?

This problem is complicated by disagreements among the "scientific" disintegrating investigators as well as between them and the metatheorists. The difficulty for an editor is to correlate two different kinds of evidence and two views of authorship. The first looks, most usefully with a certain skepticism, for gradually accumulating detail, unconscious linguistic markers and stylistic preferences pointing to one writer or another, and accepts the commonsense belief that dramatic documents were composed by individuals who had personal and discoverable histories, attitudes, and canons. The second stresses that collaboration was composition of a different kind, an additional element further constructing and constricting the agency of the individual subject. In this view collaboration led to something more like a chemical melding than a simple accumulation of parts, fundamentally undermining the possibility of an analysis that begins from the assumption of identifiable individual work. Yet even the second approach may lead in different directions. For Masten, the emphasis falls on "seeing double" and the homosocial, dispersing the authority associated in later periods with the authorial subject sought by the traditional text disintegrators. For Hirschfeld, differences may still be traced between agonistic groups of collaborators even while the internal distinctions are effaced in particular conditions of production. The appendix to Brian Vickers's new book *Shakespeare, Co-Author,* "Abolishing the Author? Theory *versus* History," which attacks attempts to move beyond positivist analysis of composition into larger questions of the nature of agency and the social construction of authorship, seems to suggest that there is no way to exist in both camps.[58]

In this atmosphere, too little attention has been paid to the different significance that collaboration had for different authors, differences that in fact suggest the value both of historical/linguistic analysis and of theoretical considerations.[59] Vickers's title carries an intentional challenge, a frisson of scandal missing from discussions of *Eastward Ho!* largely because of the lesser regard in which its authors are held four centuries later. Yet Shakespeare's coauthorship manifests a pattern immediately comprehensible for a long-term and successful attached dramatist. It seems likely that he collaborated first as a beginner, before he arrived at the Chamberlain's Men, and then later, in a period when he was both established and busy, tried out two apparently promising young men, George Wilkins and John Fletcher, who had themselves collaborated with others before having plays produced by Shakespeare's company. Perhaps predictably, only one of these attempts to enrich the stable of King's Men's authors worked out particularly well.[60] By contrast, Middleton, a freelancer all of his life, collaborated occasionally with a variety of other playwrights— Dekker, Webster, Ford, and probably Shakespeare—but clearly he, too, found some collaborators more congenial: his best working relationship proved to be with William Rowley, with whom he intermittently wrote five plays as well as the theater masque *The World Tossed at Tennis.* Rowley's repeated contribution of "fat clown" scenes, like those of Chough in *A Fair Quarrel,* has been long recognized, partly because these scenes are easily identifiable and separable—Rowley added an additional one to *A Fair Quarrel* (published in the second issue of Quarto 1) when the part proved successful. But association with Rowley also had a less easily extricable effect on Middleton's writing. In a particularly striking example, one of the most famous dramatic moments of *The Changeling,* the confrontation between De Flores and Beatrice-Joanna, is a Middleton scene echoing or imitating a Rowley scene in *A Fair Quarrel* between Jane and the physician. Both scenes are basically about unexpected blackmail for sexual favors. The relationship between Rowley and Middleton's work here goes beyond the division of *The Changeling* that yields to linguistic tests; it is a different kind of collaboration, enabled, as Masten says so often happens in these texts, by "a female body as textual corpus"; it exemplifies a variation on the homosocial "doubleness" that Masten describes and usefully complicates more limited definitions of "joint writing."[61]

I conclude by returning to Marston and *Eastward Ho!*, where collaboration once again presented differing professional and psychological challenges to the authors involved, with effects on their working methods that we may never be able entirely to reconstruct. This is true even if we do not reject all earlier attribution scholarship by claiming that "the three playwrights remove their signatures from the play altogether."[62] The irascible Jonson had deep affection and respect for one of his two collaborators: he would report to Drummond that "Chapman and Fletcher were loved of him" and "next himself, only Fletcher and Chapman could make a mask."[63] What did this mean at the time to the third member of the trio, barely readmitted to Jonson's graces? Unlike Masten's paradigmatic two gentlemen, Francis Beaumont and John Fletcher, Marston seems to have had great difficulty developing and maintaining "the socially sanctioned bonds among men within the institutions of the theatre."[64] Even Jonson, although capable of killing a fellow actor, normally honored the demands of these bonds; consider his claim that he voluntarily imprisoned himself with Chapman. Even if not true, as "spin" it reflects an expected attitude toward colleagues.[65] Marston, however, fled and most likely, as Jackson and Neill put it, "contrived to avoid arrest until the uproar was over."[66] Not surprisingly, his flight ended the reconciliation with Jonson that had preceded the dedication of *The Malcontent*. Marston's next mention of Jonson, in the note to the reader of *Sophonisba* (1606), is a satirical jab at those who transcribe authors and translate Latin prose orations, a clear attack on *Sejanus* despite the encomiastic verses Marston had previously written for that tragedy.

Marston's tortuous history with Jonson was, unfortunately, typical of his relationships with his associates. Envisioning "communities of collaboration" in the Jacobean theater—somewhat undercut by his analogy to the frequently abused dower system—William Slights attempts to insert Marston into a vision of positive filiation, a tradition of "theatrical apprenticeship that included Jonson mentoring Marston, Shakespeare Fletcher, Fletcher Massinger, and Massinger Field."[67] But this, again, is to ignore personality. No one ever called Marston "sweet" or "gentle." Rather, from the very beginning of his career he engaged in what one might call collaboration by quarrel. To inflate Joseph Hall's "almost invisible response" to being parodied in *Certaine Satyres,* in the second edition of *The Scourge of Villainie* Marston "actually quoted in full . . . the epigram that Hall had pasted into just a few copies of Marston's earlier volume."[68] Marston's role in the *poetomachia,* whether that was really the large scale conflict imagined by the Victorians or involved a more modest number of plays and dramatists, could be viewed generously as creating a kind of convivial intertextual rivalry. Probably more appropriate is its usual metaphor of war; the "mentoring" was violent and public. The events of Marston's life demonstrate a constant tendency to reject cooperation or collaboration for competition and aggression. Although there is debate about details— Bednarz has recently argued that Chrisoganus in *Histriomastix* is not a compliment that went wrong but a satire on Jonson's hubris and pedantry, which would make it an attack on an established figure parallel to the attack on Hall[69]—there is little question that Marston's relations with others almost always ended badly. As Wharton writes of the ambiguity of Chrisoganus, "Even if in any sense Marston was trying to compliment Jonson . . . he could not resist annexing him and making him speak with his own voice."[70] Rather than the equal or even friendly relations implied by collaboration, psychologically Marston seems to have been locked into an alternation between dependency and aggression. His joking pseudonym, Kinsayder (that is, Mar-stone, or "castrator's song")[71] significantly rejects male homosocial bonding for implied bodily damage.

Eastward Ho! itself, a play that begins in contrast and contest (good/ bad apprentice, social-climbing/modest daughter, flashy lover/elderly husband), ends with general reconciliation: "My sister and I are friends" (5.4.9); "Thank this worthy brother and kind friend, Francis" (5.5.125). Even old Security is assured of collaborators: "if you be a cuckold, it's an argument you have a beautiful woman to your wife . . . you shall have store of friends . . . you shall be eased of much o'your wedlock pain: others will take it for you" (5.5.170–73). Fittingly, the end of the play has not been assigned to Marston, a man who seemingly could neither compromise nor maintain a "store of friends." By 1608 Jonson, apparently the controlling hand in those final scenes, was engaged in his most successful collaboration, with

Inigo Jones, and writing masques for the same king who had brought the "industrious Scots" and the "thirty-pound knights" to court. Marston, instead, was again stubbornly and singularly engaged in satire, and this time did not escape imprisonment for his offense to the king. It is perhaps no surprise that he eventually fled the theater and, if he collaborated again, it was with his father-in-law on sermons.[72]

Notes

1. C. H. Herford and Percy and Evelyn Simpson, *Ben Jonson,* 11 vols. (Oxford: Clarendon Press, 1925-53), 1:140.

2. Albert Tricomi, *Anticourt Drama in England, 1603-42* (Charlottesville: University Press of Virginia, 1989), 44.

3. R. W. Van Fossen, ed. *Eastward Ho!* (Manchester: Manchester University Press, 1979), 218. In Appendix 2, pp. 218-25, Van Fossen reprints all ten known letters that Jonson and Chapman wrote from prison.

4. E. K. Chambers, *The Elizabethan Stage,* 4 vols. (Oxford: Oxford University Press, 1923), 3:374.

5. See Gary Taylor, "Introduction," *The Collected Works of Thomas Middleton* (Oxford University Press, forthcoming).

6. See Gerald Eades Bentley, *The Profession of Dramatist in Shakespeare's Time, 1590-1642* (Princeton: Princeton University Press, 1971), 229-30. Bentley seems to suggest that ultimately Chapman wrote all five acts but acknowledges that the relevant entries in Henslowe's diary may refer to one, two, or three plays.

7. W. David Kay, *Ben Jonson: A Literary Life* (New York: St. Martin's Press, 1995), 30.

8. W. Reavley Gair, "John Marston: A Theatrical Perspective," in *The Drama of John Marston: Critical Re-Visions,* ed. T. F. Wharton (Cambridge: Cambridge University Press, 2000), 31; Philip J. Finkelpearl, *John Marston of the Inner Temple* (Cambridge: Harvard University Press, 1969), 84.

9. Chambers, *Elizabethan Stage,* 3:428.

10. Gustav Cross, "The Authorship of *Lust's Dominion,*" *Studies in Philology* 55 (1958): 39-61.

11. Cyrus Hoy, *Introductions, Notes, and Commentaries to Texts in "The Dramatic Works of Thomas Dekker,"* 4 vols. (Cambridge: Cambridge University Press, 1980), 4:59-70.

12. Charles Cathcart, "*Lust's Dominion; or, The Lascivious Queen:* Authorship, Date, and Revision," *Review of English Studies* 52 (2001): 365.

13. MacDonald P. Jackson and Michael Neill, eds., *The Selected Works of John Marston* (Cambridge: Cambridge University Press, 1986), xii.

14. See David Lake, *The Canon of Thomas Middleton's Plays* (Cambridge: Cambridge University Press, 1975), for a fuller explanation of his method. Lake uses much of the data collected for analysis of the Middleton canon for analyzing *Histriomastix.* For discussions of the various methodologies involved, see also MacDonald P. Jackson, *Studies in Attribution* (Salzburg: Salzburg Studies, 1979); Gary Taylor, "The Canon and Chronology of Shakespeare's

Plays," in *William Shakespeare: A Textual Companion,* ed. Stanley Wells and Gary Taylor (Oxford: Oxford University Press, 1987); and Brian Vickers, *Shakespeare, Co-Author* (Oxford: Oxford University Press, 2002).

15. D. J. Lake, "*Histriomastix:* Linguistic Evidence for Authorship," *Notes and Queries* 226 (1981): 148-52. See also Anthony Caputi, *John Marston, Satirist* (Ithaca, N.Y.: Cornell University Press, 1961); Finkelpearl, *John Marston,* and Chambers, *Elizabethan Stage.*

16. Roslyn Lander Knutson, *Playing Companies and Commerce in Shakespeare's Time* (Cambridge: Cambridge University Press, 2001), 75-102.

17. James P. Bednarz, "Writing and Revenge: John Marston's *Histriomastix,*" *Comparative Drama* 36 (2002): 21-51.

18. Hoy, *Introductions,* 1:191.

19. James P. Bednarz, *Shakespeare and the Poets' War* (New York: Columbia University Press, 2001), 204.

20. Giorgio Melchiori, ed., *The Insatiate Countess* by John Marston and Others (Manchester: Manchester University Press, 1984), 9-16.

21. Lucy Munro, "Staging *The Insatiate Countess,*" unpublished paper, Shakespeare Association of America, Victoria, B.C., 2003.

22. Herford and Simpson, *Jonson,* 1:140.

23. Heather Anne Hirschfeld, " 'Work Upon That Now': The Production of Parody on the English Renaissance Stage," *Genre* 32 (1999): 185.

24. Hirschfeld, "Work," 179-80.

25. Gair, "John Marston," 41.

26. Hirschfeld, "Work," 186-87.

27. Ibid., 179, my emphasis. Hirschfeld expands her argument in *Joint Enterprises: Collaborative Drama and the Institutionalization of the English Renaissance Theater* (Amherst: University of Massachusetts Press, 2004).

28. Philip J. Finkelpearl, *Court and Country Politics in the Plays of Beaumont and Fletcher* (Princeton: Princeton University Press, 1990), 70.

29. Hirschfeld, "Work," 177.

30. Bentley, *Profession,* 228.

31. D. J. Lake, "*Eastward Ho:* Linguistic Evidence for Authorship," *Notes and Queries* 226 (1981): 166.

32. Thomas Marc Parrott, ed., *The Plays of George Chapman: The Comedies,* 2 vols. (New York: Russell and Russell, 1961), 2:838-48.

33. Bentley, *Profession,* 233; Van Fossen, *Eastward Ho!,* 10-11.

34. Herford and Simpson, *Jonson,* 9:641.

35. Van Fossen, *Eastward Ho!,* 11.

36. Our edition will follow Oliphant in the direction, "SECURITY [*appears at a grating.*]," though we acknowledge that other stagings are possible.

37. T. F. Wharton, *The Critical Fall and Rise of John Marston* (Columbia, S.C.: Camden House, 1994), 16.

38. Tom Cain, ed., *Poetaster* (Manchester: Manchester University Press, 1995), 29.

39. Lois Potter, ed., *The Two Noble Kinsmen* (London: Arden, 1997), 25.

40. Herford and Simpson, *Jonson,* 9:637.

41. Parrott, *Chapman*, 2:841.

42. Caputi, *John Marston*, 218-28.

43. Ibid., 217.

44. We will discuss the dating of the play in our Introduction. In brief, the play must date between the appearance of "that which is opposed to ours in title," *Westward Ho!*, in winter 1604-05 (entered in the Stationers Register 2 March 1605) and the entrance of *Eastward Ho!* into the Stationers Register on 4 September 1605. We believe that the play was presented, unlicensed, between 16 July and 31 August 1605 when James was on progress to Oxford with many of his courtiers. Suspecting that the unlicensed performances would rapidly be suppressed, the authors or the company quickly sold the script to the stationers Aspley and Thorpe, who in turn gave it to George Eld to print. The printing may have been begun but not completed before the authors were imprisoned.

45. Petter, *Eastward Ho!*, xlii.

46. Jeffrey Masten, *Textual Intercourse: Collaboration, Authorship, and Sexualities in Renaissance Drama* (Cambridge: Cambridge University Press, 1997), 7.

47. Petter, *Eastward Ho!*, xviii.

48. Lake, *Eastward Ho!*, 166.

49. Hirschfeld, "Work," 186.

50. Lake, *Eastward Ho!*, 164.

51. Ibid., 165.

52. Cited in Masten, *Textual*, 17.

53. Further examples will be found in the commentary notes and Textual Introduction to Suzanne Gossett and W. David Kay, eds., *Eastward Ho!*, *The Cambridge Works of Ben Jonson* (forthcoming).

54. Petter, *Eastward Ho!*, xvi; Lake, *Eastward Ho!*, 164.

55. Van Fossen, *Eastward Ho!*, 9.

56. Lake, *Eastward Ho!*, 160.

57. Masten, *Textual*, 20.

58. Vickers, *Shakespeare, Co-Author*, 506-41.

59. Jeffrey Masten comments briefly that "collaborations between (or among) writers had differing valences" and reiterates G. E. Bentley's distinctions between "regular attached professional" playwrights and freelancers such as Jonson (20-21).

60. See the Introduction to Suzanne Gossett, ed., *Pericles* (London: Arden, 2004), for further discussion of the Shakespeare-Wilkins collaboration.

61. Masten, *Textual*, 60, 42.

62. Hirschfeld, "Work," 192.

63. Chambers, *Elizabethan Stage*, 3:250.

64. Masten, *Textual*, 2.

65. Jonson's career with Inigo Jones demonstrates both collaboration at its most effective and its eventual limits and collapse.

66. Jackson and Neill, *Marston*, xiv-xv.

67. William W. E. Slights, "Dower Power: Communities of Collaboration in the Jacobean Theater," *Essays in Theatre/Études Théâtrales* 19 (2000 for 2003): 4.

68. Wharton, *Critical Fall*, 5.

69. Bednarz, *Shakespeare,* 83–92.

70. Wharton, *Critical Fall,* 13.

71. Ibid., 5.

72. This paper has greatly benefited from comments by James Bednarz, by the anonymous reader for *Renaissance Drama,* and by members of the 2003 SAA seminar on Dekker and Marston led by Ewen Fernie and William Kerwin.

Barbers and Barbary:
Early Modern Cultural Semantics

PATRICIA PARKER

Barbarie (a port, or Province, of Affrike;) also, barbarisme;
also the trade of a Barber.
> —Cotgrave, *Dictionarie of the French and English Tongues*

A half-witted Barbarism! which no Barber's art, or his balls,
will ever expunge or take out.
> —Jonson, *The Magnetic Lady*

. . . for your country's sake, which is called
Barbary, I will love all barbers and barberies . . .
> —Heywood, *Fair Maid of the West*

MUCH RECENT WORK has reoriented the focus of early modern studies toward the Ottoman Turk and the threat from the Barbary Coast, famous for its Barbary horses, sugar, and gold, but also for its exiled Moriscos, Moors, and Jews, for its Christian captives and its renegades who converted or turned Turk.[1] This work has helped to counterbalance more anachronistic approaches to a period when English power was far from established in the New World and the interior of Europe itself was threatened by the advancing empire of Islam. What I want to add to this reorientation is something that has largely escaped attention: the pervasive discursive network that conflated Barbary and the "barbarous" with barbering of all kinds, including the cut of castration or forcible circumcision and the shaving of bodily hair as a sign of slavery and availability for pathic use.

Part of the impetus for this study is my conviction that important cultural work was done in this period by associational networks that were influential even when the connections they forged were enabled only by the variability of early modern spelling or by similarities of sound. In the case of the nexus of Barbary, barbers, and beards, conflations of sound and interchangeable spellings were joined by the polyglot influence of languages in which different parts of the network were semantically or etymologically connected. The best guides here are frequently the period's own interlingual dictionaries, which are still not widely used by editors or interpreters of the period, though they are often a much better index to its historical and cultural semantics than the *OED*. John Minsheu's *Guide unto the Tongues* (1617) observes that "Barbers shoppe" appears in other languages as "Barberie" or "Barberia." Randle Cotgrave's *Dictionarie of the French and English Tongues* (1611) notes that French "Barbarie" meant simultaneously "barbarisme," "the trade of a Barber," and "a port, or Province, of Affrike." Florio's Italian-English *Worlde of Wordes* records that *Andar in barberia* meant "to go and be cured or laide of the pocks," while *Barbiera* was the name not only for "shee-barber" but for a "common harlot" (1598) or "strumpet" (1611), an important contributor to the association of Barbary with the loss of hair, as we shall see. When Ben Jonson treats of "A half-witted Barbarism! which no Barber's art, or his balls, will every expunge out," Sir John Harington combines "barbarous" Latin with "Mydas Barber," or a "harlot" is described as a "barber" or "barber's chair" in other English contexts, the nexus of associations is one that was enabled by such macaronic crossings, in a period when "barbe" was not only a verb for "cut" but the term used in English for "the beard of a man," though "barbe" and "beard" do not come from the same root.[2]

The beard itself, which Will Fisher, Elliott Horowitz, and others have reminded us was an important contemporary index of virility, was part of a broader cultural semantics influenced by classical, Roman, and biblical texts that not only associated loss of hair with "harlots" but identified the beardless chin with the youthful Ganymede and the depilated or shaven older male. Horowitz has described what he calls "the changing face of Europe" in the period, the growing fashion for beards that he argues reflected European encounters with the New World, whose male inhabitants were frequently characterized as beardless and sodomitical.[3] What I propose to do in what follows is to reorient the focus on shaving and on beards as a gendered index of virility in the direction of contemporary engagements with Islam (often in combination with Jews as the other circumcised nation). The aim of this examination is twofold: to identify an influential nexus of associations registered in representations of the Ottoman Empire and the Barbary Coast, foregrounding the complex amalgam of influences that contributed to its overdetermined historical layering; and to explore a broad spectrum of English dramatic instances, from Heywood's *Fair Maid of the West*, Daborne's *A Christian Turned Turk*, and other Barbary plots to the "Barbor" of Beaumont's *The Knight of the Burning Pestle* and

Enobarbus's description in *Antony and Cleopatra* of Antony as "barber'd ten times oer" (2.2.224).

> A murrain of these barbers of Barbary!
>
> *2 Fair Maid of the West*

> I can cut and shave. . . .
>
> *The Jew of Malta*

> It shall to' th Barbars, with your beard . . .
>
> 1623 Folio *Hamlet*

> take you in this barberous Moore . . .
>
> *Titus Andronicus* (1594 Quarto)

I begin with Heywood's *Fair Maid of the West,* whch foregrounds the "barbers of Barbary" in both of its parts, across the space of several years. In Part 1 of *Fair Maid,* the company of an English Bess whose name recalls Elizabeth the "virgin queen" travels south to make "spoil / Of the rich Spaniard and the barbarous Turk." Her ship, called the *Negro,* connects the blackness of Bess's mourning for the lover she assumes dead to the play's North African plot: "she in a Negro / Hath sail'd thus far to bosom with a Moor."[4] In the scene in which this "Fair Maid" is welcomed in "rich Barbary" (5.1.82), the apprentice Clem, who has accompanied her, appears on stage as a cultural transvestite, dressed in the clothing of a "fantastic Moor" (5.1.82). Transformed into a "courtier in the court of Fez" (5.1.115) and enamored of the wealth of the Barbary Coast (one of the motives for turning Turk in the period), this English apprentice introduces into the play the first of many variations on Barbary and "barbers" of all kinds: "CLEM. For your country's sake, which is called Barbary, I will love all barbers and barberies the better" (5.1.125-29). "Barbers" here conflates Barbary with barbers or barber-surgeons, in lines whose "barberies" denote barbershops as well as the barberries alternately spelled "barbarian" or "Barbaryn frute."[5]

Almost immediately after, this same "sudden courtier" is offered "Barbary pieces" (*1 FM* 5.1.136), the gold coins (5.1.140) that were part of the fabled "wealth of Barbary" (*2 FM* 4.1.148), familiar from Peele's *Battle of Alcazar* and other early modern texts.[6] Barbary gold is promised by the Moroccan ruler Mullisheg to Bess herself ("when th'art weary of our sunburnt clime, / Thy Negro shall be ballast home with gold," [*1 FM* 5.2.36-37]). But Clem confuses Barbary gold (or *gelt*) with the gelding or barbering that was a different part of contemporary associations with the Barbary Coast. Mullisheg proposes the clipping, cutting, or gelding of the "gentleman of England" (5.2.88) who is Bess's lover, a gelding he presents as elevation to favored status as a "eunuch" (5.2.92-93). But when Bess objects, it is the apprentice who has already gone barbarian in his clothing who is invited to "taste the razor" (5.2.103), exiting off stage in lines whose "before" calls attention to the "preferment" (5.2.127) he appears to enjoy at this North African court ("ALCADE. Come, follow. / CLEM. No, sir; I'll go before you for mine honor" [5.2.105-6]). When Clem reappears on stage, however, he is protesting the "Moorish preferment" that would "rob a man of his best jewels," calling the "barber" of Fez not "Davy" but "shavy" and resisting Barbary's "cutting honor" (5.2.126-31).

The first part of Heywood's *Fair Maid* ends with the transformed apprentice attempting to flee from such cutting. But when Part 2 opens, his complaint against the "barbers of Barbary" (*2 FM* 1.1.49-53) makes clear that he has not been able to escape. Deprived of his bodily "jewel" or "stone," the apprentice who had embraced the apparent upward mobility of a "preferment" that allowed him to "go before" (*1 FM* 5.2.105-6) confesses of his transformed bodily "case" that he can no longer go "before" a woman ("I must confess I am not her gentleman usher to go before her, for that way, as the case stands with me now, I can do her but small pleasure. I do follow her" [*2 FM* 1.1.63-65]), an inability he shares with the gentleman usher of Mason's *The Turke* (1607-8), who similarly finds his sexual function reversed ("my office is italianated, I am faine to come behinde" [5.1.2156]). The "case" of this English renegade thus joins that of Basilisco in Kyd's *Solyman and Perseda* (1592) or the renegade of Daborne's *A Christian Turn'd Turk* (1612), where the barbering that associated circumcision with the castration of the eunuch simultaneously conflated pathic sexual submission with turning Turk.[7]

Heywood's English apprentice—who has already turned Turk in his clothing—is barbered in the doubled sense of the cutting of castration or gelding (to make him a eunuch at the court of Fez) and the "sodometry" associated with the Turk and the Barbary Coast. The threat of castration hangs over both parts of this play ("If he fail / I'll have his flesh cut" [*2 FM* 1.343-44]), threatens Mullisheg to Goodlack, whose very name suggests that danger). So, simultaneously, does the threat of sodomy, as sign of English subjection to the "intemperate lust" (*2 FM* 2.1.88) of the "barbarous Moor" (2.1.4). The barbered Clem recounts his experiences at the Barbary court, where he is "tir'd" not only by "black she chimney sweepers" but by the "Morian" who "entreated me to lie with him" (2.1.17–27). By the end of the play's second half, the English apprentice who was once "Clem of Foy, the Bashaw of Barbary," has been turned again from "a courtier of Fez" into "a drawer in Florence" (*2 FM* 4.5.52–53). But he is still "a true eunuch" (4.5.100), whose gelding is irreversible ("ROUGHMAN. His master may well trust him with his maids, / For since the bashaws gelded him, he has learn'd / To run exceeding nimbly" [4.6.180–82]). His sexual case permanently "alter'd" (5.3.20), Clem calls attention to the cost of his preferment in Barbary in his own final words ("I am Bashaw of Barbary, by the same token I sold certain precious stones to purchase the place" [5.4.133–34]).

The identification of barbers with Barbary in Heywood's *Fair Maid of the West* is joined by multiple contemporary connections between barbering, Barbary, barbarisms, and the barbarian or barbarous, including iterated references to the "barbarous" (or "barberous") Moor and Turk. *Barber* in early modern English (related to *barbarius* and *barba* or beard) was repeatedly conflated with *barbarous* as well as Barbary, in ways enabled by both unstable orthographies and sound. A text of 1579 refers to "Alehouses and Barbar-shops," while the Acts of Henry VIII (1540) treat of "offences . . . against the good order of barbary or surgery" (xlii.§1). In *Othello,* a play where an "erring barbarian" (1.3.355) is assimilated to a "Barbary horse" (1.1.111), Desdemona's "maid call'd Barbary" bears a name that is alternately spelled "Barbery" in *Two Noble Kinsmen.* Barbering by "barbars"—the variant spelling reflected in the early texts of *Hamlet,* which themselves allude to the Turk and turning Turk—was part of the contemporary cultural semantics of shaving or cutting.[8] The comparison of "barbarous" Turks, Moors, and Jews—represented as forcibly circumcising or castrating Christians—to barbers who both "cut" and "shave" is part of an important textual crux in *The Jew of Malta* (whose circumcised Barabas sounds like an anagram of such associations) when either Ithamore (its "Turk") or an anonymous Moorish "slave" announces that he can "cut" and "shave."[9] In a play in which "barbarous mis-beleeving *Turkes*" (D3v) as well as "Moore" and "Jew" are all from "circumcised" nations, the cutting or shaving that here includes stealing and cutting the throat joins the threat of forcible circumcision or castration identified with all three.

Association of the barbarous with barbering or cutting appears repeatedly in Shakespeare as well as other early modern texts. In the final act of

Titus Andronicus, Aaron, the "barbarous Moor" (2.3.78; 5.3.4), who has
been linked throughout with the "barbarous Tamora" (called "Semiramis"
in 2.3.118) and "barbarous Goths" (1.1.28), taunts Lucius with the barbaric
acts the play has staged, including the cutting or "trimming" of Lavinia
by Tamora's sons, who had him as their "tutor" (5.1.94–98). Lucius's "O
barbarous" (5.1.97)—in response to the Moor's account of a trimming that
recalls (and outdoes) the cutting of Philomel's tongue by Tereus in the
barbarian East—appears as "barberous" in the Quarto texts here. A few
scenes later, the "barbarous Moor" (5.3.4) himself appears as a "barberous"
Moor in the Quarto versions, drawing attention to the variant early modern
spelling that enabled the easy conflation of barbering with Barbary and
Moors.[10]

Aaron has been critically situated primarily in relation to his blackness.
But his biblical name associates him with the high priest of the Jews (or
the other circumcised nation), supposed idolators of the golden calf made
possible by Egyptian gold; while his sending of his racially mixed son to
"*Muliteus* my Countriman" (Romanized in quartos and Folio, but emended
by Steevens to the "Muly" familiar from *The Battle of Alcazar*) at the
same time suggests a more contemporary North African Islamic resonance,
one consonant with the closing references to him as an "irreligious" and
"misbelieving Moor" (5.3.121, 143). As a name identified with Barbary
in the period, the Muly evoked by Aaron's "Muliteus" was itself part of
the network that conflated Barbary with barbering or gelding. Middleton's
Spanish Gipsy makes the connection explicit ("A beast? is't a mule? send
him to Muly Crag-a-whee in Barbary" [4.1.22–23]), identifying a "Muly"
of "Barbary" with a gelded or barbered mule.[11] Though the plot of *Titus
Andronicus* is situated within Roman history, the "barbarous" (or "barberous") Moor responsible for so much of its barbering simultaneously evokes
both Roman and early modern Moors.

By a French Barbar, [he] had all of the haire of his face miraculously shaued off. . . .
(Robert Greene, *A Disputation betweene a Hee Conny-Catcher and a
Shee Conny-Catcher*)

A barber's chair that fits all buttocks . . .
(*All's Well That Ends Well*)

The lines on the barbers of Barbary in Heywood's *Fair Maid,* and on
cutting, trimming, and shaving by "barbarians" in *The Jew of Malta* or

Titus Andronicus, provide only a few of many early modern English examples of this associational nexus. But before examining further dramatic and literary instances—as well as purportedly factual representations of Barbary and the Ottoman Turk—it is important to consider other influential contributors to this network: the contemporary lingua franca that made *barber* the term not just for the barber-surgeon but for a "common harlot" or "strumpet" and *barbarous* (or barbarous treatment) part of the familiar lexicon of sodometry in the period; and the overlay of classical and Roman with biblical influences that associated barbers and shaving with harlots and pathic subjection, as well as with thievery (or fleecing) and the treatment of captives and slaves.

We have already cited the interlingual complex in which *Barbiera* designated a "shee-barber" in these overdetermined senses and the reminder in Florio that *Andar in barberia* meant to "go and be cured or laid of the pocks." The association of harlots with barbering derived in part from the loss of hair from syphilis, the allegedly "foreign" disease ascribed not just to the French or Neapolitans but to contaminating contact with Jews, Moors, and inhabitants of the New World. Barbers in the sexual sense thus caused what the barber was supposed to cure. A bawd in Marston's *Dutch Courtesan* is described as being the "supportress of barber-surgeons" (1.2). The name "Shavem" is given to a harlot in Massinger's *City Madam,* while Davies of Hereford exploits the conflation of "hairs" and "heirs" (or "heires apparant") in warning of the "dry-shaving" to be given by a "Kate." *Barber's chair* is listed as a synonym for harlot in Motteux's *Rabelais* (1694), but the association was commonplace long before. Joseph Swetnam, in the *Araignment of Lewd, idle, froward, and unconstant women* (1615), compares a lascivious woman to "a Barbers chaire, that so soone as one knaue is out another is in," as does *All's Well That Ends Well,* where an "answer" is described as "a barber's chair that fits all buttocks" (2.2.17).[12] But it is important at the same time to observe that this contemporary vernacular of gendered connections was itself inflected by the idiom of cross-cultural encounter. "Barbarie pidgeon" and "turning Turk" (like "Guinea hen") were well-worn terms for "harlot" in early modern England, while the brothel areas on the south side of the Thames were known as the coast of Barbary or the "Turkish shore."[13]

The network aligning barbering, bodily hair, and barbarous treatment (as well as the multiple implications of cutting and shaving) was in the same period a staple of descriptions of sodomy, the notoriously capacious term that was frequently combined with circumcision as the bodily sign of turning Turk (or Jew) and the castration or gelding of the eunuch as an "eviration" or unmanning. Grammatical *barbarisms*—combined with barbers in the work of Ben Jonson and others as well as through French *Barbarie*—were associated with both Barbary and the passive male.[14] Ian Smith has demonstrated that linguistic and grammatical barbarisms were at the same time inseparable from racial and geographical reference, in descriptions such as Puttenham's of "the rude and barking language of the Affricans now called Barbarians."[15] In early modern English texts, "sodomy" was described as "barbarously diverting Nature" by "metamorphosing humane shape into bestiall forme,"[16] while narratives of captivity by Barbary pirates and the "barbarous Turk" included the threat of sodomizing among alleged barbarous practices. In John Dickenson's *Arisbas, Euphues Amidst his Slumbers; Or, Cupid's Iourney to Hell* (1594), to cite just one example, a youth of "rare beauty" recounts his captivity by pirates "amongst whome he had long led a miserable life, being most barbarously handled, they sometimes alluring him with faire promises . . . but no way able to winne him to their wills, or move him to satisfye their beastly lust." The sodometry already associated with pirates attached to renegades who turned Turk on the Barbary Coast, such as the notorious English pirate Ward, whose "Sodomie" is decried in contemporary texts. This includes Daborne's *Christian Turn'd Turk* (1612), where the cutting or circumcising that is part of Ward's conversion in Tunis is represented as his being pathically "handled" by "Mahomet" himself, in a scene whose reference to a "barber" combines all of the forms of barbering (and barbaring) to which he is subjected, including this bodily cutting and his captivation by the harlotlike "infidel" enchantress who first tempted him to turn Turk. In this play, the choice of Agar or Hagar as the name of this Islamic enchantress's sister (and wife of its renegade Jew) evokes both the mother of Ishmael (progenitor of Islam) and the "bond-woman" who was a familiar figure for the Jewish covenant, in an influential New Testament passage on Christians betwitched backwards from baptism to circumcision that was central to descriptions of the potential reversibility of conversion itself.[17]

How incensed they become if the barber gets careless, as if he were trimming a real man!

(Seneca, "On the Brevity of Life")

lovers with shaven chins and posteriors . . .
(Athenaeus, *Deipnosophists*)

barbers who pluck out the hair of these
effeminate creatures . . .
                            (Clement of Alexandria)

Antichristes shaven captaynes . . . sorcerous shavelings.
                    (Bale, *Apology agaynste a ranke papyst*)

Early modern descriptions of the sodometry as well as eunuchry or gelding
associated with barbering need also to be considered in relation to the
classical (and particularly Roman) writing on shaving, beards, and bodily
hair they so frequently invoke. Barbering of different kinds pervades the
plays of Plautus, for example, from the association of a harlot with shearing
or fleecing (*[at]tondere,* from *tonsor* or barber) in *Mercator* or *The Merchant* and the function of cutting or barbering as "a virtual leit-motif" in
Bacchides to the explicit connection with a barber shop in *Captivi* or *The
Captives.* At the same time, depilated actors and shaven buttocks are part
of other Plautine plays that draw on the figure of the *cinaedus* (or adult
male who invited penetration) as a *saltator* or transvestite male dancer,
dressed in female clothes.[18] Julius Caesar as "shaven," his "haire plucked,"
"over-curious" about "the trimming of his body," and taunted as "Queen
of Bithynia" for his alleged pathic role while with King Nicomedes in Asia
Minor was part of a Roman history familiar from Suetonius even before its
translation into English in 1606.[19] Will Fisher's work has brought to our
attention the importance of the beard in early modern writing as "the sign
of man . . . by which he appears a man," reflected in texts such as Marcus
Ulmus's *Physiologia Barbae Humanae* (1603), which argues that "Nature
gave to mankind a Beard, that it might remaine as an Index in the Face of
the Masculine generative faculty" (208). But the early modern physiognomy
and other texts that describe this "Index" also repeatedly echo classical and
Roman antecedents. In order to articulate more fully the cultural semantics
of barbering and beards in early modern writing (including the threat from
Barbary and the Turk), we need therefore to consider the influence of this
earlier archive in which early modern writers were steeped, even as such
influences were transformed or differently directed.

As the recent work of Maud W. Gleason and others has demonstrated, the
beard (together with "hairiness in general") in these earlier physiognomy
and other texts was one of the principal signs that "announce from afar, 'I
am a man.'"[20] In Roman descriptions, the smooth attractiveness of the boy
was held to end with the arrival of the beard, observed by the ceremony of
the "*depositio barbae,* in which clippings from the beard were offered

to the gods," usually around the twentieth year.[21] Shaving, cutting, or depilating were by contrast associated with the pathic or slave, or (in the case of the *cinaedus*) with the attempt to simulate the smoothness of the youthful "Ganymede."[22] Seneca's Epistle 114 (repeatedly echoed in Jonson's *Discoveries,* whose title suggests the detection dependent on such signs) compares an "effeminate" style to "those who pluck out, or thin out, their beards, or who closely shear and shave the upper lip while preserving the rest of the hair and allowing it to grow." This "train of association," Gleason observes, can be traced in Seneca's progression from a "satire on the self-conscious hairstyles of his contemporaries to an indictment of their passion for singing with unmanly inflections: 'How incensed they become if the barber gets careless, as if he were trimming a real man!' "[23]

Roman texts well known to early modern writers repeatedly associate multiple forms of barbering with the East. In Juvenal's Second Satire, the description of the depilated *cinaedi* for whom "all that remains is for them to castrate themselves like *galli* do" (115-16) combines pathic subjection with the *gallus,* gelding, or eunuch identified with the castrated devotees of Cybele, transformed like Attis from "he" to "she."[24] Both the castrated *gallus* and the penetrated *cinaedus* were frequently assimilated to Eastern practices, including the eviration or unmanning associated with depilation and shaving. The opposition of the bearded to the shaven or smooth extended even to the geopolitics of rhetorical style. Rhetoric (in contrast to "hirsute philosophy") was represented as "depilated" or "smooth," akin to the smooth or hairless body of the Eastern eunuch or eunuch rhetorician. In the influential alignment of Rome with the virility of the "Attic," the contrasting "Asiatic style," like the lack of the beard that served as the sign of transition from boy to man, was "more appropriate to young men than to mature men."[25] In one of many early modern applications of this Roman rhetorical (and orientalizing) geopolitics, Lipsius, the continental humanist who exercised such an important influence on Jonson and other English writers, proclaims that "*I have become a man,* and my tastes have changed. Asiatic feasts have ceased to please me: I prefer the Attic."[26]

The barbering identified with Asiatic excess was at the same time associated with slaves available for pathic use. Quintilian—warning against emasculating an orator's style by "the effeminate use of depilatories" and opposing a virile style to Eastern decadence and "expressions which would not be tolerated even from the effeminate youths of Alexandria" (1.2.6-8)—describes those whose oratory has become "flaccid and nerveless" (a metaphorics deriving from the *nervus* or male member) as "guilty of exactly the same offense as slave-dealers who castrate boys in order to increase the attractions of their beauty. For just as the slave-dealer regards strength and muscle, and above all, the beard [*barba*] and other natural characteristics of manhood as blemishes, and softens down all that would be sturdy if allowed to grow . . . even so we conceal the manly form of eloquence and power of speaking closely and forcibly by giving it a delicate complexion of style."[27] The adjective *glaber* ("hairless") was used to describe "young men, usually slaves, who were considered sexually attractive because of their smoothness, whether natural or artificially attained by depilation."[28] Pliny recommends the "application of ants' eggs to boys' armpits so as to prevent the growth of unsightly hairs," adding that "dealers in slave-boys, in order to keep their merchandise as marketable as possible, used blood from the testicles of castrated lambs to delay the growth of the beard."[29]

The classical and postclassical texts that influenced early modern writing include numerous other passages that made clear the overdetermined connections between different kinds of shaving. Athenaeus's *Deipnosophists,* in the midst of a section devoted to the love of boys, provides an influential discussion of beards and the origins of shaving, which begins with the smooth-shaven "favourites" of hypocritical Stoics and ends with "shaven chins and posteriors." At Rhodes, he observes, "although there is a law which forbids shaving, there is not so much as a single prosecutor who will try to stop it because everybody shaves. And in Byzantium, although a fine is imposed on the barber who has a razor, everybody makes use of one just the same."[30] Dio Chrysostom—addressing an audience at Tarsus in Cilicia—describes the degeneration that begins with trimming or cutting the beard (to make "faces . . . boyish beyond their years") and ends with removing from "private parts the hair which is distinctive of the full-grown male."[31] (In ways suggestive for Jonson's *Epicoene,* which features a "Barber" named "Cutbeard," the cutting of the "beard" is here described as leading to the unnatural "female" nature of the "epicene.") Clement of Alexandria associates shaving with "unnatural acts," in a discussion that combines classical and Roman influences with the *contra naturam* of Romans 1. "The towns are full of pitch-plasterers," he writes, "barbers who pluck the hair of these effeminate creatures" and "hunters of base pleasure" who go to barbers to get "their whole bodies made smooth" ("Is it not disgraceful that, although they are men, they have themselves shaved and their bodies rid of hair?"). In Clement's second-century treatise (which cites other biblical authorities, including the beard of Aaron and Leviticus against shaving), the "beard" is "the badge of a man" that "shows him unmistakably to be a man."[32] To barber or cut it is thus to castrate or remove the outward sign of manhood itself, just as the use of depilatories suggests practices "contrary to nature."

Early modern English writing on barbering and beards is variously inflected by such multiple influences, including the association of shaving with pathic subjection, with punishment or shaming, and with captives or slaves, as of beardlessness with the smooth attractiveness of the boy.[33] The identification of beardlessness not just with women or eunuchs but with the Ganymede or catamite appears repeatedly in English contexts. Marston's *Malcontent* (1600–1604) calls the "Dukes Ganimed" a "smooth chinned Catamite" (1.2.9), while an "Imberbis juvenis" or beardless youth (2.1.142–46) is called "Ganymede" in Middleton's *A Mad World, My Masters* (1606), the association similarly reflected in Shakespeare's *As You Like It*. In *The Knight of Malta*, Norandine professes "I love old Adams way; / Give me a diligent Eve, to wait towards bed-time, / Hang up your smooth-chinned page" (3.4.14–16), making clear the connection between the beardlessness of the "smooth-chinned" boy and the homoerotic or sodomitical, contrasted here to "old Adams way" with "Eve." Drayton's "The Moone-Calfe" refers to a "smooth-chind, plump-thigh'd, Catamite" (line 316). King James's male favorites were similarly characterized as "smooth-faced," as Harington in *Nugae Antiquae* describes Carr, the favorite portrayed by Tillières as falling from favor after he acquired *beaucoup de barbe* and by Francis Osborne as retaining his attractiveness to James "before he had either Wife or Beard."[34] At the same time, the suspicion that the beard itself may be a deceptive index is registered from Juvenal 2 and other well-known Roman texts: Martial's Epigram 7, which warns that the hirsute who invoke a traditional bearded *virilitas* may themselves be *cinaedi* ("habet tristis quoque turba cinaedos") is cited as reason for suspicion of "toute mine rebarbative" in the influential *Essais* of Montaigne translated by Florio in 1603 but circulating long before.[35]

Even the description of priests as "shavelings" in antipapist polemic compounds the Roman Church's "tonsure" (from Latin *tonsor*, or barber) with the imputation of pathic subjection from the combination of Roman and biblical texts. William Tyndale observes in *The Obedience of a Christian Man* (Antwerp, 1528) that "Shaving is borrowed of the hethen," an association strengthened by the biblical examples of the shaving of Joseph in Egypt (Genesis 41:14) and the priests of Baal as castrating or lancing themselves with "lancets" or "knives" (1 Kings 18:26). Hugh Latimer claims that papists "make the yomanry slavery and the cleargye shavery," a collocation that registers the biblical as well as Roman identification of shaving with subjection. John Bale condemns papists as "sorcerous shavelings" and "Antichristes shaven captaynes," conflating the Roman Church's tonsure with the shaving he ascribes to "sodometry" as "preposterous amor, a love out of order or a love agaynst kynde," in the unmistakable Pauline accents of Romans 1. Observing that the Roman emperor "Nero . . . gelded male chyldren to use them in stede of women" and that Aurelius "gelded hym selfe into a preposterous offyce of Venery" (Biir), the "bilious Bale" not only conflates gelding with pathic subjection but treats all such evirations as "preposterous" (reversed and unnatural) transformations of the masculine into the "feminine gendre."[36]

the battell lost, was vnto Selymus as if a man should shave his beard, which would ere long grow againe.

> Knolles, *Generall Historie of the Turkes* (1603)

Turks . . . no sooner lay hold on a Christian, but . . . [they] shave off all his hair . . .

> Dekker, *Gull's Hornbook* (1609)

The history of beards and body hair between Roman and early modern writing has already been charted by Giles Constable and others.[37] David Halperin, Mario DiGangi, and historians of sexuality in the wake (pro and contra) of Foucault have more recently described the transformations that distinguished early modern writing from the Roman influences it absorbed, including in relation to the *cinaedus* recalled in the Italian "Cinedo" (used for the name of Carlo Buffone's page in Jonson's *Every Man Out of His Humour*) or the "Cynede" of early modern physiognomy treatises.[38] What I want to concentrate on here is the cultural inflection given to these multiple influences in early modern representations of being barbered by the Turk, or new Emperor of the East, as the Sultan is called in *The Battle of Alcazar,* in the elaborate forms of princely address recorded in Hakluyt, and in Dekker's *Old Fortunatus,* where Fortunatus "revels with the Emperor of the East" in Constantinople before proceeding to Egypt, part of the North African coast already under Turkish control.[39] Egypt and the East (including Persia, associated with the barbering of

Macedonian Alexander as well as the broader reaches of the Islamic world) continued to be identified with effeminacy in ways that both iterated and renovated familiar classical and Roman descriptions. But at the same time, the Ottoman Turk as the new power of the East and the Barbary Coast was represented as not only bearded but as identifying beardlessness and shaving with pathics and slaves, including captives from Christian Europe. If, as Elliott Horowitz has argued, the "changing face of Europe" reflected in the new importance of the beard as an index of virility is related to the European conquest of the New World, with its allegedly beardless "sodomitical" inhabitants, the contemporary preoccupation with *bearding* or challenging the Turk or with the threat of barbering in Barbary simultaneously reflected identification *with* the conquering Ottoman and fear of territorial and bodily sodomizing *by* this encroaching Islamic power, as Christians were being taken captive (or turning Turk) in increasing numbers.[40]

Repeated references to the "bearded" Turk, and the association of shaving with shaming or defeat, appear in nonliterary as well as literary and dramatic texts of the period. Richard Knolles's *Generall Historie of the Turkes* (published in London in 1603)—an acknowledged influence on Shakespeare as well as other early modern writers—characterizes the temporary defeat of the Ottoman forces at the battle of Lepanto in 1571 as an only temporary shaving of the Sultan's "beard," which would soon grow back again, reflecting in its language not only the assimilation of shaving to defeat but the signifying uses of the beard as index of the loss and regaining of comparative power.[41] Balthazar in Kyd's *Spanish Tragedy* requires a stage "beard" in order to play the part of Solyman the Great Turk.[42] The multiple allusions to barbers and beards that pervade the play of *Sir Thomas More*, already related by commentators to the beheading of More (or "Moore") himself at the king's command, include reference to the shaven or polled ("poll") head of a "Sarcen" or Saracen.[43] Lyly's *Midas* (similarly filled with allusions to barbers and beards) features a ruler who has often been read as a political allegory of Spain's Philip II. But the fact that he not only wears a "great tiara on his head" (the turbanlike headdress of Ovidian and early modern descriptions) but rules over Phrygia—the territory in the East or Asia Minor associated with Ganymede, with the castrated Attis, and with the effeminately barbered Aeneas, whose Phrygian effeminacy must be left behind in his westward progress—makes this figure who seeks to rule over an empire extending from early modern Turkey a potential avatar of the Turk as well.[44]

References to the Turk figure prominently in other early modern discussions of shaving and beards, including debates over the Roman Church's tonsure. Valerian's *Pro Sacerdotum Barbis* (1533), for example, cites the historical example of "Alexander of Macedone," who "was scorned . . . bycause he wolde be shauen, to shewe hym selfe feminine." In his strenuous defense of the priestly beard, Valerian associates the shaving of priests not only with the "delycate felowes of the court of Rome" but with "priestes of Egypt" and the "womannyshe mynde" of foreign peoples.[45] In this, he both iterates and updates familiar ascriptions of effeminacy or womanishness to alleged Eastern practices. But in observing that "to this daye, all the nations of the Easte parties, where so euer they se men with suche smothe faces . . . calle them women in scorne," he simultaneously invokes the reversibility of this East-West binary and its orientalizing history. In a striking reference to territorial struggles with the Ottoman Turk, he blames Rome's desire to distinguish itself from the Eastern Church by being shaven for the losses of "all Asia" (and Jerusalem) to the "infidels" or "*Turkes,*" who value and retain the manliness of the "Bearde" (20v; 21r). In ways indicative of the contradictory determinations of many such texts of the period, Valerian's defense of the beard as a cultural as well as gendered index of virility and power simultaneously repeats the familiar characterization of shaving as an Eastern practice and blames its adoption by Rome for the losses of territory in Asia and the Middle East to this new Eastern power, which (unlike Rome) retains the "Bearde" and scorns men with smooth or shaven faces as women.

Early modern physiognomy and other treatises that bear the imprint of biblical and classical or Roman influences likewise register the transcultural, and not simply the gendered, significance of shaving and beards. John Bulwer's *Anthropometamorphosis* (1653) self-consciously echoes both classical Roman and later influences in his claim that "those who expose themselves to be shaven . . . . [are] called, in reproach, women." But his characterization of the "shaven" as a sign of being "abused against Nature" (the familiar phrase from Romans 1) at the same time includes the "beardless" or shaven inhabitants of the Americas and contemporary representations of the "bearded" Turk. Citing the ancient Roman index of the "Beard" as "the naturall Ensigne of Manhood," Bulwer iterates the familiar association of shaving, "unnaturall dipilation" and other customs "contrary to nature" with the effeminizing of "Alexander" by "Persian luxury" and with "Ægyptians," who "have many strange customs contrary to Nature."[46] He also adds to the well-known story from Pliny and Varro of the origin of Roman barbers the alleged contemporary predilections of the Turk, followed by "Fez" in Barbary, the Moroccan locus of the barbering of the English apprentice of Heywood's *Fair Maid:*

[V]erily the *Turkes,* who shave their slaves, do justly scoffe at such Christians, who cut, or naturally want a beard, as suffering themselves to be abused against Nature. The Inne-keepers of *Fez* are iustly therefore detested among the honester part of the Citizens, who go apparelled like women, and shave their Beards, and are so delighted to imitate women, that they will not only counterfeit their speech, but will also sit down and spin. With a Rasor then to go so deep as to leave no impression of haire upon the Chin, as if we would with the same Iron invade the roots, but that we feare wounds and deforming skars of the skin, is to turn Rebell, and to shew a willingnesse to avert the Law of Nature.   (199–200)

The association of shaving with pathic subjection or the familiar *contra naturam* of Romans 1—applied to shaven "slaves" but also to Christians "who cut, or naturally want [i.e., lack] a beard"—is here followed by the "Inne-keepers of Fez" who "go apparelled like women, and shave their Beards," a geographical reference for which Leo Africanus's *Historie of Africa* is cited in the margins, bringing together the "Turk" and "Fez" or "Fesse" in Barbary in relation to barbering and other practices defined as against "the Law of Nature."

Bulwer repeats Diogenes' frequently cited question to a man with "a smooth shaved Chin" ("hast thou whereof to accuse Nature for making thee a man and not a woman?"), the biblical injunction from Leviticus ("wherein we are forbidden not to corrupt the upper and lower honour of the Beard, or shave it"), and the example of the "Rhodians and Bizantines . . . who when they were forbidden by a law that no man should be shaved, all of them began against the Law to shave their Chins." Claiming that "the Beard is a singular gift of God, which who shaves away, he aimes at nothing than to become less man," he proceeds to instances of being *forcibly* shaved, as a shaming or punishment, including the contemporary example of the "Turk":

Thenet in his *Cosmography* saith, at this day in the Isle of *Candy* it is a kind of punishment to cut a man's beard. . . . The Beglerbegs and Bassas of the Sultan wore very long Beards: if the Sultan were displeased with any man he caused his beard to be cut for a punishment and shame; as Emyr Seleyman served Chassan Captaine of the Janizaries, which Chassan esteemed so great a shame unto him, that he handled the matter so, that Emyr Seleyman was entrapped and strangled.   (200-201)

Citing the familiar passage from Ulmus's *De fine Barbae Humanae* on the "Beard" as "an Index in the Face, of the Masculine generative faculty," and insisting that "The Beard being the signe of a man . . . to violate then that which is a sign of virile Nature is an impiety against the Law of Nature," Bulwer stresses that to "eradicate our Beard, or with Depilatories burn up and depopulate the Genitall matter thereof" is "to evirate ourselves" against "the Law of Nature." He then goes on to make even clearer the association with sodomy, in yet another passage devoted to the "Turkes":

Nay even the Turkes, (whom we account even but Barbarians) herein do more homage to Nature, who if a man have a faire long Beard they reverence him, and only he is a wise man, and an honourable Personage: but if they have no Beard at all, if they be young, they call them Bardasses, that is, Sodomiticall Boyes. . . . Therefore the Aghas of the Great Turke, who are most commonly five and thirty, or forty yeares of age before they are sent abroad, because they come out of the Seraglio with their Beards shaven, they are fain to stay within doores for some daies to let them grow, that they may be fit to come amongst other great men, and as soon as their Beards are grown they go abroad and begin their visits.   (208-209)

The "Turkes" noted by Bulwer as shaving their "slaves" and scoffing at "such Christians, who cut, or naturally want a beard, as suffering themselves to be abused against Nature," are here cited as reverencing the "beard" and calling beardless youths "Bardasses" or "Sodomitical Boyes." In its variable orthography in early modern English, "bardash" itself (frequently traced to Arabic *bardaj* or slave) appeared in forms that suggested the shaven, depilated, or "bared" ass of the pathic or beardless youth. "Bardasses" or "bardassoes" were part of an early modern set of associations that included shaving or barbering of all kinds. Florio (1598) cites "bardash, a buggering boy," in his definition of *Cinedo*, from the Roman *cinaedus* associated with depilatories and other forms of barbering.[47]

In a period in which the Ottoman Empire was identified both with eunuchry and with a predilection for "sodomy" and beautiful boys, cutting, shaving, and barbering in all senses—including sodomizing, castrating, and the forcible circumcising of captives—were repeatedly ascribed to the "barbarous Turk."[48] In ways indicative of the frequent conflation of the eunuch of Roman writing with early modern accounts of Ottoman courts, George Sandys (travel writer and translator of Ovid) applies Juvenal's Sixth Satire on the gelded but still sexually active eunuch ("so smooth, / so beardless to kiss. . . . What the surgeon chops will hurt nobody's trade but the barber's" [6.366–68]), to contemporary "Turkes":

Many of the children that the *Turkes* do buy (for their markets do affoord of all ages) they castrate, making all smooth as the backe of the hand, (whereof diuers do die in the cutting) who supply the vses of nature with a siluer quill, which they weare in their Turbants. In times past, they did but onely geld them: but being admitted to the free conuerse of their women, it was obserued by some, that they more then befittingly delighted in their societies. For according to the Satyre,

With feeble Eunuches some delighted are:
Kisses still soft, chins that of beards despaire:
who need force no abortments.

But others say, that *Selymus* the second, hauing seene a gelding couer a mare, brought in among them that inhumane custome.[49]

In the margin here is the Latin of Juvenal's Satire 6, on the *desperatio barbae.*

What was claimed as the Turkish custom of castrating prisoners was dramatized repeatedly on the English stage, just as smooth-chinned "eunuchs" figured prominently in descriptions of the "great Turke."[50] Mason's *The Turke* (1607–8) features a slave who was "a free borne Christians sonne in Cyprus, / When Famagusta by the Turke was sackt," but when captured was made "an Eunuch, / Disabled of those masculine functions, / Due from our sex" as well as "subiected" to "the vilde commaund" of the "imperious Turke." Massinger's *The Renegado* (1623–24) reflects reports of Christians being forcibly circumcised or gelded in Barbary (2.6.4), as well as turned "renegade" or Turk, in the plot of the servant Gazet (played by the same actor as Heywood's Clem), who considers parting with his "stones" (3.4.53–54). The play's Englishman, eunuch servant to the niece of the Ottoman emperor, has already been "made lighter / By two stone" (1.2.25–26).[51]

The association of the Turk with beards, eunuchry, and other forms of barbering appears in Shakespeare as well, though criticism has not always recognized such allusions.[52] Even the reference in the early texts of *Hamlet* to something in need of cutting ("It shall to 'th Barbars [Quarto 2 barbers] with your beard") may be part of topical allusions in those texts to contemporary as well as ancient empires, to turning Turk, piracy, and the Diet of Worms, concerned not only with the Lutheran schism but with the Ottoman threat.[53] In *All's Well That Ends Well*—immediately after the scene that invokes a "barber's chair"—youths are threatened with being sent "to the Turk to make eunuchs of" (2.3.87-88), in a play whose reference to the "Tongue" of "Bajazeth's mule" (emended to "mute" by Warburton and others) is followed by allusion to the "baring" (or shaving) of Parolles' "beard" (4.1.41-49). In *The Merchant of Venice*, where a "knife" wielded by a "Jew" evokes the imaginal threat of forcible circumcision from one circumcised nation, the Prince of Morocco's "Let us make incision for your love, / To prove whose blood is reddest" (2.1.6-7) is followed by the curious scene involving the apparently prodigious "beard" of the "Clown" who is both servant of the Jew and impregnator of a female Moor, a "bondsman" ("of Hagar's offspring" [2.5.43]) connected with both religious and racial others in the play's Venetian setting. His name (Lancelot in most modern editions but "Lancelet" in the play's early texts) recalls not only the influential biblical passages on lancing as castrating or cutting but even more specifically the name of the barber-surgeon's instrument used for incising and bloodletting.[54] Bodily cutting or incision likewise figures prominently (together with reference to beards) in *Twelfth Night*, where Viola's intention to become a "eunuch" in Illyria (1.2.56-63) suggests not just the Italian *castrato* evoked by the name of "Cesario" (from *caesus*, "cut") but—in lines that explicitly involve a "mute" (and a play that features pirates as saltwater thieves)—the eunuchry identified with the Turk, whose dominion over Illyria numerous early modern texts make clear. Malvolio (who is called a "renegado" after his fantastic change of clothes) suggests in the "C-U-T" of the letter scene the familiar sign of circumcision/castration, as well as the sodomitical associations of the "O" and "I" or "eye" that "comes behind," evoking perhaps another kind of Illyrian "backtrick" (1.3.123).[55] The "beard" that Cesario longs for (3.1.45) is not only part of the "lack" of Viola (as both woman and boy) but the beard of the older man in a pederastic relationship, at the court of Illyria where a "Cesario" (still in boys' clothes) is finally wedded to its Duke.

forceably and most violently shaven,
head and beard. . . .

"The voyage of the Jesus" (1583)

In the same period as such dramatic representations, narratives of Barbary and of bond slaves of the Turk reported the forcible shaving of Christian captives, as well as their barbering in multiple senses, including circumcising, gelding, and sodomizing or pathic subjection. Georgijevic's *Ofspring of the House of Ottomanno* (1569) describes the eradication of "manlines" from the "bodyes" of young captives subjected to the Turk's "unnatural lust and lecherye" or ("their comly bewtye wearynge away") made "Eunuches, to serue matrones, and dames."[56] The barbering of Christian captives by the Turk was a staple of early modern accounts of the Barbary Coast. Hakluyt includes a voyage to Tripolis in "Barbarie" in 1583, in "a ship called the Jesus," in which Englishmen were not only taken captive but violently barbered, or shaved, in an account that simultaneously suggests their sodomitical use.[57] The narrative by Thomas Sanders tells of "Turks" from "Barbarie" who board the *Jesus* and take the Englishmen captive (5.297-99), joined by "Christian caitifes" already under the Turk, who "made spoyle of our goods" and "used us as ill as the Turkes did." After a cheating French factor (who "protested to turne Turke, hoping thereby to have saved his life" [5.300]) is hanged, the English captives put in bondage to these "infidels" in "Barbarie" (5.299) are condemned to be "slaves perpetually unto the great Turke" (5.301). As a sign of their "slaverie" and subjection to the Turk, they are "forceably and most violently shaven, head and beard" (5.301).

This violent shaving is followed by the threat of sodomy and forced circumcision, in an account that inverts the Prospero-Caliban relationship of European master and slave with origins in Barbary, as English "slaves" are sent to "fetch wood" (5.302). The son of the king of Tripoli—"ruler in an Island called Berbi"—"greatly fancied Richard Burges" the "Purser" and James Smith, both "yong men" whom he was "desirous" to have "turne Turkes." These young English men refuse to "yeeld" to the "desire" of this Barbary "Turke" and beseech "the king that they might not be inforced thereunto." But after they are shown another Englishman "whom the kings sonne had inforced to turne Turke," they are forcibly "circumcised," dressed (in the case of Burges) in the "habite of a Turke," and "violently used" (5.304-6). Here, not in a literary or dramatic treatment but in a purportedly factual account of Christian "slaves" who are forceably "shaven, head and beard" (5.301), on the Barbary Coast, the cut of circumcision and the threat of sodomizing provide what might be seen as the historical counterpart to the comically deflected "barbering" of Heywood's apprentice.

The treatment of these English "slaves" caused a major international incident—prompting the intervention of Elizabeth's ambassador in Constantinople to redeem them from "captivitie" in "Barbarie." Hakluyt reproduces not only Sanders's account of the shaving of the English captives but the "Queenes letters to the Turke" on behalf of "the English captives detained in Tripolie in Barbarie, and for certaine other prisoners in Argier" (5.311), the Barbary port that (with Tunis) figures so prominently in the Mediterranean geography of *The Tempest*. The address in Elizabeth's letter on the captives' behalf—to "The most valiant and invincible Prince, Zultan Murad Can, the most mightie ruler of the kingdome of Muselman, and of the East Empire" (*imperiique Orientis Monarchae* in the Latin original)— makes clear not only the power of the sultan or Great Turk in "Barbarie" but his standing as the new emperor of the East. The violent shaving of English Christians on the Barbary Coast and the forced circumcision of "yong men" subject to the sodomitical "desire" of the "Turke" are given in Hakluyt's rendering an ultimately redemptive biblical ending. The "plagues and punishments" it describes as visited on "Barberie" (5.308) recall the plagues on Egypt prior to the Exodus deliverance—conflating "Barbary" with "Egypt" in ways that were frequently repeated in early modern accounts of Alexandria and other parts of Egypt and North Africa under Ottoman control. Elizabeth's "Ambassador with the Grand Signor" in Constantinople challenges an Englishman who has become a "eunuch" in Barbary to be like "Joseph" in "Egypt," keeping his "true christian mind & English heart" free from Turkish "vices," notwithstanding that "your body be subject to Turkish thraldom."[58] As Jonathan Burton points out with regard to Sanders's redemptive ending, however, this liberation of English captives not only flies in the face of other early modern realities (including the numbers of Christians who remained under the Turk) but leaves traces of its reverse, describing an unhappy English "boy" who *voluntarily* turns Turk, like thousands of "renegades" who chose never to return from Egypt or Barbary.[59]

Alexandria—under Ottoman rule from the early sixteenth century— provides the locus of other captivity narratives that conflated the biblical Egypt with the "captivitie of the Turkes," including another account in which Christian captives are forcibly barbered or shaved.[60] In the version printed in the 1589 edition of Hakluyt—entitled "The woorthy enterprise of John Foxe an Englishman in delivering 266. Christians out of the captivitie of the Turkes at Alexandria, the 3. of Januarie 1577" (5.153-64)— Englishmen in a ship bound from Portsmouth to Seville in 1563 are "beset round with eight gallies of the Turkes" (5.152). Despite "manfully" resisting (an emphasis on English "manhood" the account repeatedly stresses), they are captured by the attacking "Turkes" and "caried prisoners unto an Haven nere Alexandria" (5.156). Hakluyt's narrative of their Alexandrian captivity focuses on the figure of "John Fox, who . . . being somewhat skilfull in the craft of a Barbour, by reason thereof made great shifting in helping his fare now and then with a good meale" (5.156). The account quickly becomes one of barbering in reverse—as this English "Barbour" (with the help of "an olde rustie sword blade, without either hilt or pomell, which he made to serve his turne" [5.158]) rescues his fellow captives from "thraldome and bondage" (5.163) to the "Infidells" in Alexandria, in a narrative of release from Turkish "thraldom" that again invokes the Exodus from Egypt. When the redemption wrought by this English "Barbour" is retold in the version attributed to Munday in 1608, the account calls explicit attention to the initial barbering of the captives by the Turk. As a sign of their subjection as "slaves" to this "barbarous . . . tyrant" (before their deliverance from "so barbarous a thraldome"), the "first villany and indignitie that was done to them" was "the shauing off of all of the hayre both of heade and beard."[61]

Narratives of the shaving of English captives contributed in turn to more literary accounts of the association of "barbers" with Barbary and the "barbarous" Turk. Dekker's *Gull's Hornbook* (1609), which devotes an entire section to "Long Hair," rails against "base barbarous barbers" in a passage that anticipates references later to an "abominable shaving," associated both with catamites or ingles and with the thievery identified with Ward, the renegade pirate of Tunis.[62] Treating of the "hoary beards" of "Saturnists," in ways that reflect the influence of Roman writing on the use of the beard to conceal secret practices, Dekker protests disgust for what he calls "this polling and shaving world" (31–32). He then describes the barbering to which Christian slaves are subjected by the "Mohammedan cruelty" of the "Turks," who (he claims) "no sooner lay hold on a Christian, but the first mark they set upon him, to make him know he's a slave, is to shave off all his hair close to the skull" (30–31). The shaving of Christians by Turks—and the association of "base barbarous barbers" with the Barbary Coast—is soon after retroactively glossed by the opening sentence of the next chapter, which professes to be "weary with sailing up and down alongst these shores of Barbaria" (33).

puppets in Turkish dress, whose red-bearded captain was finally devoured by the flames . . .

                                        Hans Sachs on Barbarossa

That son of Barbarossa (*Barbarroja*) . . . savagely mistreated his captives.
Don Quijote ("The Captive's Tale")

What fond unknowing wight is this? that dares
So rudely knocke at *Barbarossa*'s Cell,
Where no man comes but leaves his fleece behind?
The Knight of the Burning Pestle

The most notorious beard of "Barbaria" and enslaver of Christian captives from the Barbary Coast was the figure known as Barbarossa (or Redbeard), the younger of two red-bearded brothers from a family of reputed renegade Christians (Khaired-din and his elder brother Aruj), thought to be originally pirates from Cilicia or Mytilene.[63] Khaired-din (Defender of the Faith)—the more famous of the Barbarossa brothers—was described as "very hairy with a beard extremely bushy."[64] Beginning in Egypt and succeeding the brother with whom he extended the power of the Turkish Sultanate from Alexandria to Tunis and other ports on the Barbary Coast, he made Algiers into a haven for renegades as well as a base for the taking of Christian captives. He was thus instrumental not only in extending the Ottoman Empire but in creating the Barbary port that would be described by Nicholas de Nicholay as filled with Christians who have "reneid [i.e., become renegades] or turned Turk," condemned by Samuel Purchas as "the Throne of Pyracie" and "Receptacle of Renegadoes," and identified with the North African origins of Sycorax in *The Tempest*.[65] In a contemporary account of this Barbarossa of Barbary, his name in English was alternately spelled "Barbarus."[66]

The red-beard Barbarossa was famous throughout early modern Europe. When Charles V retook Tunis in 1535, his victory was commemorated by "a new order of crusading chivalry" whose motto was *Barbaria*. According to Hans Sachs, the conquest of Tunis by this new "Roman" emperor was celebrated by a pageant featuring the "capture of a model fortress manned by puppets in Turkish dress, whose red-bearded captain was finally devoured by the flames amid the cheers of the spectators."[67] The celebration of Barbarossa's demise, however, was only wishful thinking. Not only had he escaped the slaughter, he made immediate reprisal raids elsewhere, capturing and enslaving thousands of Christians, making Charles's vaunted conquest of Tunis of little consequence as long as this Barbary "Turk" remained master of the seas.[68]

In the struggle between Ottoman power and Charles's revived Roman

Empire, which was plagued by defections, betrayals, and disunity within the forces of the Christian West, Barbarossa was also the victor at a new Battle of Actium, fought at Prevesa on the site of Actium itself in 1538.[69] Barbarossa—wooed repeatedly by the new Roman emperor to defect to the side of Rome—is said to have followed "exactly the course taken fifteen hundred years earlier by Octavian, the future Augustus Caesar, in preparation for his defeat of Anthony, with Cleopatra, in the battle of Actium,"[70] while Andrea Doria (commander of the temporarily unified Christian fleet) inexplicably retreated, putting the Western forces in the ignominious position of the retreating Anthony. This reversal at another Actium—compounded by the opening of a new naval front by Suleiman the Eunuch, pasha of Egypt—had momentous consequences, marking "a significant turning point in Mediterranean history."[71] In the wake of this Actium victory, Barbarossa ravaged the coasts of Naples and Sicily, causing panic in Rome and carrying off the wife of the governor of Reggio di Calabria, whose parents gave her in marriage to the Barbary corsair in exchange for their own release.

Barbarossa (or "Barbarus"), the renegade whose striking red beard was the visual marker by which he was known, not only captured Christian slaves but made incursions into the interior of Christian Europe. Following his raids on Naples and Sicily, he landed in Marseilles and turned the French port Toulon into a "second Constantinople," full of "San-Jacobeis" (or sanjak beys), imams reciting the Koran, "turbanned Moslems pacing the decks and Christian slaves—Italians, Germans, and even some Frenchmen—chained to the benches of the galleys," replenished by raids into nearby French villages from which the "Turks" carried off "peasants to serve in the galleys, while Christian captives were openly sold in the market."[72] The aftermath of the Ottoman victory at a new battle at Actium was thus that East conquered West, rather than the reverse, putting the West in a defensive position very different from the perspective that has anachronistically portrayed sixteenth-century Europe and England as conqueror and colonizer of the New World. Even Barbarossa's death in 1546 brought no respite to Europe, as his protégé Dragut, Uchali, and others continued to attack Christendom from strongholds in Barbary, and Hassan Barbarossa, the son who continued this famous Redbeard name, took twelve thousand Spanish prisoners at Oran.[73]

Both Khaired-din Barbarossa and his victory at this new Actium were vivid memories well into the seventeenth century. Minsheu's entry in 1599 on "*Barbaroxa,* a famous pyrate among the Moores which had a red beard," notes the "figure of a great beard" or "barba roxa" painted on drinking vessels; in 1617 he again cites the pirate famous "among the Moors" (*inter Mauros*), so-called because of his red beard (*propter barbae ruborem*).[74] Knolles's *Historie of the Turkes* (1603)—already an acknowledged influence on *Othello*—tells at length not only of "Hariadenus" Barbarossa's early years and his reception by the Sultan in Constantinople (though he was "borne of a renegat Greeke, and had from his youth liued as a mercilesse pyrat") but also of Charles V's siege of Tunis (635–69), of the Christian captive in Tunis who had been Barbarossa's "minion" (666), of the "demie man" or "eunuch of *Solymans* court, sent by him as *Barbarussa* his companion" (688), and of the Bassa married to Solyman's sister, who "after the vnnnaturall manner of those barbarous people kept in his house a most delicat youth, in whom he took more pleasure than in his wife" (675–76), in a passage that refers to him as a "Cynaedo" (676). Knolles narrates at length the major encounter with this Redbeard renegade and sea captain at "ACTIVM" (687), or Prevesa, describing the retreat of Andrea Doria (689–90) as "so disorderly and in such hast" that "it seemed rather a shamefull flight than an orderly retreat" and recording the scorn of "Barbarussa" at this western commander's loss of "honour" in so "shamefull a flight." Knolles's account then proceeds to recount the subsequent history of a "sonne" taken captive with his father at this new Actium, a "yong gentleman . . . beautifull with all the good gifts of nature, who afterwards presented to *Solyman,* turned Turke; and growing in credit in *Solymans* chamber, after three yeares miserable imprisonment, obtained his poore fathers libertie, and sent him well rewarded home againe into SPAINE" (689), a Joseph-in-Egypt story in which the Egyptianized son gains redemption for his family but does not himself return home.

The Barbarossa who appeared as "Barbarus" in the early English account and as "Barbarussa" in Knolles almost a century later was not only identified with the threat from Algiers, Tunis, and other parts of the Barbary Coast but was incorporated into the discursive network of Barbary, barbers, and beards in the period. "Barbarroja" (as he was known in Spanish) appears in the Captive's Tale of *Don Quijote,* where Charles V's conquest of Tunis is part of a narrative of conflicts with the Turk that evokes the history of captives taken to the Barbary Coast, from the generation of Barbarossa to the treatment of captives by his son.[75] This Captive's Tale first celebrates the Christian victory at Lepanto. But that temporary celebration is soon dampened by the narrator's own capture, when—like Hamlet taken by pirates—he boards the ship of the new pirate-king of Algiers (Barbarossa's successor Uchali or Uluj Ali, an Italian who had turned Turk) and is separated from his ship, commanded by Andrea Doria's son.

The tale of this captive famously recalls the experience of Cervantes himself, who "lost the use of his left hand while fighting against the Turks at Lepanto (1571), was seized by Barbary Coast pirates en route home from the wars, and spent over five years as a captive in an Algerian *bagnio*."[76] In *Don Quijote*—whose first part appeared in 1605 and became an immediate success in Europe, England, and the New World—the "Barbarroja" or Redbeard referred to in the Captive's Tale, by a writer who was also a barber-surgeon's son, is at the same time a reprise of the longer narrative's already-established nexus of associations between barbers, beards, and Barbary or *Berberia*. The first part of *Don Quijote* features not only the episode (1.21) in which the Don mistakes a barber's basin said to be capable of making a *barba* or "beard" for the helmet of a famous Moor but the disguise of the barber (*barbero*) named Nicolas in a huge borrowed red beard (*barba roja*), recalled in the later references to Barbarroja (400) or Barbarossa. Cervantes' text—which repeatedly exploits the homophonic affinities of *barbero* and *Berberia*—is filled with reminders of the beard as a prosthetic as well an alleged natural sign of masculinity, in the barber's detachable beard in Part 1 and the episode of the bearded ladies (or *dueñas barbudas*) of Part 2 who turn out to be men in disguise. As Barbara Fuchs has argued, both become part of a transvestism or cross-dressing that is not only transgendered but transcultural, crossing the boundaries between Christian and Moor, in ways reflective of the shifting identities of renegades, Marranos, and Moriscos in the period.[77] In one of the most striking episodes involving the barber's detachable beard—when it is kicked off by a *mula* or "mule" (echoed homophonically in the "Muley" of Barbary in the Captive's Tale)—the curate reattaches Nicolas's prosthetic red beard, rendering him as "bushy-bearded" (*bien barbado*) as he had been before.[78] He goes on to tell of the "robbers" or "galley slaves" who "attacked us and stripped us to our beards," and then took "those off, too, so the barber had to get himself a false beard" (1.29), an account that once again evokes the barbering or shaving of Christian captives. The references throughout Part 1 to barbers and detachable beards provide Cervantes with "an opportunity to examine the construction of masculinity," as Fuchs points out (24). But in the larger context she describes—of the Cervantine undermining of essentializing identifiers of religion and race as well as of gender—they simultaneously apply the barbering associated with captivity in Barbary or *Berberia* to something within the borders of Spain itself.

The fact that Cervantes' barber or *barbero*—transformed by the *barba roja* that connects him with Barbarossa—is named Nicolas or Nick furnishes him with a name that resonates in English with the nicking or cutting associated with Barbary and the threat of circumcision, castration, or shaving by the Turk. In *The Knight of Malta*, Norandine, fighting against the Ottoman, gives thanks for help he describes as coming "i' the nick" ("My Turke had Turk'd me else"), in lines that make clear that to be "Turk'd" is to be "circumcis'd" (2.1.14-25) or gelded, and that "nick" includes both the nick of time and other kinds of nicking or cutting. "Nick" as cutting "short" appears in Shakespeare's *Comedy of Errors* ("His man with scissors nicks him like a fool" [5.1.175]), implying that the "itch of his affection" has emasculated him, in a play whose Ephesus (in Turkey or Asia Minor) and Mediterranean-Aegean geographies suggest both ancient and early modern worlds. The Bottom of *A Midsummer Night's Dream,* who proclaims that he must go to the "barber's" because he is "hairy about the face," is also named Nick, a "Nick Bottom" here under the spell of an enchantress associated with the East, in a play that recalls both Babylon and Semiramis, the first to favor eunuchs.[79] This Athenian "rude mechanical"—in a period when "mechanical" was already a source of Nashean wordplay on the *mechanus* or pilgrim to Mecca—is spared such a nicking perhaps, as part of his upward mobility at the court of this Fairy Queen. But the final act's reference to an "Athenian eunuch" (5.1.45)—in a play that invokes an "Ethiope" and "tawny Tartar"—may serve as a contemporary reminder of the "barbarous" occupation that had overtaken Athens itself.[80]

In the same period as the barbering of Heywood's apprentice by the barbers of Barbary and the identification of the "shores of Barbaria" with "barbarous barbers" in Dekker's *Gull's Hornbook,* the name of Barbarossa himself appears in relation to barbering in *The Knight of the Burning Pestle.* In Beaumont's play (which has been dated as early as 1607-8, or close to Mason's *The Turke, Pericles,* and *Antony and Cleopatra*) another barber named Nick—disguised as a "Barberoso" who keeps captives in his cave—calls himself "Barbarossa." The name has often been excised or misunderstood by editors. But it is clear from the plot and the play's Cervantine echoes that this "Barbarossa" is neither a textual mistake nor the medieval Emperor Frederick I (also named Barbarossa), as frequently

assumed, but rather the notorious Barbary corsair, already identified with
the taking of captives as well as with barbers and the threat of nicking on
the Barbary Coast. Beaumont's play—which explicitly invokes the nicking
or gelding associated with Barbary in its description of a Barbary horse
as a "double gelding" of the "Barbarian kind" (1.192)—provides its own
plot of barbers, barbarians, and the Barbarossa or Barberoso against which
its apprentice crusades, in its parody not only of romances but of the
apprentice plays of Heywood himself.[81] "*Nick* the *Barbor*" (3.2.78) here
has a red beard that recalls Barbarossa's, as well as the red of the barber's
pole that stands for another kind of bloodletting, in a play whose "Burning
Pestle" evokes syphilis as well as the romances' Knight of the Burning
Sword. This red-bearded "Barbor" or Barbarossa is the bearer not only of
a barber's "bason" (like the one identified with a Moor and the making of
beards in *Don Quijote*) but of a "naked lance" (3.2.99) or "prickant spear"
that is a phallic euphemism for the barber's pole, joining the "balls" that
figured both the soap balls of the barber and the bodily appendage that
could be barbered or gelded.[82]

In a play that invokes "infidels" (1.1.69), "treacherous Sarazens" (3.2.19),
the "Sophy of Persia" (4.1.33), and the "great Turke" himself (Interact 1),
the captives of Barbary are explicitly recalled in the cave of this barber
alternately named "Barberoso" and "Barbarossa," in lines where fleecing
suggests not just the thievery associated with Barbary pirates but shaving
or cutting by "Barbars" of all kinds: "What fond unknowing wight is this?
that dares / So rudely knocke at *Barbarossa*'s Cell, / Where no man
comes but leaves his fleece behind?" (3.3.15–17). The threat of "*Nicke
the Barbor*" summons both the shaving that was a synonym for piracy
and the "nicking" or circumcising of a phallic "pestle," associated with
the Barbarossa who took Christian captives and inspired (or forced) so
many to turn Turk. Beaumont's English apprentice defeats "Barbarossa"
and frees his captives—in a scene that conflates the captives of a "barber"
who "under pretence of killing the itch" of syphilis or pox, is described
as having "cut away" the "beard" (3.3.67–69), with Barbary captives who
are "cut" as well as "fleeced." Hope is expressed that this Barbarossa might
be "convert[ed]" (3.3.116), in a scene where the disguised barber Nick—
claiming "I do recant my ill"—swears upon and kisses the apprentices'
"burning pestle" (3.3.154–59), promising that he "henceforth never gentle
bloud will spill" (3.3.154–55). The plot of this "Barber" satirically combines
the contemporary association of barbers and shaving with syphilis or pox

with accounts of captives of Barbarossa and others on the Barbary Coast, in a play in which captives are freed and a "Barbor" apparently converted, as in the (wishful) providential narratives of redemption from captivity in Barbary.

The Turk in early modern accounts was thus simultaneously represented as part of an "effeminate" East (associated with eunuchry and "sodome-trye") and as a bearded conqueror who expressed disgust for the clean shaven as bardashes or pathics. Given the ambiguous status of a Europe that was not yet a conqueror (as, in the Americas, it would later become) but was repeatedly invaded and threatened by this expanding Ottoman power, the new fashion for the beard as a masculine index in early modern Europe may have been both a complex emulation and a fear of assuming the visual appearance of the beardless *glaber* in its early modern form, when European captives were being "barbered" and shaved as a sign of pathic subjection or turning Turk. At the same time, this alleged natural sign was notoriously unreliable—in contexts where natural and constructed dizzyingly interact, complicating the very opposition of "hirsute" and "smooth."[83] The stage beard was a detachable marker not only of gender (or the passage from boy to man) but of assumed cultural and religious identity, enabling an English player to turn Turk by wearing the great "beard" of Barbarossa or of Solyman himself. For all of the rhetoric of definitive "Index" (or "pointer"), in the discourse of physiognomy as in other accounts, the binaries involved were not only reversible but unstable.

> by Jupiter,
> Were I the wearer of Antonio's beard,
> I would not shave'it to-day. . . .
> Our courteous Antony . . .
> Being barbered ten times o'er . . .
>
> *Antony and Cleopatra*

> On th'other part with all *Barbaria* force of diuerse armes
> Anthonius drags his traine of nacions thick. . . .
>
> *Aeneid,* trans. Thomas Phaer (1573)

Barbary and North Africa continued to be associated with barbering into at least the early eighteenth century: an account in 1704 reports a barber's shaving of a Christian slave in Algiers as an instance of the "barbarous cruelty" of a master who forces him to "turn Mussulman" or "Turk."[84] I want to end my examination of this nexus in earlier English drama, however, with

Antony and Cleopatra, set in the Roman frame of the original Actium battle
but staged at a time when Alexandria and Egypt (like Actium itself) had
long been identified with the new power of the East and renegades who
never returned. In Thomas Phaer's influential translation of the *Aeneid*
(1573), where Dido's African suitor is aligned with "the Turkes," the forces
on the side of Antony and his "*Gyptian* wife" at Actium are described
as "all *Barbaria,*" overlaying the ancient battle with the new geopolitics
of North Africa and the East. Phaer's culturally translated *Aeneid* pictures
Aeneas himself in Carthage in terms that align him with the Moriscos and
renegades of Tunis and the Barbary Coast: "in roabe of *Moorishe* purple,
mantle wise, / Hae stood, and from his shoulders down it hing *Morisco*
gise."[85] The counterpart in *Antony and Cleopatra* is the scene in which
Cleopatra's "tires and mantles" (2.5.22), worn by Antony in Egypt, evoke
not just attire but the turbanlike Eastern or "Turkish Tires" familiar from
Lyly's *Midas,* from the "tyres of the head" of Babylonian "harlots," and from
the exotic headresses (including a "tire of Venetian admittance") contrasted
with "plain" English dress in *Merry Wives* (3.3.56–58).[86]

Antony is described at his first meeting with Cleopatra on the Cydnus
as "barber'd ten times o'er" (2.2.224), in lines that sound the familiar
homophone of barbaring for this famous encounter in Asia Minor and
the *Barbaria* of more contemporary renegade plots. "Barber'd" manages
at the same time to convey its Roman overtones—curling the hair in an
effeminate fashion (recalled in the "curled Antony" of act 5); depilating,
shaving, and the eunuchry associated with Egypt or the East; and the
potential pathic subjection registered both in orientalizing descriptions
and in the Roman reputation of Antony as the "catamite" or male "bride"
of Curio, the charge leveled in Cicero's *Philippics* that led to the Roman
orator's own barbaric death. Antony's later description of Cleopatra as a
"triple-turn'd whore" (4.12.13) identifies her with the infidelity of harlots
(or "shee-barbers"), with unfaithful or renegade turning in religion, and
with the infidel enchantresses with whom she had already been conflated
in early modern writing. Here, in the retroactive description of Antony as
"barber'd" in Cilicia or early modern Turkey, the description of his heart as
"pursed" (2.2.86–87) casts Cleopatra as a pirate taking him captive, in a play
whose ancient pirates inevitably recall their contemporary equivalents.[87]

Antony and Cleopatra repeatedly foregrounds barbering, unhairing,
cutting, and gelding as the traditional currency of internecine rivalry but
also of eunuchry or unmanning in the familiar binary opposition between

Rome and Egypt, in a play in which the Folio's conflation of "haires" and "heires" is compounded by the racialized metaphorics of mingled "white" and "brown," lawful and unlawful "heirs" (3.11.12–15). The description of Antony as barbered and barbared in this historic encounter on the Cydnus is prefaced by the potential shaving of "Antonio's beard" in Rome itself: "Let Antony look over Caesar's head / And speak as loud as Mars. By Jupiter, / Were I the wearer of Antonio's beard, / I would not shave't to-day" (2.2.5–8). The lines invoke the emblems of Roman *virilitas* on the threshold of another pivotally decisive meeting—between Antony and the "boy" Octavius or "scarce-bearded Caesar" (1.1.22), who after Actium (where Antony's "ships" are "not well manned" and his own "captainship" is "nicked") would ultimately triumph as Virgil's Emperor Augustus. Here, however, in a context in which beardedness and shaving traditionally figure as indices of masculinity and comparative power, "Were I the *wearer* of Antonio's beard" simultaneously foregrounds this outward sign as a theatrical or prosthetic prop.

No treatment of the combination of barbering and barbaring in this play could ignore the fact that both the warning against the shaving of "Antonio's beard" in Rome and the description of Antony as "barber'd" on the Cydnus are delivered by Enobarbus, whose own Redbeard name (shortened elsewhere to "Enobarbe") calls striking attention not only to the *barbus,* beard, or "barbe" so important in the play but to the red beard he himself may have worn on stage. The red beard and defection of this Enobarbus (as his "place i' th' story" [3.12.46]) have been identified with Judas and the stage beard of the Jew.[88] But, as a potential renegade in Egypt who finally does return to Rome, his name could as readily evoke the most famous Redbeard of the other circumcised nation, the renegade who was wooed to return to the side of the new Rome but instead reversed the ancient Roman victory at the new Actium battle described in the influential *Historie of the Turkes* used for *Othello* only a few years before. Enobarbus and Barbarossa—as "Redbeards" from both Roman and early modern worlds—were directly aligned in Camden's *Remains Concerning Britain* (1605), which comments on "*Aenobarbus* of the Latines, or *Barbarossa* of the Italians," as simply different forms of the same name. Within the same two- or three-year period as *Antony and Cleopatra*, "Barbarossa" was used as the name of an actual stage character for the first time in English and as the assumed name of the "Barber" named "Nick" in *The Knight of the Burning Pestle*.[89] In a Roman plot in which multiple forms of barbering are evoked in a North African setting already associated with the "barbarous Turk," and the pair of its title are themselves contemporized in the Folio's "Anthonio" and tawny "Gypsy," this Roman Redbeard might well have summoned reminders (with Actium itself) of the more recent history in which this other Redbeard so prominently figured, as a renegade or defector in the opposite direction.

Whether or not Shakespeare's Enobarbe evokes his early modern name-sake or this more recent reversal, Enobarbus had a well-known "place i' th' story" of Rome's own history, as of the history of barbering and beards. It is a fiction of *Antony and Cleopatra* criticism that Antony's "Domitius Enobarbus" was a historically obscure or little-known figure, created from only scattered hints in Plutarch's *Life of Mark Antony*. In fact, his place in this story was well known, as was his reputation as an experienced sea captain—familiar from Tacitus, for example, already an acknowledged source of the more skeptical view of Augustus within this play. Plutarch's *Life* goes out of its way to highlight the imperial history in which Antony's Enobarbus was a pivotal figure: the marriage of his son to the daughter of Antony and Octavia and the mingling or intermarriage of the heirs of Antony, Enobarbus, and Octavius or Augustus that produced the ultimate "Domitius Enobarbus"—the emperor Nero. The larger "story" of Antony's Enobarbus was thus one in which even the ancient victory at Actium was ironically reversed by an imperial Enobarbus who brought Alexandrian revels—and theatricality—into the very center of Rome.

In Suetonius's *Life of Nero*—already an influence on *Hamlet* and other plays before its translation by Philemon Holland in 1606—this Enobarbus story parallels the course of Roman history itself, from the Redbeard origin of the name and the bearded *Ahenobarbi* of an older "virile" Rome (opposed to the introduction of eastern practices and championing Cato and the republican cause against the rise of Caesar), through the pivotal "place" of Antony's lieutenant (commander of a fleet who fought on the republican side before changing to Antony's), to the theatrical Enobarbus who issued not from the "unlawful" or Egyptian but from Octavius and Antony's "lawful" race, the "villanous out-of-tune fiddler AENOBARBVS" referred to in Jonson's *Poetaster* (1601), and the Enobarbus who was father of Nero, a riotous adulterer and reveler.[90]

The well-known history of Antony's Enobarbus—issuing in the barbaring of Rome by the ultimate "Domitius Enobarbus" who was heir not of a (barbarous) Egyptian but of the Octavian or Augustan imperial line—calls repeated attention to barbering and beards, as well as to shaving, gelding, and pathic subjection. Romans objecting to Nero's importing entertainers from Alexandria place a "curl" on his statue, memorializing the long hair worn by this imperial "Ahenobarbus" on his trip to the East and taunting him as a *Gallus* (devotee of the castrated Attis as well as a Roman from Gaul, red-bearded origin of the Enobarbus line). The chapters on his bringing Alexandrian revels into Rome picture him wearing what Holland glosses as "counterfeit hair," immediately before his "unnaturall abusing of boyes freeborne."[91] The future emperor compares the cutting of "the tender downe of his beard new budding forth" to cutting off the life of a member of his Domitian family. Notorious for gelding the "boy" Sporus in order to "transforme him into the nature of a woman" as his male "bride" and for subjecting his "owne body" to "bee abused" by his servant or "freed-man," this imperial Domitius Enobarbus is said to have had as his "tutors" not only a *saltator* or dancer (term for a transvestite performer in Plautus) but a *tonsor* or "Barber" (Holland, 1606). When Tacitus records the "Juvenalia" in celebration of the first shaving of Nero's beard (*Annals* XIV.xv), it is in a passage on the obscene gestures, or "postures," he encouraged Roman actors to assume, described as "never meant for the male sex" (*ad gestus modosque haud virilis*).

The "place i' th' story" of Antony's Enobarbus—who delivers the speeches on "Antonio's beard" and on Antony "barber'd" by Cleopatra—thus stresses the larger imperial history in which the binary oppositions of Roman orientalizing break down and the East is brought into Rome, including the theatricality that Shakespeare's Octavius emulates as well as condemns.[92] As in *Titus Andronicus,* where "thou art a Roman, be not barbarous," voices an opposition the larger play undoes, it is finally unclear which side is the inverse. This Roman play (like the earlier one of a "barbarous" and "barberous" Moor) participates in both ancient and early modern registers at once. But the historical palimpsest that dresses Roman Antony in Eastern or Islamic "tires" has in the staging of this renegade play yet another transcultural twist, and even more striking transvestite performance. "Salt Cleopatra"—"triple-turn'd whore" and emblem of the "Gypsies Lust" by which Antony or Antonio is "barber'd"—is famously neither female nor Egyptian, neither tawny nor Turk, but a transvestite English boy, in the "posture" of a "whore," on the English stage itself.

Notes

1. In addition to work cited in the notes below, see the recent bibliography in Daniel J. Vitkus, *Turning Turk* (New York: Palgrave, 2003).

2. See John Florio, *A Worlde of Wordes* (London, 1598), and *Queen Anna's Worlde of Wordes* (London, 1611); Sir John Harington, *A New Discourse of a Stale Subject Called the Metamorphosis of Ajax*, ed. Elizabeth Story Donno (New York: Columbia University Press, 1962), 65; *Ben Jonson*, ed. C. H. Herford and P. and E. Simpson (Oxford: Clarendon Press, 1938), 6:545. Minsheu's 1599 Spanish dictionary notes that *Barbacana* was used for "graie-bearded" as for "a yarde about a house, a barricado made of barrels filled with earth, & c. to defend soldiers with"; Florio gives for its Italian counterpart "a toole that chirurgions use to pull out teeth," one of the functions of the barber-surgeon, as well as "a ietty or out nooke in any building called a Barbicane" or "a toole that Masons and Carpenters vse." In Jonson, see (inter alia) *The Staple of News;* the barber "Cutbeard" of *Epicoene; Cynthia's Revels* (4.3.134–36); the "beard" of Face (who becomes "smooth Jeremy") and Surley, who swears by his "beard" in 4.3.92 before meeting the harlot Dol Common in *The Alchemist* (4.3.92).

3. Elliott Horowitz, "The New World and the Changing Face of Europe," *The Sixteenth Century Journal* 28 (Winter 1997): 1181–1201. Will Fisher examines this alleged natural sign of masculinity, prosthetic genders, and stage beards in "The Renaissance Beard: Masculinity in Early Modern England and Europe," *Renaissance Quarterly* 54(1) (2001): 155–87, and in "'His Majesty the Beard': Facial Hair and Masculinity on the Early Modern Stage," in *Staged Properties*, ed. Natasha Korda and Jonathan Gil Harris (Cambridge: Cambridge University Press, 2002).

4. See Thomas Heywood, *The Fair Maid of the West, Parts I and II*, ed. Robert K. Turner Jr. (Lincoln: University of Nebraska Press, 1967), Part 1, 4.5.7–8, 5.1.8–9, and 5.1.87–102. See also Jean E. Howard, "An English Lass Amid the Moors: Gender, Race, Sexuality, and National Identity in Heywood's *The Fair Maid of the West*," in *Women, "Race," and Writing in the Early Modern Period*, ed. Margo Hendricks and Patricia Parker (London: Routledge, 1994), 101–17; Barbara Fuchs, *Mimesis and Empire* (Cambridge: Cambridge University Press, 2001), 129–34; Jonathan Burton, "English Anxiety and the Muslim Power of Conversion: Five Perspectives on 'Turning Turk' in Early Modern Texts," *JEMCS* 2(1) (2002): 35–67, esp. 53–59; Vitkus, *Turning Turk;* on "Barbary," George Abbot, *A briefe description of the whole worlde* (London, 1599), ciiii ("from the confines of Cirene vnto the West, as farre as Hercules his pillars, is called Barbary"), and Christopher Lloyd's *English Corsairs on the Barbary Coast* (London: Collins, 1981), 21, which notes that "Turks" was a collective designation that included Muslims in Barbary. Part 1 of *Fair Maid* is usually dated between 1597 and 1603, though it may be later. Part 2's date is also uncertain, though it has been suggested to belong to the 1630s.

5. Heywood, *Fair Maid*, 82. On barber-surgeons, see Ian Burn, ed., *The Company of Barbers and Surgeons* (London: Farrand, 2000); Jessie Dobson and R. Milnes Walker, *Barbers and Barber-Surgeons of London* (Oxford: Blackwell Scientific Publications, 1979); Sidney Young, *The Annals of the Barber-Surgeons of London* (New York: AMS Press, 1978). References to their teeth-extracting function appear frequently in contemporary literature, often combined with shaving, hair-cutting, and bloodletting.

6. On Barbary gold, see Robert Ralston Cawley, *The Voyagers and Elizabethan Drama* (London: Oxford University Press, 1938). Heywood's conversion of a "noble Moor" to Chris-

tianity (*2 FM* 5.4.184-87) is one of many such wishful conversions, in contrast to the greater number of Christians turning Turk in the period: see Nabil Matar, *Islam in Britain, 1558-1685* (Cambridge: Cambridge University Press, 1998), 17.

7. See Gordon Williams, *A Dictionary of Sexual Language and Imagery in Shakespearean and Stuart Literature,* 3 vols. (London: Athlone Press, 1994), 1:593-94 ("gentleman usher") and 1:720-21 ("Italian fashion"), with Heywood, *Fair Maid,* 100.

8. See *Othello,* 4.3.26, and *Two Noble Kinsmen,* 3.5.26 (Folio "Barbary"; Quarto "Barbery"), in *The Riverside Shakespeare,* ed. G. Blakemore Evans et al. (Boston: Houghton Mifflin, 1974), which is the source of all Shakespeare citations unless otherwise noted; *The Three-Text Hamlet: Parallel Texts of the First and Second Quartos and First Folio* (New York: AMS Press, 1991), 112-13 (Quartos 1 and 2, "barbers"; Folio, "Barbars"); "barbars his beard to shave" in Richard Edwards's *Damon and Pithias: A Critical Old-Spelling Edition,* ed. D. Jerry White (New York: Garland Publishing, 1980), 68.

9. Although the 1633 Quarto (for which Heywood wrote prologues) gives this line to Ithamore, editors frequently assign it to an anonymous Turkish "Slave." Barabas's "under colour of shaving, thou'lt cut my throat for my goods" (2.3.120-21) combines shaving as thievery with its other senses here.

10. See Jonathan Bate's Arden 3 *Titus Andronicus* (London: Routledge, 1995), 249, on the "possible pun on 'barber'" in Quarto 1's "O barberous" with my remarks on barbering in *Titus Andronicus* and other plays in *Shakespeare from the Margins* (Chicago: University of Chicago Press, 1996), 5, 276; and Arthur J. Little Jr., *Shakespeare Jungle Fever* (Stanford: Stanford University Press, 2000), esp. 57-58, 63-64. See also the discussion of the play's complication of binaries of all kinds in Francesca T. Royster, "White-Limed Walls: Whiteness and Gothic Extremism in Shakespeare's *Titus Andronicus,*" *Shakespeare Quarterly* 51(4) (2000): 432-55, including p. 442 on Aaron's biblical name.

11. See Bate, *Titus,* 228, on Steevens's "Muly"; Jack D'Amico, *The Moor in English Renaissance Drama* (Tampa: University of South Florida Press, 1991), 141, who notes "Muly" as an "Islamic name" though he does not examine these Islamic implications; A. H. Bullen, ed., *The Works of Thomas Middleton,* 8 vols. (Boston: Houghton Mifflin, 1985), 6:184; the further association of mules with "Mulatto" mixture in Margo Hendricks, "'Obscured by dreams': Race, Empire, and Shakespeare's *A Midsummer Night's Dream,*" *Shakespeare Quarterly* 47 (1996): 37-60, esp. 56-60.

12. *All's Well* may be exploiting Latin *anser* (or the "goose" that was familiar slang for harlot), as in *Loves Labours Lost* (3.1.90-124). See Philip Massinger, *City Madam* (1632); John Davies of Hereford, *Scourge of Folly* (1610), *Complete Works,* 2 vols., ed. A. B. Grosart (Blackburn: Chertsey Worthies' Library, 1878), 2.8; Williams, *Dictionary,* 1:69-70; François Rabelais, *The Lives . . . of Gargantua and . . . Pantagruel,* trans. Sir Thomas Urquhart and Peter Le Motteux, ed. M. Le Du Chat et al., (1784; reprint, Navarre Society, 1931), 4v; Joseph Swetnam, *Araignment of Lewd, idle, froward, and unconstant women* (London, 1615), 29; Robert Greene, *A Disputation betweene a Hee Conny-Catcher and a Shee Conny-Catcher* (1592, 10:226).

13. See Williams, *Dictionary,* 3:1439-40 ("Turk"); and "She can turn, and turn" (*Othello* 4.1.253) in Vitkus, "Turning Turk in *Othello:* The Conversion and Damnation of the Moor," *Shakespeare Quarterly* 48(2) (1997): 145-76, esp. 154, 157-58.

14. On linguistic barbarisms (in Pliny, *contra naturam*) and the passive male role, see Jan Ziolkowski, *Alan of Lille's Grammar of Sex* (Cambridge, Mass.: The Medieval Academy of America, 1985), 15-17, 20 ("epicoene"), 22; Alexandre Leupin, *Barbarolexus*, trans. Kate M. Cooper (Cambridge: Harvard University Press, 1989), 60-64, 76; and the *barbarus* of Alan of Lille's influential *De planctu natura*, where the "bewitching" of male into female is also a blackening *(denigrat)* in Metre 1.15-20 (cited in Ziolkowski, *Alan*, 15).

15. Ian Smith, "Barbarian Errors: Performing Race in Early Modern England," *Shakespeare Quarterly* 49 (1998): 168-86. In "When We Were Capital, Or Lessons in Language: Finding Caliban's Roots," *Shakespeare Studies,* 28 (2000): 252-54, Smith discusses representations of the " 'barbarous' debased speech of Africans" and the derivation of "Barbary" from "Barbar, signifying in their Language an uncertain murmur."

16. The quotation here is from I. H, *This World's Folly, or a Warning-Peece Discharge upon the Wickednesse thereof* (1615).

17. See respectively John Dickenson, *Arisbas, Euphues Amidst his Slumbers; Or, Cupid's Iourney to Hell* (London, 1594), sig. D2; Robert Daborne, *A Christian Turn'd Turk* (1612), 13.52-72, in *Three Turk Plays from Early Modern England,* ed. Daniel J. Vitkus (New York: Columbia University Press, 2000); Andrew Barker, *A True and Certaine Report of the Beginning, Proceedings, Ouerthrowes, and now present Estate of Captaine Ward and Danseker, the two late famous Pirates* (London, 1609), sig. A3r and sig. C2r, on the "Sodomie" of Ward's company; and my "Preposterous Conversions: Turning Turk, and Its 'Pauline' Rerighting," *JEMCS* 2(1) (2002): 1-34.

18. See Elaine Fantham, *Comparative Studies in Republican Latin Imagery* (Toronto: University of Toronto Press, 1972), 103-4, for Plautus's *Mer.* 524-25; *Bacchides;* and *Captivi* 266-69; with Plaut. *Men.* 513-14; *Asin.* 402; Thomas Cooper's *Thesaurus Linguae Romae & Britannicae* (London, 1565): "Cinaedi, Dictu sunt apud veteres, saltatores. Plaut. wanton daunsers," in an entry whose "One abused agaynst nature. Improbi cinaedi. Catul." combines Catullus with the influence of Romans 1:26-27.

19. See Philemon Holland's 1606 translation of Suetonius's *History of Twelve Caesars,* ed. Charles Whibley, 2 vols. (London: David Nutt, 1899), 1.45 (49), 1.49 (51), 1.48-49, 16.

20. Maud W. Gleason, *Making Men* (Princeton: Princeton University Press, 1995), 68-69, citing Epictetus, *Discourses,* 1.16.11.

21. See Craig A. Williams, *Roman Homosexuality* (Oxford: Oxford University Press, 1999), 73; Horace's *Odes* (Book 4.10); Martial, *Epigrams,* 1:49 (Epigram 1.31) and 1:331 (Epigram 5.48) on a slave-boy; Catullus 61.134-36.

22. See Anthony Corbeill, *Controlling Laughter* (Princeton: Princeton University Press, 1996), chap. 4, esp. 145-73; Catherine Edwards, *The Politics of Immorality in Ancient Rome* (Cambridge: Cambridge University Press, 1993), 68-69, 77, 81-82, 93-96; Gleason, *Making Men,* 68-70, 76, 109; Amy Richlin, *The Garden of Priapus* (Oxford: Oxford University Press, 1992), 41, 93, 137, 168, 188-89; Williams, *Roman Homosexuality,* 26, 129-32; Martial, *Epigrams,* 2.29, 2.62, 9.28; Juvenal, *Satires,* 2.8-13, 8.114-15, 9.1-15; Persius, *Satire,* 4.1-16 and 4.33-42 (with Gleason, *Making Men,* 76n.94). Depilatories and curling the hair are cited from Ovid's influential *Art of Love* in Bruce R. Smith, *Homosexual Desire in Shakespeare's England* (Chicago: University of Chicago Press, 1991), 169.

23. Gleason, *Making Men,* 113, citing Seneca, "On the Brevity of Life," 12.3. For Epistle 114, see Seneca's *Ad Lucilium Epistulae Morales,* trans. Richard M. Gummere, 3 vols. (London: Heinemann, 1952), 315.

24. For Attis, see Catullus 63. On the *cinaedus,* see (in addition to work by Gleason, Edwards, Richlin, Williams, and Corbeill cited above), David M. Halperin, "Forgetting Foucault: Acts, Identities, and the History of Sexuality," *Representations* 63 (Summer 1998): 93-120; Judith P. Hallett and Marilyn B. Skinner, eds., *Roman Sexualities* (Princeton: Princeton University Press, 1997), 15, 17, 21, 14, 48, 51-58, 60, 63, 101, 105, 114, 118, 121, 135, 146; Amy Richlin, "Not Before Homosexuality: The Materiality of the *Cinaedus* and the Roman Law against Love between Men," *Journal of the History of Sexuality* 3(4) (1993): 523-73; Carlin A. Barton, *The Sorrows of the Ancient Romans: The Gladiator and the Monster* (Princeton: Princeton University Press, 1993), 72, 139, 161, 167; and John J. Winkler, *The Constraints of Desire* (London: Routledge, 1990), esp. 45-47, 50-54, on the Greek *kinaidos.* For identification of castrated galli with sodomites, see Gary Taylor, *Castration* (New York: Routledge, 2000), 149-53 (which includes a section on "Beards").

25. Cicero, *Brutus,* 325-27. On "hirsute philosophy and depilated rhetoric," see Gleason, *Making Men,* 72-73. On "Asiatic style," see William J. Dominik, ed., *Roman Eloquence* (New York: Routledge, 1993), 9, 17, 36-37, 41-46, 84-87, 91-107, 132; and Cicero, *Brutus,* 51, 284-91, 325-33; Cicero, *Orator,* 23-32, 57, 75-90; Tacitus, *Dialogus,* 15.3, 18; Quintilian, *Institutes,* 11.3.57-60, 12.10.12-26, 12.1.22, 12.6.7, 12.10.12-26.

26. Justus Lipsius, *Epp. Misc.,* 2:10, and *Inst. Epist.,* 14-15.

27. This last is Quintilian, *Inst.,* 5.12.17-18, *The Institutio Oratoria of Quintilian,* trans. H. E. Butler, 4 vols. (London: Heinemann, 1921), 2:307. See also Herodotus, *Histories,* 2.33-37, on Egyptian shaving, reversed gender roles, and circumcision. Effeminate rhetoric and beardless chin are combined in Shakespeare's *1 Henry IV,* 1.3.33-48.

28. Williams, *Roman Homosexuality,* 73.

29. Ibid., 26, citing from Pliny, *Natural History,* 30.41 and 30.132-34, trans. W. H. S. Jones, 10 vols. (London: Heinemann, 1963), 8:304-5, 8:364-65.

30. Athenaeus, *The Deipnosophists,* trans. C. B. Gulick, 7 vols. (London: Heinemann, 1959), 6:50-55.

31. Chrysostom's *Discourse,* 33.62-64, cited from *Dio Chrysostom,* trans. J. W. Cohoon and H. Lamar Crosby, 5 vols. (London: Heinemann, 1951), 3:330-33.

32. See *Paidagogus,* Book 3, chap. 3, in *Clement of Alexandria: Christ the Educator,* trans. Simon P. Wood (New York: Fathers of the Church, Inc., 1954), 212-14, with chaps. 3, 4, and 11 (esp. pp. 246-48, 256, 258, on beards, hair, and barbers); Ramsay MacMullen, "What Difference Did Christianity Make?" *Historia* 35 (1986): 322-43; Gleason, *Making Men,* 68-70.

33. Huloet in 1552 defines *pubeo* as to "berden, or begyn to have a berd" (beard). On shaving as shaming or punishment (including of captives) and on "bearding," pulling or taking by the beard, see Giles Constable's Introduction to Burchard's *Apologia de Barbis,* ed. R. B. C. Huygens, Corpus Christianorum: Continatio Mediaevalis, 62 (Turnholt: Brepols, 1985), 62-64, 72, 74, 77, 80-81, with 56-59; Horowitz, "New World," 1190-91; W[illiam] Ewing, "Beard," in *Dictionary of the Bible,* ed. James Hastings, 4 vols. (New York: Charles

Scribner's Sons, 1911), 260; Reynolds, *Beards* (Garden City, N.Y.: Doubleday, 1949), 9, 31, 41, 51, 57-61 (including on shaving and servitude in the Ottoman court), 66, 69-71; Fangé, *Mémoires,* e.g., 187-88.

34. See J. William Hebel, ed., *The Works of Michael Drayton,* Vol. 3 (Oxford: Basil Blackwell, 1961), 170; *The Knight of Malta,* in Fredson Bowers, ed., *The Dramatic Works in the Beaumont and Fletcher Canon* (Cambridge: Cambridge University Press, 1992), 8:416; Fisher, "Renaissance Beard," esp. 176-77, 181; Mario DiGangi, *The Homoerotics of Early Modern Drama* (Cambridge: Cambridge University Press, 1997), esp. 50-62. On James's "smooth-faced" male favorites, see Michael B. Young, *King James and the History of Homosexuality* (New York: New York University Press, 2000), 74, citing Harington, *Nugae Antiquae* (London, 1804), 1:395; M. C. Hippeau, ed., *Mémoires Inédits du Comte Leveneur de Tillières* (Paris, 1862), 1-4, 6; Caroline Bingham, *James I of England* (London: Weidenfeld and Nicolson, 1981), 159.

35. Montaigne's *Essais,* 3.5, in *Oeuvres Complètes de Montaigne,* ed. Albert Thibaudet and Maurice Rat (Paris: Éditions Gallimard, 1962), 822. On secret *cinaedi* or *cinaedi latentes,* described as concealing hidden practices behind a hirsute exterior (or the persona of the bearded philosopher), see Gleason, *Making Men,* 67, 77-81; Williams, *Roman Homosexuality,* 188-93; Richlin, "Not Before Homosexuality"; the opening of Juvenal's *Satire* 2; Martial, *Epigrams,* 7.58.7-8.

36. See *The apology of Iohan Bale agaynste a ranke papyst* (London, 1550), ffo. ciii, and *The actes of Englysh votaryes* (Antwerp, 1546), Preface, and Biir; and for Latimer, Reynolds, *Beards,* 188. On the Roman tonsure, see Constable's Introduction, esp. 55, 62, 70-75, 103-6, 112-19.

37. Constable (47-130) examines influential writing on beards as virile signs, including Augustine, *The City of God,* 22.24.4; Tertullian, *De cultu feminarum,* 2.8.2; and *De spectaculis,* 23.3; Isidore of Seville, *Etymologiae,* 11.1.45, ed. W. M. Lindsay (Oxford, 1911) [*Barbam veteres vocant, quod virorum sit, non mulierum*], Cyprian, Lactantius, Epiphanius, Clement, Bede, Hildegard of Bingen, Walter Map and others, with biblical texts on beards including Leviticus 19:26-27, Psalm 132:2-3 on the beard of Aaron, and the beard of David in 1 Kings 21:13. See also Richard Corson, *Fashions in Hair* (New York: Owen, 1965); Reynolds, *Beards,* esp. 109-10 on depilation and shaving and 110 on Tertullian's association of shaving with Bacchus and Isis; E. Clodd, "Beard," in *Encyclopedia of Religion and Ethics,* ed. James Hastings (New York: Charles Scribner's Sons, 1910), 2:441-43; H. Leclerq, "Barbe," in *Dictionnaire d'archéologie chrétienne et de liturgie* 2, 1 (Paris, 1925), 478-94; Augustin Fangé, *Mémoires pour servir à l'Histoire de la Barbe de L' Homme* (Liege, 1774); J.-A. Dulaure, *Pogonologia; or, a Philosophical and Historical Essay on Beards* (Exeter: R. Thorn, 1786).

38. See Halperin, "Forgetting Foucault"; DiGangi, *Homoerotics,* 70-72; on Jonson's "Cinedo," the "Cinedo" entry in Florio, *A Worlde of Wordes* (London, 1598), and the "lewd Cinaedian" and "fair Cinaedian boys" of Marston's *The Scourge of Villainy,* Satire 1, line 59, and Satire 3, line 49; Williams, *Dictionary,* 1 ("cynede"), which cites the "Cynoedus" of Philip Stubbes's *Anatomy of Abuses* (1598), 1.154; "Cyneds regiment" in Joseph's Hall's *Virgidemiarum* 4 (1598), 1.130; and "Cynedus" in Fynes Moryson's *Itinerary* (1617), 3.459. Jonson calls his detractors *cinaedi* in "To the Reader" (ll. 63-67) of *Poetaster* (excerpting *Improbior satyram scribente cinaedo* from Juvenal's *Satire* 4.106).

39. *The Battell of Alcazar, Fought in Barbarie* (London, 1594), sig. B4r (Amurath "mightie Emperor of the East"); Thomas Dekker, *Old Fortunatus,* Act 2 Chorus, in Fredson Bowers, ed., *The Dramatic Works of Thomas Dekker* (Cambridge: Cambridge University Press, 1953; repr. 1970), 1:136.

40. See Robert C. Davis, "Counting European Slaves on the Barbary Coast," *Past & Present* 172 (August 2001): 87–124; Matar's *Islam in Britain,* 4–19, and his Introduction to Daniel Vitkus, ed., *Piracy, Slavery, and Redemption: Barbary Captivity Narratives from Early Modern England* (New York: Columbia University Press, 2001); M. Epstein, *The Early History of the Levant Company* (London: George Routledge, 1908; repr. 1968), 241–42, on the appeal to Elizabeth by East Levant Company representatives to "preserve her subjects . . . from future captivity" by the Turk; Roslyn K. Knutson, "Elizabethan Documents, Captivity Narratives, and the Market for Foreign History Plays," *English Literary Renaissance* 26 (1996): 75–110; Shakespeare's *Henry V,* on a son who will "go to Constantinople and take the Turk by the beard" (5.2.210), in histories whose references to infidels and Turks simultaneously suggest the danger of infidels within.

41. See Richard Knolles, *The Generall Historie of the Turkes* (1603), sig. F fff 5 ("the battell lost, was unto *Selymus* as if a man should shave his beard, which would ere long growe againe," sig. F fff 5), cited in relation to *Othello* and beards in David C. McPherson, *Shakespeare, Jonson, and the Myth of Venice* (Newark: University of Delaware Press, 1990), 79; Emrys Jones, "*Othello, Lepanto,* and the Cyprus Wars," *Shakespeare Survey* 21 (1968): 47–52.

42. See Thomas Kyd, *The Spanish Tragedy,* ed. Philip Edwards (London: Methuen, 1959), 4.3.18; and its echo in the "beard half-off, half on" of Marston's *Antonio's Revenge* (2.1), with R. E. R. Madelaine, "Boys' Beards and Balurdo," *Notes and Queries* (April 1983): 148–50.

43. See Vittorio Gabrieli and Giorgio Melchiori, ed., *Sir Thomas More* (Manchester: Manchester University Press, 1990), 137; Charles Clay Doyle, "The Hair and Beard of Thomas More," *Moreana* 18(71–72) (Nov. 1981): 5–14; Fisher, " 'His Majesty the Beard." Given the spelling of More as "Moore" and the Moor's head on More's seal, this shaven "Sarcen" may also be another of the ironic avatars within the play of More himself.

44. Florio (1598) has for "Tiara, a turbant, or round wreath of linen for the head such as the Turks vse to weare." As David Bevington notes in his Revels edition of *Midas* (Manchester: Manchester University Press, 2002), which provides valuable commentary on the importance of beards, barbers, and hair in this and other plays, Midas's "great tiara" could also suggest the papal tiara, which was already part of the Protestant conflation of Papist and Turk (233).

45. Johan Valerian (Giovanni Pierio Valeriano Bolzani), *A treatise writen by Iohan Valerian a greatte clerke of Italie, which is intitled in latin Pro sacerdotum barbis, translated into Englysshe* (London, 1533), 29r, 22v, 11v.

46. John Bulwer, *Anthropometamorphosis: Man Transform'd* (London, 1653), 193, 98, 53, 199. Bulwer (201–5) also cites reports from Peter Martyr, John Smith, and others on the inhabitants of the Americas who use "depilatories," are "beardlesse," or who pluck out the beard, calling them "Scoffers of Nature."

47. See also Florio (1598) "Cinedulare" as "to bugger, to bardash, to ingle"; Thomas's 1548 Dictionary on "Zanzeri, bardasses"; 1600 *O.F. Repli. Libel* 1.2.43 ("bardasses and concubines"); William Lithgow, *The Totall Discourse, Of the Rare Adventures and Painful Pere-*

grinations of long nineteene Yeares Trauayles (London, 1632), 335 ("Bardassoes, whoorish boyes").

48. See, inter alia, Nabil Matar, *Turks, Moors, and Englishmen in the Age of Discovery* (New York: Columbia University Press, 1999), esp. chap. 4; Williams, *Dictionary,* 3:1438-40 ("Turk"); my "Preposterous Conversions"; *Sir Thomas Sherley his Trauailes* (1607) on the "Turke" as "the most inhumane of all other Barbarians" and "all Pagans, and Infidels, Sodomites, and Liars." On multiple (and conflicting) images of the "barbarous" Turk, see also Nancy Bisaha, " 'New Barbarian' or Worthy Adversary? Humanist Constructs of the Ottoman Turks in Fifteenth-Century Italy," in *Western Views of Islam in Medieval and Early Modern Europe,* ed. David R. Blanks and Michael Frassetto (London: Macmillan, 1999) 185-205, 207-30.

49. George Sandys, *A Relation of a Journey Begun An: Dom: 1610: Foure bookes* (London, 1615), 70.

50. See John Davies of Hereford, *Wits Bedlam* (1617), C2, on the gelding of "stones" from a "Purse," with Vitkus, *Three Turk Plays,* 5; Fuchs, *Mimesis and Empire,* chap. 5; the Sultan's eunuchs in Richard Hakluyt, *The Principal Navigations Voyages Traffiques & Discoveries of the English Nation,* 12 vols. (New York: Macmillan, 1904), 5:107.

51. See *The Turke,* C2; Massinger's *The Renegado* (1.1.38-58, 2.6.4-7, 40; 3.4.51-52), cited here from Vitkus, *Three Turk Plays;* and on Gazet, Clem, and such comic deflections of fears of the Turk, see Burton, "English Anxiety," 50-59.

52. In addition to recent work already cited, others have begun to remedy this, including Richard Hillman, " 'Not Amurath an Amurath Succeeds': Playing Doubles in Shakespeare's Henriad," *English Literary Renaissance* 21(2) (1991): 161-89; Virginia Mason Vaughan, *Othello: A Contextual History* (Cambridge: Cambridge University Press, 1994); Julia Reinhard Lupton, "*Othello* Circumcised: Shakespeare and the Pauline Discourse of Nations," *Representations* 57 (Winter 1997); Barbara Fuchs, "Conquering Islands: Contextualizing *The Tempest,*" *Shakespeare Quarterly* 48(1) (1997): 45-62; Richard Wilson, "Voyage to Tunis: New History and the Old World of *The Tempest,*" *English Literary History* 64 (1997): 333-57; and the special issue on "Representations of Islam and the East" of *JEMCS* 2(1) (2002).

53. See Dorothy M. Vaughan, *Europe and the Turk: A Pattern of Alliances, 1350-1700* (Liverpool: Liverpool University Press, 1954), 108, on the Diet of Worms; my "Black *Hamlet:* Battening on the Moor," *Shakespeare Studies* 31 (2003): 127-64; on *Hamlet* in relation to piracy and the Turk, Lois Potter, "Pirates and 'Turning Turk' in Renaissance Drama," in *Travel and Drama in Shakespeare's Time,* ed. Jean-Pierre Maquerlot and Michèle Willems (Cambridge: Cambridge University Press, 1996), 125-40.

54. In addition to the phallic overtones inseparable from "lance," "Lancelet" was a familiar synonym for the "lancet" used in the Geneva (1560) version of 1 Kings 18:28 (on priests of Baal incising or lancing themselves). See Minsheu: "a Launcelot, or Lancelot, a fleame or chirurgians instrument which is used in letting blood," related to Latin *"scalper, scalprum, a scalpendo,"* and Greek *Phlebotomum* (from the Greek words for "vena" and "incido"); Thomas Thomas's *Dictionarium Linguae Latinae et Anglicanae* (1587) on *"Scalper . . .* Any kinde of instrument or yron toole, to make incision, to scrape, cut, or grave with a graving yron, a lancelot, scissers"; *"Scalprum . . .* a surgeons toole to take away corrupt flesh from the bones, a barbars or surgeons lance: a graving yron, a shauing knife or raser . . . *Scalprum*

chirurgicum, Cels. A lancet, a fleeme to open a veine or let blood"; John Baret's *Alvearie* (1573), 77: "A Lancelette or like instrument, scalprum chirurgicum"; G. Harvey *New Letter* (1593), 12: "Pierces Supererogation . . . is less beholding to the penknife: Nashes S. Fame hath somewhat more of the launcelet." Barbara Mowat and Paul Werstine, in the New Folger edition of *The Merchant of Venice*, print "Lancelet" as his name (suggesting a connection with "lancet" or "small lance" as a weapon or man-at-arms). The threat of castration and forcible circumcision is foregrounded in James Shapiro's *Shakespeare and the Jews* (New York: Columbia University Press, 1996), though it does not mention Lancelet in relation to the centrality of knives and incisions in this play.

55. See *Twelfth Night,* 3.2.7 ("a very renegado"), and 2.5.86-88, 130-38; on Illyria and the Turk, see Samuel C. Chew, *The Crescent and the Rose* (New York: Oxford University Press, 1937), 132, citing John Foxe (1570) on the growing dominion of the Turk, including "the Empire of Constantinople, Greece, Illyria, with almost all Hungary and much of Austria"; *Tamburlaine 2* (3.1.1-4), where the territories of "Callapinus, Emperor of Turkey," include Illyria. On *caesus*/cut, *castrati,* and eunuchry in *Twelfth Night,* see Keir Elam, "The Fertile Eunuch: *Twelfth Night,* Early Modern Intercourse, and the Fruits of Castration," *Shakespeare Quarterly* 47(1) (Spring 1996): 1-36; John Astington, "Malvolio and the Eunuchs: Texts and Revels in *Twelfth Night,*" *Shakespeare Survey* 46 (1994): 23-34; Stephen Orgel, *Impersonations* (Cambridge: Cambridge University Press, 1996), 53-57; Taylor, *Castration,* 41, 114, 151, 260; Constance C. Relihan, "Erasing the East from *Twelfth Night,*" in *Race, Ethnicity, and Power in the Renaissance,* ed. Joyce Green MacDonald (London: Associated University Presses, 1997), 80-94. "Cesario" was also a familiar early modern spelling of Caesarion, the reputed son of Julius Caesar and Cleopatra.

56. Bartholomeus Georgijevic, *Ofspring of the House of Ottomanno,* trans. Hugh Goughe (London, 1569), Gviir (on how the emperor "disposeth his captives").

57. Cited here from Hakluyt, *Principal Navigations,* 5:292-319. Hakluyt also records more positive interaction between England and Barbary, as in Elizabeth's reference to the beneficial "mutuall traffic" or trade by which "the East may be joyned and knit to the West" with the reminder to the Sultan of the "dispensation" granted "to our Subjects of England" for safe passage in the Mediterranean (5:313).

58. See Hakluyt, *Principal Navigations,* 5:282-83; "Joseph in Egypt" cited in Matar's Introduction to Vitkus, *Piracy, Slavery, and Redemption,* 37. The application of Joseph's captivity (and rise) in Egypt to early modern contexts must also take into account the shaving of Joseph in Egypt in Genesis 41:14 (Reynolds, *Beards,* 24-25).

59. Burton, "English Anxiety," esp. 43-45. Though he does not mention the forcible shaving that was part of the *Jesus* story, Burton argues that this and other narratives were comically deflected on the stage, including in *Fair Maid.*

60. On Ottoman Alexandria, see Hakluyt, *Principal Navigations,* 5:160, 230, 329, 331; Abbot, *Brief Description* (1599), describes "Ægypt" as now "wholy vnder the Turke" (ciiii).

61. See *The Admirable Deliverance of 266. Christians by Iohn Reynard Englishman from the captiuitie of the Turkes, who had been Gally slaues many yeares in Alexandria* (London, 1608), attributed to Anthony Munday, sig. B2r. As Donna Hamilton has pointed out to me, Munday notes in *A briefe chronicle of the processe of times,* sig. Y5r-v, that "the Romans were known to shave the hair of [those] they subdued in sign of servitude."

62. Thomas Dekker, *The Gull's Hornbook*, ed. R. B. McKerrow (London: De La More Press, 1904), 3:28–30. "Abominable shaving" (7:61) refers to thievery or cheating, but with "player" and "ingle" (8:65) it retains its other contemporary senses. See also barbers in 8:66 of this edition, "shaving" as usury (or "jewish interest") in *Seven Deadly Sins* (1606), and *If This Be Not a Good Play, the Devil is In It* (1612) on the shaving of merchants by the Barbary renegado pirate Ward (5.4.90–94).

63. Fernand Braudel, *The Mediterranean and the Mediterranean World in the Age of Philip II* (New York: Harper and Row, 1973), 1:116; Chew, *Crescent and the Rose*, 341–42; S. Soucek, "The Rise of the Barbarossas in North Africa," *Archivum Ottomanicum* 3 (1971): 238–50, who cites divergences in early modern accounts, including the *Epitome de los Reyes de Argel* by the Spanish monk Diego de Haedo, published as the second of five parts of his *Topographia e historia general de Argel* (Valladolid, 1612) and two early Turkish sources, the *Kitabi-i bahriye* by Piri Reis and *Gazavat-i Hayreddin Pasa*, a semiautobiography by the younger Barbarossa brother (243).

64. Lloyd, *English Corsairs*, 22.

65. See Braudel, *Mediterranean*, II:855, 884–85; John B. Wolf, *The Barbary Coast: Algiers under the Turks, 1500 to 1830* (New York: W. W. Norton, 1979), esp. 9ff.; Andrew C. Hess, *The Forgotten Frontier: A History of the Sixteenth-Century Ibero-African Frontier* (Chicago: University of Chicago Press, 1978), 61–73; Vaughan, *Europe and the Turk*, 97ff.; Chew, *Crescent and the Rose*, 344, with 341–42; Lloyd, *English Corsairs*, 17; Matar, *Islam in Britain*, 22ff; Davis, "Barbary Coast," 90, 95–97, 117–19; *The Navigations, Peregrinations and Voyages Made into Turkie by Nicholas Nicholay*, 8r ("renied christians in Alger"); Father Dan's *Histoire de Barbarie et de ses corsairs* (1637), for example, chap. 1, titled "Corsaires de Barbarie héritiers de malediction de la terre de Cham (ie Ham)."

66. *The copye of the goyng away of the chefe Captayne of the Turke called Barbarossa, oute of Fraunce*, translated . . . into English (London, ca. 1545), sig. Ciiir.

67. Vaughan, *Europe and the Turk*, 120–21. On Charles's conquest of Tunis and the competing identification with Roman and other imperial figures by the Sultan as well as Charles V and Francis I, see Lisa Jardine and Jerry Brotton, *Global Interests* (Ithaca, N.Y.: Cornell University Press, 2000), esp. 48, 58, 76–78, 87, and 82–115.

68. See Lord Kinross, *The Ottoman Centuries: The Rise and Fall of the Turkish Empire* (London: Jonathan Cape, 1977), 221; on Ottoman sea power, see Palmira Brummett, *Ottoman Seapower and Levantine Diplomacy in the Age of Discovery* (Albany: SUNY Press, 1994), esp. chap. 4, 109, on Selim's emulation of Julius Caesar and Alexander the Great; Jerry Brotton, *Trading Territories: Mapping the Early Modern World* (Ithaca, N.Y.: Cornell University Press, 1997), 103–14; Braudel, *Mediterranean*, 2:1142.

69. See John F. Guilmartin Jr., *Gunpowder and Galleys: Changing Technology and Mediterranean Warfare at Sea in the Sixteenth Century* (Cambridge: Cambridge University Press, 1974), esp. 20–26, 42–56; Brummett, *Ottoman Seapower*, esp. 96; Lloyd, *Corsairs*, 22; Kinross, *Ottoman*, 223–27; Vaughan, *Europe and the Turk*, 117ff.; Paul Coles, *The Ottoman Impact on Europe* (New York: Harcourt, Brace, and World, 1968), 93ff.

70. Kinross, *Ottoman*, 223. On Charles V's (ultimately unsuccessful) wooing of Barbarossa to defect to the side of the new "Rome" and the importance of this new Battle of Actium at Prevesa, see Braudel, *Mediterranean*, 2:905–6; Vaughan, *Europe*, 123ff., with the map

including Prevesa (148); Coles, *Ottoman Impact,* 93; Guilmartin, *Gunpowder,* 43, 20-26, 32, 36, 42-56, 75, 261, 267.

71. Guilmartin, *Gunpowder,* 42.

72. Kinross, *Ottoman,* 227-28; Vaughan, *Europe,* 127; with Knolles, *Historie of the Turke* (1603), 744, 749ff.

73. See Braudel, *Mediterranean,* 2:905-6, 972; Lloyd, *Corsairs,* 23; Coles, *Ottoman Impact,* 95.

74. *A Dictionarie in Spanish and English, first published into the English tongue by R. Perciuale Gent. . . . Now enlarged and amplified . . . by Iohn Minsheu Professor of Languages in London* (London, 1599); *Vocabvlarivm Hispanicolatinvm et Anglicum* or "Most Copious Spanish Dictionarie, with Latine and English," bound with Minsheu's *Guide unto the Tongues* (1617).

75. See Part 1, chaps. 39-43, of Miguel de Cervantes Saavedra, *Don Quijote de la Mancha,* ed. Martín de Riquer (Barcelona: Editorial Juventud, 1955), esp. 398-402; Burton Raffel, trans., *The History of That Ingenious Gentleman Don Quijote de la Mancha* (New York and London: W. W. Norton, 1995), 258-60.

76. Diana de Armas Wilson, Introduction to Raffel, *History of That Ingenious Gentleman,* viii.

77. See Barbara Fuchs, *Passing for Spain* (Urbana: University of Illinois Press, 2003), 23-30 (which also discusses the sexual overtones of the hostess's beard/tail), with *Don Quijote,* Part 1, esp. chaps. 21-22, 27, 29, 32, 39-43.

78. *Don Quijote* 1.29; Riquer ed., 298-300; Raffel English trans., 187-88.

79. See *A Midsummer Night's Dream,* 4.1.24-25; with the face/*fesse* (buttocks) pun in relation to the shaving of "Captain Face" in Jonson's *Alchemist* (4.7.127-33); Sandys, *Relation,* 70 ("The first that euer made Eunuch, was *Semyramis*"). That "bottom" (e.g., in the "tailor" scene of *The Taming of the Shrew* [4.3.137] or *Two Gentlemen of Verona* [3.2.51-53]) has phallic connotations makes "Nick" Bottom resonate with the nicking or castrating of other contemporary allusions. Bottom's "barber" is connected to barbering and beards in Harvey and Nashe, in J. J. M. Tobin's "Have with You to Athens' Woods," *Notes and Queries* 248 (March 2003): 32-35; and reflects the influence of Lyly's *Midas,* adding barbering to the preoccupation elsewhere in the play with beards as stage props or prosthetic indices of manhood (discussed in Fisher's "Renaissance Beard").

80. On Athens under the "barbarous" Turk, see Robert Schwoebel, *The Shadow of the Crescent: The Renaissance Image of the Turk (1453-1517)* (Nieuwkoop: B. de Graaf, 1967), 63; Chew, *Crescent and the Rose,* 62-64. For "mechanical" (*mechanicus*) and Latin *moechus* (fornicator or adulterer) compounded with *mechanus* or pilgrim to Mecca, see Thomas Nashe, *The Unfortunate Traveller* (1593), 2:249 ("Mechanicall men they call vs . . . most of vs being Maechi, that is, cuckoldes and whooremasters, fetch our antiquitie from the temple of Maecha, where Mahomet was hung vp").

81. For its parody of Heywood's *Four Prentices of London,* see, for example, *Pestle* 4.1.53, with pp. 3-4 of Andrew Gurr, ed., *The Knight of the Burning Pestle* (Berkeley: University of California Press, 1968), used for all citations. The Folio and all three Quartos have "Barbarossa" (rather than the "Barbaroso" it is sometimes editorially emended to), for the lines on "Barbarossa's cell, / Where no man comes but leaves his fleece behind" (3.3.28),

a "fleece" that is both "beard" and "money" or "hide." S. P. Zitner, ed., *The Knight of the Burning Pestle* (Manchester: Manchester University Press, 1984), 116, identifies "Barbarossa" as Frederick I. On links with *Don Quijote* (translated into French in 1607, and circulating in Shelton's English translation years before its publication in 1612), see Gurr, *Knight,* 3, and Michael Hattaway's Norton edition (New York: W. W. Norton, 1969), 3. For barber's "teeth," see *Pestle* (3.3.27) with Beaumont's *The Woman Hater* (3.3.108-10).

82. In addition to Jonson's *Magnetic Lady* (2.7.51-52), see Dekker, *Noble Spanish Soldier* (ca. 1626), 5.4.143 ("Shee loves no Barbars washing . . . My Balls are sav'd then"); with other examples in Williams, *Dictionary,* I:62-63.

83. Gleason, *Making Men,* 73, characterizing this influence from Roman writing.

84. Joseph Pitts, "A True and Faithful Account of the Religion and Manners of the Mohammetans, with an Account of the Author's Being Taken Captive" (1704), in Vitkus, *Piracy,* 307-13. For beards in later eighteenth-century racial contexts, see also Londa Schiebinger, *Nature's Body: Gender in the Making of Modern Science* (Boston: Beacon Press, 1993).

85. See Jerry Brotton, " 'This Tunis, sir, was Carthage': Contesting colonialism in *The Tempest,*" in *Post-Colonial Shakespeares,* ed. Ania Loomba and Martin Orkin (London and New York: Routledge, 1998), 23-42, 41; *The Aeneid of Thomas Phaer and Thomas Twyne,* ed. Steven Lally (New York and London: Garland Publishing, 1987) IV.377 (p. 80) and IV.377 (p. 82); David Quint, *Epic and Empire* (Princeton: Princeton University Press, 1993), 24, on the *ope barbarica* of Virgil's Actium description (in a discussion that details the Islamic as well as New World updating given to the *Aeneid* and Cleopatra).

86. See *OED* (1560 BIBLE [Geneva] Isa. iii. 18, 20 ["tyres of the head"]; 1653 J. HALL *Paradoxes* 67 ["Turkish Tires"]); Minsheu (1617): "The word *Attire* in English commeth from the Latine word *Tiara,* which is an ornament of the heads of the Persian Kings, Priests, and Women," described in his Spanish Dictionary as "a round rolle of linnen . . . such as the Turkes weare at this day"; Cotgrave (1611) on "Tiare" as "A round and wreathed Ornament for the head (somewhat resembling the Turkish Turbant) worne, in old time, by the Princes, Priests, and women of Persia."

87. See Little, *Shakespeare Jungle Fever* (for the *Philippics* charge) and Potter, "Pirates."

88. R. MacG. Dawson's influential "But Why Enobarbus?" *Notes and Queries* (June 1987): 216-17.

89. See Camden, *Remains,* 76. Barnabe Barnes's *The Devil's Charter* (1607)—often used to date *Antony and Cleopatra* because of its echoes of the latter—has an Italian "Barbarossa" in its plot of a pope closely identified with the Turk.

90. See the Loeb edition of *Suetonius,* trans. J. C. Rolfe, 2 vols. (London: William Heinemann, 1914), 2:86. Nero as "Domitius Enobarbus" is also highlighted in Thomas May's *Brittanicus.*

91. See Suetonius (trans. Holland), II:123; II:130-31; chap. 43; chap. 12; II:108; II:272; II.122.

92. See Jonathan Gil Harris, " 'Narcissus in thy face': Roman Desire and the Difference It Fakes in *Antony and Cleopatra,*" *Shakespeare Quarterly* 45 (1994): 408-25.

Notes on Contributors

AMANDA BAILEY is a visiting assistant professor of English at the University of North Carolina at Chapel Hill. She has published on Elizabethan clothing laws, playhouse practices, and same-sex desire in the early modern period. She is currently completing a book entitled *Embodied Politics: Fashion, Theatricality, and the Meaning of Style in Early Modern England,* which explores how gentle-born but economically disenfranchised young men negotiated their ambivalent position to late sixteenth-century culture through style.

HARRY BERGER JR., professor emeritus of literature and art history at the University of California, Santa Cruz, has published widely on a variety of topics in classical and Renaissance literature, art history, and theory. His most recent books are *Fictions of the Pose: Rembrandt against the Italian Renaissance* and *The Absence of Grace: Sprezzatura and Suspicion in Two Renaissance Courtesy Books,* both published in 2000 by Stanford University Press.

ROBERT DARCY is an assistant professor of English at the University of Nebraska at Omaha. He has contributed an essay on printing and Marlowe to the *Journal for Early Modern Cultural Studies* and on incest and *The Merchant of Venice* to the book collection *Money and the Age of Shakespeare,* edited by Linda Woodbridge. He is currently working on a book project about misanthropy and social flight in Renaissance England.

SUZANNE GOSSETT is a professor of English at Loyola University Chicago. With W. David Kay she has recently completed an edition of *Eastward Ho!* for the *Cambridge Works of Ben Jonson.* Her Arden 3 edition of *Pericles* appeared in 2004. She has also edited or co-edited Ben Jonson's *Bartholomew Fair,* Thomas Middleton's *A Fair Quarrel,* and Lady Mary Wroth's *Urania.* Her recent articles concern *Pericles,* Middleton, feminist editing, and the treatment of earlier conjectures in current editions. She is one of the general editors of Arden Early Modern Drama.

PHILIPPA KELLY is a senior research fellow at the University of New South Wales (and a visiting scholar at UC Berkeley through June 2004). She has published a monograph on *King Lear* and a recent edition of the play (Halstead Press) and was a contributor to *The Cambridge King Lear CD ROM.* She has published a collection of papers, *The Touch of the Real: Communing with the Living and the Dead.* Her recent articles include "Surpassing Glass: Shakespeare's Mirrors" in the *Journal of Early Modern Literary Studies,* "Teaching Shakespeare in Locked Facilities" in the *Australasian Drama Studies,* " 'Make Not Your Thoughts Your Prisons': Shakespeare in a Different Place" in *Shakespeare Magazine,* and "New Faces for Shakespeare in Contemporary Australia" in *Shakespeare Matters.*

JAMES LOXLEY is a senior lecturer in English in the School of Languages, Literatures, and Cultures at the University of Edinburgh. He is the author of *Royalism and Poetry in the English Civil Wars, The Complete Critical Guide to Ben Jonson,* and a number of articles on seventeenth-century poetry. He is currently writing a book for Routledge on performativity from Austin to Butler.

PATRICIA PARKER is the Margery Bailey Chair of English and Dramatic Literature and professor of comparative literature at Stanford University. She is the author of *Shakespeare from the Margins* and co-editor, with Margo Hendricks, of *Women, "Race," and Writing in the Early Modern Period.* She is currently at work on Norton Critical editions of *Twelfth Night* and *Much Ado about Nothing* and a new Arden edition of *A Midsummer Night's Dream.*

ADAM ZUCKER is an assistant professor of English at the University of Massachusetts, Amherst. He is co-editing a collection of essays titled *Localizing Caroline Drama, 1625–1642,* and is at work on a book on the relationship between urban space, social status, and comic form in early modern England.